Advance Praise for *When I Knew Al*

"In these days of privilege, selfishness, greed and entitled movies stars, a book comes along about Al Pacino and his less fortunate childhood pal Ed De Leo. Cheers to Al Pacino for reaching out to his friend and fellow actor!"
– Richard Herd, Actor (*The Cabinet of Dr. Caligari*, *Midnight in the Garden of Good and Evil*, *The China Syndrome*)

"David Sheldon and Joan McCall present an easy to read book filled with the complexities, vulnerabilities and ambitions of these men – a true example of rational intelligence vs. spiritual intelligence."
– Gary Quinn, International bestselling author of *May the Angels Be With You* and *Living in the Spiritual Zone*

"Al Pacino is one of America's greatest actors. Edward De Leo, I had never heard of. Through the alchemy of a dual biography, David Sheldon and Joan McCall admit us to a hidden world of struggle where actors have to make choices … It's an exciting read!
– Kelly Lange, Former TV news anchor/reporter for Los Angeles NBC affiliate, author *Graveyard Shift*, *Dead File*, *The Reporter*

"Acting is a profession that requires selling yourself with artistry. This book shows how Al Pacino achieves superstar status while his mentor does not, despite Pacino's help – an inside look at the internal demons that each man faces even with the rewards and challenges that success and failure bring each of them."
– John Livesay, Author of *The 7 Most Powerful Selling Secrets*, motivational speaker

More Advance Praise for *When I Knew Al*

"My wife refused to be told how the book ends until she finished reading it herself … she knew Al Pacino was a superstar, but wanted to find out for herself what happens to Edward De Leo and why. So, the book also works as a mystery."
– James G. Hirsch, Writer, producer *The Incredible Hulk*, *Rome*, *The Blue Knight*, *Nash Bridges*, *Hart to Hart*

"This biography of Al Pacino through the eyes of Ed De Leo is both an absorbing narrative and an acute assessment of Pacino and his impact on the movie-going public. I knew De Leo – Sheldon and McCall skillfully capture his lifelong struggle."
– Harvey Flaxman, Fairleigh Dickinson University professor of theater and film, motion picture producer, screenwriter

When I Knew Al

The Untold Story of Al Pacino

When I Knew Al

The Untold Story of Al Pacino

David Sheldon
&
Joan McCall

As told by Ed De Leo

HH
HARBOR
HOUSE
AUGUSTA

WHEN I KNEW AL
By David Sheldon and Joan McCall
A Harbor House Book/2005

For information address:
HARBOR HOUSE
111 TENTH STREET
AUGUSTA, GEORGIA 30901

Cover photo used with permission from Corbis

Library of Congress Cataloging-in-Publication Data

De Leo, Edward.
When I knew Al / David Sheldon, Joan McCall ; as told by Ed De Leo.
p. cm.
Rev. ed. of: Al Pacino-- and me.
ISBN 1-891799-31-2 (alk. paper)
1. Pacino, Al, 1940- 2. Motion picture actors and actresses--United States--Biography. 3. De Leo, Edward. 4. Acting teachers--United States--Biography. I. Sheldon, David. II. McCall, Joan. III. De Leo, Edward. Al Pacino-- and me. IV. Title.
PN2287.P18D5 2005
791.4302'8'092--dc22

2005015131

Printed in the United States of America

10 9 8 7 6 5 4 3 2 1

ACKNOWLEDGEMENTS

Many friends, associates and other professionals have made special contributions to the development of this book. We acknowledge them with deep gratitude:

Right up front we wish to thank publishers Randall Floyd and Carrie McCullough for their vision and confidence in the concept of this book.

For their cooperation with our research and access to archives and interviews we thank the Academy of Motion Picture Arts and Sciences, The Actors Studio, Backstage, "The Barbara Walters Show," the Beverly Hills Public Library, Columbia Pictures, *Cosmopolitan*, the Directors Guild of America, *Empire* magazine, *Esquire*, *GQ*, HB Studio, the High School of the Performing Arts, *Hollywood Reporter*, *London* magazine, *L.A. Weekly*, the *Los Angeles Times*, *Marquee*, *The New York Times*, Paramount Pictures, *People* Magazine, *Photoplay*, *Playboy*, *Premiere* magazine, *Rolling Stone*, *Saga*, the Screen Actors Guild, *Toronto Star*, Twentieth Century Fox, United Artists, Universal Pictures, *Vanity Fair*, *Variety*, *Venice*, *The Village Voice*, Warner Brothers, and The Writers Guild of America.

David Sheldon and Joan McCall

To attorney Michael Mayro and actor Vee Gentile for their generous support and assistance in the creation of this book. A former acting student of Ed De Leo, Vee commuted from Reading, *Pennsylvania, to Manhattan to train with him. They believed in our unique approach to this biography and encouraged us to continue when the odds seemed to be against us. When many publishers expressed interest in the book only if it was exclusively about Al Pacino, Mayro and Gentile kept us committed to telling the story through the eyes of Ed, one of Al Pacino's lifelong friends.*

FOREWORD

Success is a matter of consciousness. In almost every case, the person who succeeds believes he or she can and will succced. This book illustrates how to attain that consciousness and the work it takes to make that dream a concrete reality.

Most of us come into this life carrying a dream nestled deep within us, a calling that has meaning perhaps only to us. Only we can answer that call. Nobody else can pursue our goals for us. Like the old-time gospel hymn says:

You gotta walk that lonesome valley.
You gotta walk it by yourself.
Ain't no one can walk it for you.
You gotta walk it all alone.

Putting the blinders on, as Al Pacino did, and pursuing our dreams is the only way to achieve our goals. It's a matter of reaching for what most people would say was unattainable rather than settling for what appears to be easily attainable.

One of Al Pacino's favorite quotes is from a poem by Robert Browning: "... a man's reach should exceed his grasp; or what's a heaven for?"

We are living in a shortcut society. Most people fail by not only taking short cuts, but by seeking them out, rather than taking the high road and doing the personal work high goals require. Those who stay on the high road are the ones who arrive at their destination.

Once we start compromising and taking side roads, we lose sight of our purpose and find our lives and careers stuck in mires of confusion and regret. Those who stay on the high road develop confidence through the work they do. They cultivate authenticity and by doing so, remain unique. For the most part, they grow and prosper.

Unfortunately our everyday lives are often in conflict with our dreams. Mommy and Daddy are no longer around to support us while we attempt to manifest our dreams. We're on our own. We have to make choices. Sometimes those choices include poverty and rejection for the short term and that makes us extremely uncomfortable. So we choose an easier path because we fear the poverty and rejection.

We avoid taking risks because we worry about what will happen if we fail. We delay and procrastinate, hoping for a "lucky break" or a short cut, or a boost up the ladder by someone who's already climbed it. In other words, we seek the comfortable and the known.

Success is attained by living our dreams... living them every step of the way. A career is not a dream. It's what we do with the career that counts.

There are many artists, but few Rembrandts, many composers but few Mozarts. Why is this? What do the masters have what others lack? Is it simply talent? I don't think so. There are many talented people driving taxis and waiting on tables, waiting for that lucky break.

Al Pacino is the kind of actor who is willing to go all the way to the edge. He will do whatever he feels is necessary for the part he is playing.

In his private life, however, he has been known to be shy. Earlier in his career, he would arrive at a party, find a quiet corner and sit there the entire night. He would talk to anyone who approached him, but otherwise he would simply stare at the floor.

His dread of interviews, too, is well-known. He has come a long way, however. He is quite eloquent now and has a great sense of humor.

Mr. Pacino divides his energies between the stage and screen, as well as between acting, directing and producing. He has played an amazing variety of roles – television producer, football coach, mafia don, the devil, short order cook, hit men, junkies, war heroes, gamblers, kings, race-car drivers, undercover cops, and power-brokers.

No matter what role he plays, he is unique and always able to add pathos, power, humor and poetry to his characterizations. Critics have called his performances masterful, passionate, and spellbinding. I agree.

When I Knew Al illustrates, through the lives of two people, the meaning of success and its requirements. There are no lesson plans, no formulas. We simply follow these lives as one achieves and the other falters.

Patte Barham
Bestselling Author of *Marilyn: The Last Take* and
Rasputin: The Man Behind the Myth,
Hollywood journalist and talk show host

INTRODUCTION

It seems no matter what dreams some people have they continue to struggle. They can't get the work they want, their bills are mounting, their relationships are falling apart; or they've been acclaimed in their professions but can't seem to top it with a new project. It might be their personal lives are pure hell. Friends and relatives try to rescue them from drowning, but they resent the help.

Perhaps they enjoy swimming against the tide, against unfavorable circumstances. In a way, they expect and welcome the tidal waves. Staying afloat in spite of it all makes them feel like "survivors." It energizes them.

On the other hand there are people who start out in hostile environments with overwhelming odds stacked against them, and they succeed by swimming away from the muck. They know what they want, they make the right choices, and they achieve their inner goals.

The theme intrigued us. What happens when people with similar backgrounds start out together pursuing the same dream? Why will some become survivors and others achievers?

Two people, for example, can have the same dream. The same prediction of success is made for both of them. One dream comes true, because his course has been steady. His journey has been difficult, but his eyes have has remained on the target. The other has deviated from his goal, taken many turns, many side roads. His direction has been oblique.

The future, in our opinion, is not destiny, but something created every moment. Futures can be predicted, and the outcome will prove faithful to the prediction, if people are consistent with who and what they are at every moment. If they take their eyes off their goals, their futures will be altered and their dreams will either not come true or be delayed. For that reason, all of us have the ability at any moment to change the direction and thus the outcome of our lives.

Feeling sorry for oneself has a lethal effect on wellbeing and self-esteem. If people believe others owe them something, it is usually true they won't forget about it until the debt is settled. Resentment motivates and feeds their desire for a payoff.

Thinking of themselves as deserving constant repayment for a deed done years ago enables them to avoid the conflict and competition that results as one makes his own unique way up the ladder of success.

By harboring jealousy of another's success, a person defines himself as an outsider or a loser. When one person measures his success by another's, he has taken his eye off his own goal.

Envy and jealousy might be natural, but too much time spent indulging in those emotions is detrimental to one's success. Acknowledging another person's greatness is acknowledging one's own potential greatness.

It takes a large heart and a generous spirit to do that – and everyone can't find it in themselves to do it – but it is an affirmation of one's own power and ability to rise to his own unique greatness. By praising and acknowledging success, he is identifying with success, not failure. A climate for positive things to happen has been created in consciousness.

The old saying goes: Everybody loves a winner. People, out of self-protection, instinctively avoid losers.

We first met Ed De Leo in the late 1970s. We were in the process of assembling talent and financing for two motion pictures *Leviathan* and *The Concision*, for which we already had more than half of the financing in place, as well as commitments from actors Cliff Robertson and Maximilian Schell.

Ed had written the screenplay *The Playmaker* for him to star in, and he was seeking a producer. We were impressed when he told us he knew Al Pacino and had coached him in his early years.

Ed's script was appealing, but rough, and needed a major rewrite. He told us he had several investors who were not interested in backing his own project but who might be interested in our projects. We told him if his people liked our projects and agreed to contribute the balance of the financing, we would rewrite Ed's script and include it in a three-film package.

Ed's sources, unfortunately, turned out to be flakes — one was a cigar-chewing drugstore Mafioso, one an immigrant barber who carried around his life-savings in a shoebox, and the third, a tax-shelter scam artist working out of Germany.

At the time, Ed lived with his mother in a Bronx walk-up apartment, and did substitute teaching in a Bronx public school. Even though nothing worked out, Ed stayed in touch over the years.

He eventually moved to Hollywood and we became friends. His private life was hellish; he was getting very little work as an actor, and his relationship with Al Pacino was becoming strained, to say the least.

Listening to Ed and his tales started an idea brewing. What an interesting book could be written about Ed De Leo and Al Pacino, starting out together, one remaining an outsider, the other becoming a mainstream star.

Thus *When I Knew Al* was born. We would tell about the journey to stardom through the eyes of someone who hasn't made it, like Hamlet through the eyes of Rosencranz and Guildenstern.

We picked Ed's brain, listened to hours of tapes, read transcripts and did endless research.

When we submitted the completed book to the major publishing companies such as HarperCollins, Houghton Mifflin, Simon & Schuster, St. Martins Press and Alfred A. Knopf, their editors read it with interest and complimented us with words such as "unique," "well-written," "fascinating," "intriguing," "compelling," "of great interest," "forthright, and honest narrative style," and also "very tight."

None of them, however, was willing to take it on. A few advised us to work with a small publisher that could give the book the personal attention it deserved.

The first and only smaller publisher we went to was Harbor House, which, according to *Publishers Weekly*, is one of the top 15 small publishing companies in America. The publisher Randall Floyd loved the concept.

We tell the story as Ed De Leo told it to us, often changing subjects quickly from paragraph to paragraph. He loved the first draft of the book and kept hoping it would get published.

He continued to tell his story until his unfortunate death in June 2004.

David Sheldon and Joan McCall
Los Angeles, June 15, 2005

ACT I

"Man, unlike any other thing organic or inorganic
in the universe, grows beyond his work,
walks up the stairs of his concepts,
emerges ahead of his accomplishments."

— John Steinbeck
The Grapes of Wrath

WHEN I FIRST MET AL

I KNEW AL before he was the famous Al Pacino. His rise to stardom did not happen overnight. I know. We started out together and we paid our dues together. Although we have gone in different directions, we have remained friends over the years.

By the fall of 1958, I had been studying acting for two years with the renowned Viennese actor and teacher, Herbert Berghof. He operated a popular acting school in Manhattan. I was in the advanced class, but I also participated in his Scene Study Class with new students.

In one of the opening sessions, I watched a short, Italian-looking young man perform a scene from the Broadway play, Mr. Roberts. It was Al Pacino, age 18.

Good-looking, he had dark, penetrating eyes and a wiry build. Acting with him in the scene was a kid from Brooklyn, Joe LaBrese, also 18. They had both attended the High School of The Performing Arts for two years and dropped out. This class at Berghof's was for new students, as well as advanced students.

Mr. Roberts was a big Broadway hit, as well as a successful movie. Al and Joe looked good in the roles, but they were very green, too inexperienced to tackle such mature, complex characters. Al tackled Ensign Pulver, the role played by Jack Lemmon in the movie version. Joe La-Brese assaulted the Henry Fonda role.

After the scene was finished, Al sulked off to the back of the class. Berghof, as I anticipated, reprimanded both Al and Joe for attempting such a difficult scene. It had revealed their inexperience. He told them they weren't mature enough for such dramatic material. How could they be at 18? He advised Al to consider taking some basic technique classes.

"Vhy you people try to approach zuch a difficult scene the first time?" He said, "Go und take zum classes in Technique, and ven you're more mature, you tackle ziss kinds uff parts."

Al and Joe left very depressed. They didn't understand this was part of Berghof's modus operandi, to shake up the students so the next time they'd select material more close to type, something with which they could identify.

Berghof's style was to critique his students so harshly he had them crying and feeling bad, so they would then work harder on their next scenes.

I felt sorry for Al and Joe because of the severe criticism in front of the class. I sympathized, having experienced the same treatment when I first started with Berghof. I sensed Al and Joe felt emotionally beaten. It was a familiar feeling. I had been in Berghof's class for two years and had gotten my share of tongue-lashings.

That was my introduction to Al Pacino. While I was watching him, he reminded me of myself when I was 18. It was obvious to me he was very inhibited. In fact, he was so nervous, he was turning ghostly white in the scene. His acting partner, Joe, was the opposite. He had screamed his head off in the scene. Berghof called it "overacting," the other extreme.

It troubled me. If only somebody could take these aspiring actors and tell them what it's all about. Since I had been in the class such a long time, I knew how such criticism could shake up young guys like Al and Joe. I had the same feeling I had for a classmate in elementary school, Norman Jacoby.

These kids needed help; they were hurting.

Al had been as tense doing that scene as I had been when I first started. I thought if someone could calm him down and instill some confidence in him, something very interesting might develop.

After the class was over, I smiled at Al and introduced myself. Joe, too, shook my hand.

"Were we really that bad?" he asked.

"Oh, don't worry," I said to Al. "I've been sitting in this class for a couple of years. Herbert's bark is worse than his bite. I'll explain to you what he's trying to say."

Al's eyes lit up. He was warm and friendly, anxious to learn. "Thanks," he said.

We went across the street to Martin's Restaurant and Bar on 23rd Street and Sixth Avenue for corned beef. The guys had soft drinks and I had hot tea.

While we listened to Danny and the Juniors sing "Rock & Roll Is Here To Stay," we kept talking about acting, HB Studio, our backgrounds, our ambitions. We discussed our mutual addiction to acting, and how much fun it was to escape the so-called "real" world, and how we all aspired to achieve fame and fortune on the stage and in motion pictures.

When we heard Preston Epps do "Bongo Rock," Al started to tap rhythm on the table with his fingers, saying he had his own bongo drum at home.

I learned that Al, like myself, lived in the Bronx.

He suggested we ride home on the train together. It was a long, boring ride if you had nobody to talk to or nothing to read. Taking the subway home together meant we could continue discussing the class.

"Great," I said, and that's just what we did.

We rode back together that night and many nights after that. We became good friends. He told me about his family.

SONNY

AL'S FATHER, Salvatore Pacino, an insurance agent in East Harlem, married Rose Gerard, a 20-year-old, second generation Italian beauty, in 1939. It was the year of the New York World's Fair, Gone With The Wind, Wuthering Heights and Goodbye, Mr. Chips.

On April 25, 1940, Alfredo James Pacino was born.

Sal abandoned Rose and "Sonny" two years later. From then on, it was a struggle for Rose to raise her son. She was forced to leave Sonny with her parents, Kate and James Gerard, in their small apartment in the South Bronx while she looked for work. James, Sonny's grandfather, had immigrated to the Bronx from Corleone, Sicily. He had trained to be a carpenter but became a plasterer.

Being separated so early from his mother, as well as from his father, was an emotional jolt for Sonny, leaving him feeling abandoned. He would sit on the table all day long with his mother and father's pictures and talk to them, pretending they were talking to him. And Kate, his grandmother, would comment how cute that was.

"We were poor as hell," Al has said.

His mother had to work to make ends meet. His grandfather, in Al's eyes, was a great man, the greatest man who ever lived. He worshipped him. James was an emotional man with an incredible wit and a strong image to little

Sonny, the chief guiding force in his life.

Also packed in the three-room apartment were five aunts and uncles. Al described it as "a lousy back apartment in a scummy, bad neighborhood." Unable to afford a place of her own, Rose was forced to crowd in with her parents and her siblings.

Sonny was extremely shy. When he was about three years old, to get away from the crowd, his mother began taking him to the movies, night after night. The next day, all by himself, he would re-enact all the parts of the movies before a mirror.

Though his grandmother was there, she was usually off doing chores in another room of the apartment. "Sonny likes to talk to himself," she would say; but she assured herself, "He's doing OK."

Sonny lived a rather solitary existence those first seven years of his life. "I used to go steady with a broom," he later joked, "or maybe it was a mop."

Until he was 6 years old, Sonny was made to stay mostly indoors. It wasn't safe in the streets, Kate warned.

"They were afraid of what might happen."

He was overprotected, and as a result, Sonny was neither as "street smart" as the other neighborhood boys were, nor did he belong to the gangs.

Lack of interaction with his peers made him reticent. His inhibitions made him a reserved student in school, and unable to interact freely with other kids his age in the neighborhood. But Sonny developed a resolute character that wouldn't take no for an answer.

The other kids called him "Little Dude" because Kate habitually dressed him neatly in fresh clothes. His neatness further alienated him from the other kids who were invariably ragged and dirty from life in the streets.

Sonny feared getting beat up by the other, tougher

neighborhood boys. Even the girls were tough. Often, they overpowered him and battered him. Poor Sonny's survival tactic was to throw up or fall over before they beat him too severely. Later, he learned to lash back defensively, or distract them with wild stories.

He perfected a good imitation of Humphrey Bogart. "My Bogart kept me out of fights. Some of the kids thought maybe I really was that tough."

Acting was second nature. It was almost as if he were born in the theater — the theater being movies. He had Al Jolson down pat and when he was six years old he could do the whole scene from Lost Weekend in which Ray Milland tried to remember where he had hidden the bottle and tore up the house looking for it.

When Sonny would do Milland for the family, they would laugh, though he could never understand why. To 6-year-old Sonny, it was serious stuff.

One day a strange and subtle thing happened. He was playing a character from some movie he had just seen. He was all alone, as usual, and suddenly he stopped. "This is wrong," he said to himself. "I'm too good, nobody's this good!"

Sonny's first sexual experience was a startling encounter with a girl when he was around 9. The girl took off her blouse and showed him she had breasts. He thought she might have been older than him. He put his hands on her breasts and she giggled.

She was standing in front of a mattress spring when suddenly Sonny pushed her. She bounced off the spring and they repeated the moves three or four times. From this action, Sonny concluded he had been "laid." He hurried out and bought a pack of prophylactics.

"You used to carry them around in your wallet. You didn't know what they did, but ..."

Al started smoking cigarettes at 9. At 11, more sophisticated, he converted to smoking a pipe.

When he was 12, his friend, Bruce Cohen, slipped off some rocks at a construction site and Sonny, risking his own life, pulled him to safety, rescuing him.

The pair of young heroes were invited to appear on "Wheel of Fortune," a daytime television show on which good Samaritans, people who had done good deeds, appeared. Prizes were awarded according to the spinning of the wheel and the nature of the good deeds, and a bonus of $1,000 was awarded to whoever answered a special question asked by the host, Todd Russell. This was big money in 1952, especially for kids.

Al and Bruce won several thousand dollars in cash and prizes. This was Al's first experience with professional show business and was, in a sense, his first appearance in front of a camera.

Another friend, Cliffy, was precociously mature and bragged he knew all about sex. Cliffy looked like a cross between Richard Burton and Marlon Brando. He was a Jewish kid who wanted to be a Catholic, and one of the toughest guys Sonny ever knew.

He had unusual charisma, an aura that puzzled the other kids, as if he knew some secret. He was reading Dostoevsky at 14 and told Sonny how terrific this writer was, who wrote *Crime and Punishment* in the 1800s.

Cliffy had an active libido. One day, at the apartment, he tried to feel-up Rose, Sonny's mother. Sonny noticed and was shocked at Cliffy's bravado. Rose tactfully removed Cliffy's hands and laughed it off. She seemed to understand what was going on. Al thought Rose seemed almost flattered by his young friend's attempt at a pass.

Cliffy had criminal tendencies as well. One day, he hijacked a bus filled with passengers. Another time, he stole a garbage truck and parked it outside his tenement. One night, he kicked in a store window and gifted Sonny with a pair of shoes he took from the display.

School was too regimented for Sonny and he rebelled. He took to practical jokes, like knocking over books in the school library. As punishment, he was put into a class with emotionally disturbed kids. His aversion to studying resulted in his mother being repeatedly called to the school.

Sonny's shenanigans finally got him accepted into a gang. He tore his lip playing in a vacant lot with a toy gun. He ran into a barbed wire fence which snagged his lip. He howled with pain. Another escapade found him trying to walk on a wire. He slipped and straddled it. Again, he suffered great agony.

As a kid, Sonny's playground was up on the roof of the apartment building. There, he used to jump from roof to roof. There was a whole, unique world for him up on the roofs. It was quieter than down on the street. It was almost like a desert, very peaceful.

The roof was like a penthouse. His grandfather would come home from work, go up to the roof, read his paper, and he and Sonny would talk.

Al loved to hear his grandfather tell stories about what it was like in New York in East Harlem in the early 1900s. Al could make him talk more than anybody else could. James didn't think anybody else was interested.

Al's granddaddy would spin endless stories. Al would spend nights up there, with his grandfather running on and on. It was "like a grandfather and grandson on a fishing boat, but we were in the South Bronx, on a roof."

He'd talk about his immigration to the United States, how his mother came over first, what New York was like then. His mother died when he was four. He quit school and went to work at nine on a coal truck.

When he'd come home from work, Al would be playing in the lot waiting for him to come by. Al would ask him for a nickel. Grandpa would always "kvetch" about it, but he'd bend way down, as if he was going into his shoe and he would come up with this nickel.

Al wondered, "How did he finger the nickel?"

Al's grandfather was a hero to him as well as a provider. Work, any kind of work, was the joy of James' life. So Al grew up having a healthy relationship to work. Work was something he respected.

Every time Al came home, he would fall down on the floor as if he were dead. He got a kick out of making sensational entrances into the apartment.

Lonely, bright and bored, Sonny concocted a colorful and mysterious past to impress his classmates, and he entertained his grandparents by acting out all the roles from movies he'd seen.

Since Al was always telling stories and imitating scenes from movies at school, he frequently got cast in school plays. Those early years, Rose was proud of him and did what she could to nurture his talent. She began taking him to plays on Broadway.

Embarrassed by the name Pacino, Al decided his stage name would be Sonny Scott.

He ran away from home a few times to get attention. He also liked to play the piano and bang on bongo drums. During school breaks he worked for a fruit farm sorting red and green tomatoes. He loved playing baseball. He wanted to be a professional ballplayer, since it came so naturally to him, but he wasn't quite good enough. Disappointed, he didn't know what to do with his life.

He had a lot of energy bottled up, looking for an outlet. He was a fairly happy kid, even though he had problems in school. In the eighth grade, the drama teacher wrote his mother a letter saying she should encourage him in dramatics.

He learned to recite *The Rhyme of the Ancient Mariner*, and he would read from the Bible in the school auditorium.

He was in a play once and one of the other students said, "Hey, Marlon Brando — this guy acts like Marlon Brando."

That was the first time he had heard of Marlon Brando. He was supposed to get sick on stage and he actually got sick every time he performed the play. The realism might have made him come off like Brando.

By 12, he was sure of his future as an actor and the kids in the neighborhood called him "The Actor." He would sign autographs for them as Sonny Scott. He assured them the name would be famous.

In the beginning, his mother encouraged his interest in the theater. She herself had a theatrical flair and a love of the theater. It was due to his mother's influence that he never drifted the way of some of his friends. A couple of them later died from drugs. Rose Pacino was a well-read woman, but she had deep problems and was hypersensitive, leading her to years in analysis.

Al's took his first drink in a play, with his family watching. He slurped it up and started coaxing adults to buy liquor for him. It made him feel separate from other people, above them.

In junior high, he was voted "most likely to succeed," because of his acting.

One thing that inspired him to be an actor was seeing a Chekhov play, *The Sea Gull*, in the Bronx, when he was 14. A traveling troupe performed the play in a huge movie house. There were about 15 people in the audience. It was a stunning experience for Al, making a deep impression on him.

At J.H.S. 98, he was cast in several plays. The first production portrayed America as a melting pot.

"I was the melting pot from Italy. I had to stir myself with a spoon. I also played Jewish kids."

Al's scholastic level was not high, but acting kept him in school. Still, he was never as happy performing as he was playing baseball. If he made a catch at third base, he would do a double somersault and sprawl out on the ground. He was still acting — overacting.

"Instead of O.D.ing, I O.A.ed."

Al saw Marlon Brando perform in *On the Waterfront.* He thought, What a great actor! He stayed in the theater to see it again. He was riveted to his seat. He couldn't leave. He had never seen anything like it. Brando's performance boggled his mind, as did the play.

At P.S. 115, since he excelled only in dramatics, his teacher urged his mother to enroll him in the High School of The Performing Arts, a special public high school for students living in any of the five boroughs who were talented in art, music, or drama. No other school would accept him because of his poor scholastic record. He applied and was accepted.

Performing Arts taught the Stanislavski approach to acting. Al thought the whole deal about "the Method" and serious acting, having to "feel" it, was crazy.

In one of his classes, he had to act out being alone in his own room. Since he never had a room to himself, he had to make it up. His teacher told him his acting was "natural," but he didn't know what that meant.

Once, after he had improvised something at school, one of his drama teachers, an advocate of Stanislavski, told him, "You have the fire of the great Sicilian actors!"

She called Al's mother; but Rose, unexpectedly reversed her earlier support, and insisted acting was for rich people. Al, she said, should go out and get a job.

He continued to resist studying. His mother's condition had worsened, a nervous debility which analysis hadn't cured. Her health deteriorated rapidly, and Al, only 16, had to quit school at the end of his sophomore year to go to work. His earnings would be added to his grandfather's income to support the family.

Though he dropped out of school, he couldn't forget how "natural" the teacher had said his acting was. He went around all the time trying to be natural. He didn't yet know the difference between being natural and being real.

"What do I know from Stanislavski? He's Russian, I'm from the Bronx."

The one person he most related to was James Dean. He grew up, fed on the Dean mystique. Rebel Without A Cause had a very powerful effect on him. It really got him hooked on wanting to be an actor.

He worked as a messenger, an attendant in a rest home, a shoeshine boy, a supermarket checker, a mover of furniture, an office boy, a fruit picker, and a newsboy.

The longest job he held was office boy at Commentary magazine. It exposed him to what he called "highbrow" people. High-profile people, such as Norman Podhoretz and Susan Sontag in particular, found him proficient and pleasant. They even shot craps with him. For Al, the highlight of those days was getting smashed at their parties.

But Al soon became restless and resentful. He moved out of the apartment and in with a girl who lived elsewhere in the Bronx. He sent money home to the family when he could and enjoyed his new freedom. He made many friends once he was out on his own.

He couldn't wait to earn enough money to take professional acting classes. In an attempt to follow in Marlon Brando and James Dean's footsteps, he auditioned for the Actors Studio and passed the preliminary. But on his second try he was rejected.

Finally, at the age of 18, he decided to enroll at the Herbert Berghof Studio.

ME AND AL

AL WAS 5 feet 7 inches, but powerfully built. When he sat he appeared larger because of his broad shoulders and long face. He had a mop of thick black hair, piercing eyes that watched and absorbed, and a classic roman nose.

He always appeared to be in motion, even when he was still. He invariably wore a brooding expression, emulating classical actors like John Barrymore, Edmund Kean and John Gielgud. He felt it made him look vulnerable and sensitive.

He didn't let his lack of height deter him. Because he had done poorly in school and dropped out after two years of high school, he lacked education. This deficiency made him even more determined to learn his craft as an actor and motivated him to read more to make up for it.

He worried out loud to me that his height might negatively affect his acting career, but I reassured him.

"Look at Claude Rains," I said. "He was once told he should quit acting because of his height, but he went on to become a big star. So did Alan Ladd."

Though Al had natural talent, he had some bad habits. He had no insight about what he was doing.

From that first class, I took a personal interest in him. He had raw talent, but it needed to be channeled and cultivated through technique. I told him acting was not just saying the words. Confidence was what he needed most, and I suggested roles more suitable for him.

Berghof invariably made it more difficult for them than

he needed to. I decided to coach Al and Joe on the side, as I had done earlier with the ball players. I was confident I could have a good effect.

One day, Berghof asked me if I could coach Al on the side, as well as Joe. I agreed without hesitation. I was relieved, because I really didn't want to coach them behind Berghof's back. My goal was to make sure they were guided in the right direction to become fine actors. Especially Al. I could see the possibilities in him.

Since I'd been attending so many classes and had been giving so much private coaching, I itched to share this knowledge with them. Berghof didn't usually teach privately. It was too expensive for most students who were struggling even to pay for their tuition.

My imagination shifted into high gear. I thought of great scenes we could do together, such as Arthur Miller's Death of a Salesman. I would play Willy Loman and Joe and Al Willy's sons, Hap and Biff. Or I could play Biff with Al portraying his younger brother, Hap.

Al was a lot like James Dean. Both of them haunted Greenwich Village, both lived in the city. Both were driven to act.

Al and I continued classes with Berghof where our scenes were critiqued by him or the other teachers. Afterwards, we would ride home on the subway and analyze our performances. Often we would meet in the Bronx at a park to work on our scenes or he would come up to my apartment to talk about acting.

We met frequently at a school yard in his neighborhood, in another part of the Bronx. I had to take two buses to get there. I would critique his scenes and he would offer his opinion about mine. We were both learning.

I did a monologue from a short play, The Valiant, in one class. The character was a prisoner on death row.

Berghof directed me to use another actor to play to. Since I wanted Al to watch, I asked Joe to sit with me and be the priest who's listening to me.

When I finished the monologue, Berghof said, "You were very real, but the moment before the scene ended, you did a fake, theatrical gesture. I want five minutes of life."

Actually, the scene had been finished and I was only clowning around. I didn't argue.

Joe told me his family name was Calabrese, but he dropped the first two letters to use LaBrese as a stage name. I told him there was a Calabrese in my family. It turned out my cousin Grace was married to Joe's uncle, Mike.

I accompanied Al to the High School of The Performing Arts where he wanted to show me the kind of work they did. He had a couple of tickets to an all-girl production of *Twelve Angry Men.* They called it *Twelve Angry Women.* I would have called it *Twelve Disturbed Teenagers.*

Afterwards Al asked me, "What did you think of it?"

"There was one girl up there who was really alive. "She was a stand out." And I talked about why.

Al turned to eye me. "Boy, you know your stuff, don't you?"

"I hope so," I said. "I mean, that girl was living the role. The others were 'acting.'"

Natural ability may be something you're born with. I'm inclined to think a lot of it is inherited. When we see someone who has it, we call him a natural actor. Some people go through life not knowing they have this talent.

Al toiled to cover his expenses. Most of his jobs paid poorly. One of his stints was as a stock boy in a factory that made trimmings. He did things like packing boxes of drapes. It was heavy, back-breaking work.

Al audited several of my classes, one of which was

taught by Lee Grant. Her teaching impressed him. In one of the classes I performed a scene from Tennessee Williams' Summer and Smoke, playing the doctor.

Lee interrupted the scene and gave each of us secret directions. What she whispered into the ear of the actress playing the role of Alma, I don't know, but immediately into the scene, "Alma" shook me up by crying hysterically.

Emotionally shaken, I gave her prop pills. Al was watching intently. I was so jarred out of my "plans" that my lines emerged from me spontaneously and freshly. To tell the truth, I had forgotten them and reacted to the moment, saying whatever came to me.

After the class, Al complimented me.

"You know, Ed, you really have talent."

I was deeply touched. I told him, "If you want to learn what acting is all about, watch other actors."

In retrospect, I don't really know what it was I did in that scene. I do know I was beginning to learn to be myself and apply my improvisational techniques.

Al wanted to get more involved in improvisation. He later told me, "Improvisation really frees the actor."

Anthony Mannino, my improvisation teacher, broke away from the Berghof Studio and started his own school on 20th Street and Fifth Avenue. Since I had been profiting greatly from his classes, I decided to continue studying with him. Al accompanied me several times, sitting in on some of Mannino's classes as an observer.

Al and I searched the library shelves and the play catalogs at Samuel French and the Drama Book Shop to find two- and three-character scenes to do together. We also did monologues using each other to talk to on stage for eye contact and someone to react to.

Herbert Berghof really laid into Al after one of his scenes. Always very perceptive, he was attempting to break the protective shell Al wore. Prodded beyond endurance, Al snarled at him, which is exactly the reaction Berghof wanted. Al's face flushed and he became deeply agitated. It was a beautiful, "real" moment for him.

Later I said to Al, "So that's what Berghof's trying to get from you. Some real emotions, not..."

Al interrupted with, "I can get angry on my own!"

"Sure, but it was so real. You'd have such emotional power if you'd just loosen up, let go ..."

"Let go? Is that all there is to it? Just let go?"

"That's a big part of it," I said. "The real emotion wasn't in the scene. It was there when you got angry, defending the scene. You see, what they taught you at Performing Arts was helpful at the time, but now you need to go deeper."

"What do you mean?"

"When you were defending the scene, you gave Berghof exactly what he wanted to see in the scene," I said. "That's what acting's about. Breaking down 'the wall.' Most actors try to hold onto lines and squeeze the life out of them, but emotion is not with the lines, but within you, what you bring besides the lines. You'd be great if you just let go and let loose during your scenes."

By breaking down the wall, I meant the imaginary wall between the actors and the audience. A good actor ignores that wall and creates reality by living moment to moment up there in the scene.

Al said, "I guess I have a lot of work to do."

"If you want, I'll let you know when you're being honest in a scene or when you're not."

Berghof's criticism and our talk marked a major breakthrough for Al. We continued to grow as actors.

I found a three-character play, Crime in the Streets, by Reginald Rose, which proved to be an excellent "vehicle" for Al, Joe and myself. After class one day, Joe suggested we all chip in and rent a room at the Chelsea Hotel to rehearse it.

The play concerned three hoodlums. I played Lou, a dumb bully, a physical guy. Al chose the role of Baby, the younger guy, an innocent kid growing up in a bad neighborhood who was forced to join the gang. Joe took the role of Frankie, the leader of the gang.

In one scene, the three of us were on a roof top with a lot of conflict going on between us. Joe, as Frankie, was a sick kid, pathological. He couldn't stand to be touched. He'd been abused as a child. He would go berserk if anyone even touched him.

The scene called for me to touch Frankie by mistake, and Frankie to go bananas. We started wrestling. Baby (Al) grabbed my arm to try to break up the fight. I stopped, but Frankie (Joe) panicked thinking Baby and Lou were teaming up against him.

It was a highly dramatic scene. It became utterly real to us. To prepare, we discussed street crime in character, relating it to what was going on with us personally.

We performed the scene at the Studio on 23rd Street. Berghof began his critique by saying we had totally captured the rooftop atmosphere. We had immersed ourselves in the characters. He was pleased.

"You guys have been practicing this scene, I can tell."

I replied, "Yeah, we went over to the studio and rehearsed it quite a few times."

We did this same sort of thing in other classes. We'd rent our own space and rehearse.

During the rooftop scene, Al had been very real, but Joe was still "acting." I realized that Al was beginning to break out, to find his freedom. He could relate to the problems of his character and to others in the scene. Berghof praised all three of us.

Al came up to my apartment on Valentine Avenue at 183rd Street. My mother took one look at skinny Al and said to my sister, Joan, who was still living at home, "I'll make him a nice Italian meal."

She made spaghetti and meatballs, which turned out not to be one of Al's favorite dishes. Cissy Connors a friend of Joan's, lived in the apartment next door. We introduced her to Al and invited her to join us, but she took one look at his dark, intimidating features and declined. I'll bet she regrets it to this day.

Al once said, "I appreciate the time you're taking with me, Ed. You're like a father to me."

Slightly insulted, I said, "I'm only nine years older than you, Al. I'll be a big brother, but, please, not a father."

Al didn't have brothers or sisters, nor had he had a real father since he was two years old. So, in a way, we were like father and son. He looked to me for direction and I enjoyed guiding him.

As a child, I seemed to need a title or designation. In school, the teachers would invariably appoint me as the class monitor. So once again, I found myself forced into the role of "monitor."

Father image, big-brother image, what did it matter?

"Let's just be friends," I suggested.

It seemed to suit Al. He opened up about his family soon after, confiding his father had moved to California, taken up with another woman and married her.

Al met the woman and her family, but felt very uncomfortable with them at first. He deeply resented his father for his betrayal, for leaving his mother virtually destitute, and forcing her to live with her parents in the Bronx. His mother was very ill now and constantly in pain, always taking pills for relief.

Success as an actor was destined for Al Pacino. He longed for it with all his heart. If a person wants something badly enough, they focus on it and take steps to make it happen, wearing blinders to everything else. That's what Al did.

I sensed Al could be great, with the right teachers and good direction. I was already a teacher, teaching in private schools, and I had an empathetic awareness of young people's needs. I thought I might be able to mold Al; at least to guide and encourage him.

I was reading a lot of psychology and success books such as Napoleon Hill's *Law of Success*. I shared the ideas with Al. Napoleon Hill asserts there's no hope for success unless a person decides on and aims for a definite goal.

I told Al, "If you really go after your objective, you can get it."

After every scene together at the Berghof Studio, we would analyze our own work. I offered Al suggestions and he was always eagerly receptive. He began to rely on me and my opinions, seemingly appreciating my ideas.

Joe LaBrese, too, had a lot of raw potential and, as with Al, I treated him like a kid brother. Actors who are friends and work together quickly become like a family. Joe lived in Brooklyn, but we always found a mutually convenient place to get together to rehearse scenes.

The long subway ride was always an opportunity for Al and me to talk.

THE SAME ROOTS

MY FATHER was a mailman, born Louis De Leo, on January 1, 1900, in New York City. His parents came from Salerno, immigrating to the U.S. a few years earlier.

Finding jobs to put food on the table was not easy, so Pa had to go to work as a boot black at the age of 12. He didn't graduate high school, but he learned a lot from reading books, magazines and newspapers.

He enlisted in the Navy during World War I and became a boxer. Legend has it he hurt some people so bad he had to quit. He had a killer punch.

My mother, Matilda Leone, was born December 14, 1901. Like dad, she was a native of New York City. Her mother was born in Naples, Italy, and her father was from Salerno. They immigrated to the United States before the turn of the century and met in New York City where Grandpa worked as a longshoreman. Both of them died before I was born.

To support herself, my mom was forced to quit high school and go to work alongside her sisters in a candy factory. They rolled candy and sealed it in wrappers.

My mother and father met in New York and married in 1926. My sister, Gloria, was born in 1927, the year Pa went to work for the U.S. Postal Service as a mail carrier.

I was born four years later October 16, 1931. We lived on 138th Street and Willis Avenue in the Bronx. We moved to Brooklyn for a year or two so my father wouldn't have to commute to work, and we moved back to the Bronx when he was transferred. The apartment was at 2060 Grand Concourse, at 180th Street.

My mother was a kind, gentle person. Everyone called her Tillie. She did housework with enthusiasm, singing while she worked. She enjoyed entertaining at home. She had a great sense of humor and a voice good enough to allow her to sing professionally. Her sisters, Lizzie, Lucy, Dolly, and Annie, told me Mom had star quality. They begged her to go on the stage.

"Tillie has talent," they would say. "She's a natural." There was even a man who wanted to finance her career. She was tempted, but taking care of her family was more important. Her children meant more to her than a career.

I loved to hear her sing "Poor Little Beggar Boy," which she sang to me frequently.

I'm a poor little beggar boy.
My mother, she is dead.
My father, he's a drunkard,
And won't give me a piece of bread.
I sit by the window,
And hear the organ play;
It sounds so like my mother;
But she's far, far away.

I would cry after I heard it. "Ma, why are you singing such a sad song?"

"Oh, you'll know," she would say. "One day you'll know why I'm singing it."

I guess she was trying to prepare me for what was ahead.

My mother always stood out in a crowd. A friend of mine said, "Boy, when your mom is with those aunts of yours, she's the one everyone notices. You don't wanna look at anybody else but her."

"What're you talking about?" I replied. "Of all the sisters, she's not the prettiest one."

"No, but she has something extra. Look at her. She radiates a quality of some kind. Like she's lit up inside."

I studied her as if I'd never seen her before and I saw what he meant. Ma did radiate some kind of energy and light towards which everyone gravitated.

Both of my parents were caring people. They had arguments, but they were mainly about money. There was never enough. But my father was ever hopeful.

He believed in the power of positive thinking and was a fan of Norman Vincent Peale. He listened to him on the radio. He would also bring home pamphlets from church with messages about giving and helping others. He always gave to the poor.

"What you give comes back double," he'd say.

I was circumcised at the age of four. The operation was performed at my uncle Nick's house, around 102nd Street off Madison where he had a delicatessen. Uncle Nicky was called "Curly."

When I was under the ether, a voice in my mind said, "You're not going to go to sleep. You're going to remember this and hear me throughout your life. Years from now, you will remember this incident."

I had never heard a disembodied voice, separate from my own thoughts. I didn't know what to make of it. I stayed awake in spite of the ether, though I didn't feel anything. The operation itself was nothing. My concern was this voice. I asked my mother if she heard it. She smiled and told me I was probably just dreaming.

This was the early 1930s and the country was deep in a depression. The streets teemed with beggars and panhandlers, and people stood in line at soup kitchens. Most people were struggling to make a living, but my father had the good fortune to be working for the U.S. Post Office and earned a steady salary. He was able even to move the family to a nicer apartment on Valentine Avenue, a three-bedroom walk-up on the fifth floor.

In 1937, I started elementary school, P.S. 115, Bronx. In first grade, I appeared in my first play, Hansel and Gretel. I played a woodsman, who had one line.

When I heard my cue, I raised my arms to speak, and my costume ripped apart. I was totally unaware of what had occurred, and exulted when the audience howled and applauded loudly. I puffed up with pride that I had made them do that. That day I decided to be an actor.

I started going to movies. I couldn't get enough of them after seeing *Three Comrades*, starring Margaret Sullavan, Robert Young, Robert Taylor and Franchot Tone. That movie made a big impression on me.

It was about three men who were in love with the same young woman dying of tuberculosis. It took place in the 1920s in Germany and hinted at the Nazi threat. I was too young to know who Hitler was and what it all meant.

My sister, Gloria, took me to another movie, *Under Twenty-One*, that had a profound effect on me. It was about two sisters down on their luck. One of them, who was under 21, was played by Mary Anderson. One sister let the other sister eat the only donut. It was about love and sacrifice, and it touched me deeply.

In 1939, the movie everyone was talking about was *Gone With the Wind*. It was touted as the biggest blockbuster in the history of the motion picture industry.

I was crazy to see it. Clark Gable was starring! He was

one of my idols, and I wanted to be just like him. The English actress, Vivien Leigh, was playing Scarlett O'Hara. She looked so beautiful in the newspaper ads. But my mother wouldn't let me go because the movie was over three-and-a-half hours long.

I was eight years old, in the third grade at P.S. 106, when Mrs. Sullivan asked me to read my composition. I had written about seeing someone getting murdered. A woman screamed, "Somebody's trying to kill me!" Then when I opened the back door and looked out, I saw it was a movie set and a film was being shot.

Mrs. Sullivan said I had a lot of imagination.

That fall, 1939, my parents took Gloria and me to the New York World's Fair in Flushing Meadows. My father believed in developing a child's imagination. We went by subway. My imagination worked overtime when I viewed the automobile show, which demonstrated how highways of the future would be double-deckers.

The exhibit showed a vast landscape in miniature with expressways full of futuristic cars. My father explained a future like that would come from intelligent people fulfilling their goals.

He said, "Whatever you want to do in life, never quit. Life is education. Education is Life."

Pa, along with his brothers, Jimmy and Nick, opened a boot black stall and barber shop at 711 Fifth Avenue in Manhattan. He continued working for the Postal Service and worked the concession between shifts.

In 1940, nine years after I was born, my mother gave birth to my sister, Joan. I was allowed to pick her name, first narrowing it down to Joan, Jean or Helen.

Suddenly I was no longer the baby, but the middle child. All "middle children" get confused, I was later told. This was to prove all too true in later years. Being neither the youngest nor the oldest makes the middle child play an ambiguous role in the family.

Several years in a row, my sister, Gloria, was voted the most beautiful girl in her class. She had long, black hair and always managed to be well-dressed, even on a tight budget. Guys would come up to me and tell me how beautiful she was. She was so good, never tardy, on the honor role, never absent from class, and willingly helped out at home.

War broke out in 1941 when Pearl Harbor was bombed. We heard it on the radio on Sunday, December 7. It scared us that another country would want to attack the United States. My father was 41 and very concerned he might be recalled. Luckily the combination of his age and the size of his family exempted him.

My exposure to the war was limited to newsreels in the theaters when I went to the movies. Hollywood was turning out propaganda movies for the war effort. I saw films like Wake Island with Brian Donlevy, and God Is My Co-Pilot with Dennis Morgan. They kept me abreast of who the good guys were and who the bad guys were.

Churchill was good; Hitler was bad. I was never sure about Stalin.

I was so troubled by the killing in the movies and so anguished at seeing people lose their loved ones, I couldn't sleep afterwards; so I switched to comedies and musicals. I could escape by watching Joan Crawford, Ginger Rogers, and Judy Garland. I begged to take lessons so I could sing and dance like Fred Astaire or Gene Kelly.

Every day we read about our favorite male movie stars joining the military. James Stewart joined the U.S. Army Air Force, Robert Montgomery the U.S. Navy, and Tyrone Power went off to the U.S. Marines. Others like Bob Hope, Paulette Goddard and Al Jolson supported the war effort by entertaining the troops overseas.

Wartime was rough on everyone. Food was rationed, no one sold anything that contained rubber or metal, which was allocated to the military to build tanks and planes.

Children saved pennies from our allowances to buy war stamps. If you had enough war stamps you could trade them in for government bonds. My father bought war bonds for me and my sisters, with the promise they would be worth $25 each in 10 years.

Father was a stamp collector. He had a large coffee table size book of stamps from all over the world. He had been collecting them since he was a kid. Each stamp had a history and he loved telling us about each one.

I was bored. Stamps didn't appeal to me. I was obsessed with one thing: acting. I tried out for and acted in every school play I could, and I loved it. I became more sure all the time that acting was what I wanted to do professionally.

I heard a voice in my head again when I was 10. I was at my cousin's wedding reception and my uncle Jimmy asked me what I wanted to be when I grew up.

My own voice said to me, "Say you want to be a writer. It will impress everybody."

My father, who was standing next to me, eating cannolli, turned to look at me. The little voice contradicted my own voice, saying, "Don't just say writer, say writer and actor."

So I said, "I want to be an actor — and a writer."

My father beamed. "An actor is a very difficult career to pursue, for many reasons. But writing? That's possible."

I was relieved I had gone on record. He continued, "It's a tough world out there, Ed. Make sure you get an education before you do anything else. Without a good job, life can be cruel."

But acting was what I really had my heart set on. I confessed to him.

"Well, whatever you do, I want you to finish high school and college. And then you'll have my blessing." He already had my future planned.

When I was 12, my father began taking me to basketball games at Madison Square Garden in Manhattan and to baseball games at Ebbetts Field in Brooklyn. He once took me to the Polo Grounds, to a New York Giants game. Before the game, a major movie star, Carol Landis, made an appearance to promote war bonds. Her enthusiastic speech earned her an ovation. Her beauty and that speech started me going to the "war movies."

When I was 13, I started seventh grade at Creston Junior High School. By then I was a healthy, extroverted kid who had been voted president of the class and chosen as captain of the basketball team.

In a school musical, I was cast in a small speaking part as The Sandman. I wore an outrageous costume that looked like a large body diaper. Suddenly, one of the kids went up on his lines. I covered for him by grabbing an alarm clock, winding it quickly, and making it ring.

I shouted to the others actors on stage, "It's time to go to bed!" The lights dimmed and the curtain came down. My teacher told me I had saved the play. Boy, was I proud!

My father had a natural musical talent. He played the piano and accordion nicely by ear. His favorite songs were "Anchors Away," "Come Back To Sorrento," and "By Mir Bis Du Shoen." He also was fond of Gene Autry songs, such as "I'm Back in the Saddle Again."

I asked to take piano lessons so I could read music and play any song I wanted to. I learned quickly and began writing my own songs.

I went to see the movie, *Abbott & Costello in Hollywood*, an adventure that took place mostly in a movie studio and ended with a wild roller coaster ride. But I didn't like slapstick like the other kids did. I thought it was pretty silly.

What I did like, and do seriously, was to flirt with the girls. They called me "Casanova," though I didn't know what the term meant. "Romeo," or "Lover Boy," I could have understood.

My first girlfriend was Robin Corelli, whom I used to sneak and meet after school. Next came Jean Salinger who was as nutty for the movies as I was. All of our "dates" were spent in the dark of the theater. My father found out and warned me to give them up and concentrate on my school work.

One of my friends, Walter Eisenberg, introduced me to his girlfriend, Elaine, who'd had a nose job which had transformed her from a gawky girl to a beauty. Walter and Elaine introduced me to a lot of girls.

One of them was Muriel Samek, a redhead. I sneaked over to her apartment when nobody was home. Hot to trot, we shucked our clothes, dove onto the bed and started making out, hugging and kissing; but the voice in my head startled me by saying, "No!"

I hustled myself out of there and she never spoke to me again.

One day, my teachers announced there would be a competition among the students to write a school song. I volunteered enthusiastically. I wrote one in a week's time and played it for Miss Gray, the music teacher.

"It's very nice," she said, "but we need something that's more of a march. Your song is too romantic."

I didn't win.

I was learning to reverse negative conditions. It was a game for me, because of my father's teachings. When people said something or someone was terrible, I reversed the idea and tried to do something to change it.

One of my teachers, Dr. Leonard, once introduced me

to a poor, special education-type child.

"Ed," he said, "this is Norman Jacoby. I want you to help him."

"I will," I replied, without batting an eyelash.

It was a natural task for me. Norman was a bit overweight and had a speech problem. His Russian immigrant parents had instilled a lot of fear in him. He was scared of everything. In contrast, I was fearless, Mr. Personality, an all-American boy.

I accepted the challenge and took him under my wing. I became Norman's protector and mentor, making sure none of the other kids picked on him. I encouraged him and coached him academically. He really blossomed and did well, making me proud.

Helping the underdog was as enjoyable to me as basketball. I was always sympathetic to other people's feelings and could empathize with them.

Always short of cash, I collected soda bottles and turned them in to earn money for the movies. I think theater admission for a minor was about 12 cents at that time. I savored double-features like *The Pride of the Yankees* on the bill with *Citizen Kane*, or *Yankee Doodle Dandy* showing with *Sergeant York*.

My mother would sigh, "That boy lives in the movies."

But she never worried. Asked where I was, she'd say, "Oh, he's either at the movies or playing basketball."

When I came home, I'd act out one of the characters from whichever movie I had seen, and recreate my own fantasy world. I'd imitate James Cagney, and tap-dance to You're a Grand Old Flag, the musical accompaniment only in my head.

My mother loved the radio and listened faithfully to *One Man's Family*, *Stella Dallas*, and *Young Doctor Malone*. Her favorite character was Reggie on *I Love a Mystery*.

My father routinely encountered many Hollywood and Broadway stars at his concession and often brought home autographed pictures of actresses like Joan Bennett. We were all star-struck.

My cousin Tony De Leon, whose father was my Uncle Jimmy, was an avid fan of Marie Wilson. He told me she was performing with Don Red Barry, who was a favorite of mine. We went together to see them perform.

Uncle Jimmy had added an "n" to the end of De Leo because of discrimination against Italians.

My sister, Gloria, dated Charley Guttermyer, a blonde guy with blue eyes, who was a cousin of a next-door neighbor. She met him while he was home on leave from the Navy. It could have turned into something, but when she discovered he drank heavily, she broke it off.

Deep into adolescence, I was mad about girls but feared getting one pregnant. I didn't want to wreck my life, so I stayed celibate as long as I could. However, I had my eye on an attractive girl in my class, Teddy. I was strongly attracted to her, but she was also a good friend. I was reluctant to try anything with her.

It really confused and frustrated me, battling the urge to bed every girl I was attracted to. I was envious of other guys going out with girls while I was sublimating my urges by playing basketball and acting. I wanted a career, but it was hard to keep focused with all those nubile girls flirting with me. I was weakening fast.

My mother was full of dire warnings to stay away from them. It only made me want them more. I resented her caution and felt she was trying to suppress me emotionally. It was a very troubling period for me.

Walter, my friend, was seeing a therapist, a Dr. Berger. I asked my parents to let me see him, too, and they agreed.

It was a total waste of time. After a few sessions he told me the best cure for my frustration was intense study and cold showers.

I learned the war was over when I heard shouting in the streets. People were laughing, crying and hugging each other. Total strangers seemed to bond instantly. Hitler was dead and "the boys were coming home." My whole family watched the parade on Fifth Avenue. We sat on the ledge of my father's shop on the second floor of the building at 711 Fifth Avenue. It was a great view.

The streets were full of streamers and flags. Soldiers, sailors and marines were marching. Drum and bugle corps were blasting away and twirling batons. War heroes were sitting up in the backs of convertibles. My whole family sang along when one of the bands played "When Johnny Comes Marching Home."

During the fall of 1946, I matriculated to St. Simon High School on an athletic scholarship from Creston. I tried out for the basketball team and made the first string.

I went to see Lee Grant, Chester Morris and Joseph Wiseman in *Detective Story*, a play by Sidney Kingsley. They were performing it at the Windsor Theater on Fordham Road. Lee Grant played a shoplifter.

The movie was made in 1951 with Kirk Douglas and Eleanor Parker in the leads, but Lee Grant and Joseph Wiseman repeated their stage roles. Lee Grant got nominated for an Academy Award. I saw a classic, old school actor, Francis Lederer, play there, too.

I met vivacious, 15-year-old, Nancy Saragetti, in an ice cream parlor. We were both ripe and ready. By the time we finished our ice-cream cones, we had only one thing on our minds. She invited me to her house, telling me her parents were out for the evening. I didn't know her last name and we were making out like jack rabbits.

My mother was very selective about the girls in my life. "You don't want an Irish girl. They all drink," or "Stay away from that one because she's... whatever." She always had a reason and it made me angry.

"Who am I ever gonna get who'll please you, Ma?"

She had no answer.

When I was 16, I went to see the movie, *Good News*, a musical written by Betty Comden and Adolph Green. It starred Peter Lawford and June Alyson. It bowled me over and I sat through it twice. I knew the song "Pass That Peace Pipe" backward and forward.

My father knew of my continued inclination toward dramatics, but he cautioned that the life of a teacher would be wiser for me.

"I see you shaping a lot of young minds. Did you ever think of teaching?"

I said, "Sometimes."

But I thought of acting more. In truth, I was a natura teacher from my earliest years and had enjoyed it. But it seemed dull and tame beside acting.

I excelled at athletics and was an expert basketball player. I won the All City award and got a write-up in the *New York World Telegram*, a popular daily newspaper at the time.

The kids at school called me "Eddie." I hated it. So I made up different names. Czar Modak. I liked names with K in it. My cousin, Tony, suggested Kurt Klondike.

Tommy Jordan, a popular kid in the neighborhood, was studying to be an actor at the American Academy of Dramatic Arts. He informed me that Spencer Tracy, who was one of my favorite actors, had studied there. He encouraged me to enroll, but I knew my family could never afford the tuition, and I certainly couldn't.

"That's OK," Tommy said. "They take older people.

You can go there later in life, like after college."

There was a 24-year-old guy, Joe Green, who hung out with our gang. He was 6 feet 6 inches and could run and fight like a pro. He came from a religious family. His brother was a priest, his sister a nun. He was a great athlete. Kids would pepper him with questions, like, "Is there anyone in the neighborhood you're afraid of?"

There were 12 kids standing around listening.

He said, "There's only one: Ed De Leo. He's quiet, but I'm afraid if he got angry, he'd kill me."

My cousin Tony was there and told me about it later. Joe took to betting. Later he became a fixer, got in trouble with the law, and did time.

I graduated high school with honors in June, 1949, at the age of 17. At the commencement party, when I spoke about my dreams and ambitions, a friend remarked I was a complicated person.

Another friend, Tommy Levy, said , "Ed's a simple guy with complex thoughts."

At the time, both remarks confused me. They do no longer.

In the fall, I turned 18. While I enjoyed playing basketball, I still wanted to become an actor. I decided to work for a year before deciding on a college.

My father, through a contact, got me a job in the mail room at WMGM radio. The station was headquartered at 711 Fifth Avenue, where my father had his shoe and barber concession.

It couldn't have been a better place to work. I'd duck out of work to watch radio plays in rehearsal, then in performance on the air. I could get seats to any broadcast or performance I chose. Famous stars were doing radio shows there. I was awed by them and wanted to emulate them in life and work.

I met young Alan Alda when his father, Robert Alda, was performing a radio play with Arlene Dahl, Brian Donlevy and Lex Barker.

I said to him, "It's amazing how well they can act."

Alan replied, "There's nothing to it. All they do is read the lines."

That didn't sound too hard to me.

My father got us tickets to see *South Pacific* with Mary Martin and Ezio Pinza, at the Majestic Theater. Juanita Hall was a knockout as Bloody Mary. We were amused there was an actor listed in the Playbill whose last name was De Leon.

South Pacific was staged by Joshua Logan and the sets were designed by Jo Mielziner. I had never seen Jo spelled that way before. I didn't know whether it was a man or a woman.

How these names stuck with me. I soon became a walking encyclopedia of theater trivia. I even knew the names of the stage managers. After the show, and for weeks to come, I drove my parents to distraction singing "Some Enchanted Evening" like Pinza.

My sister, Gloria, got married in 1953 to Ben Sarnicola and moved to California. She later had twin boys and two girls.

I was 19 and at my peak, I thought. Even though I felt like a stud, I was still shy. Eddie and Joey fixed me up with Joey's sister. She was short and wore glasses, but she had a great body.

We had a date at a rooming house. This time, I was the one who wanted to go all the way. I did it and it was OK, but no bells started to ring. I wanted sex, but with the right girl, someone I cared about.

I applied to several colleges and used my high school basketball record to try to get a scholarship. I won a scholarship to Iona College, in New Rochelle, but their basketball team wasn't good enough, so I didn't take it.

I also won a scholarship to Columbia University, but I was intimidated by their academic standards. I turned down St. Johns in Brooklyn because I didn't want to ride the subway. Finally, I decided to go to Long Island University where I received a basketball scholarship.

I attended Long Island University through June 1951, but left after the first year when a basketball scandal was exposed. It involved the seniors and, since I was on the freshman team, it didn't affect me.

I decided to change colleges because, although I knew basketball was going to be part of my life, I now was certain I wanted an acting career.

Even though I knew this very early in life, I had kept suppressing it as an impossible dream because of my parents' discouragement. I decided to work for a while and save some money so I would have a degree of freedom as I continued my studies.

I took a job ushering at Loew's Paradise Theater on Grand Concourse and Fordham Road. I saw many, many movies, like *All The Kings Men* with Broderick Crawford; *Twelve O'clock High* with Dean Jagger, and *The Adventures of Don Juan* with Errol Flynn.

And there were movies with Gail Russell, Brian Donlevy, Veronica Lake, Alan Ladd, Arlene Dahl. I fell in love with Hedy Lamar and saw her in everything she did. I watched *On the Town* with Gene Kelly and Frank Sinatra 25 times.

I went home and imitated the actors. I did a great Billy Eckstein. I would sing "Bring Back the Thrill" and "Cottage For Sale."

I worried about my appearance. I had always had a bump on my nose which made me self-conscious. I thought it might hurt me as an actor, so I decided to do something about it. I had my nose "fixed" in a hospital at 126th Street in Manhattan.

While my nose was still swollen from the operation, my uncle Jimmy drove me out to Islip, Long Island to visit my cousin, Sonny, who'd had a nervous breakdown and was confined to an institution. He cracked up when a girl rejected him. I couldn't understand it. To my way of thinking, there were hundreds of girls all over the place. Why go to pieces over losing one? He had been high school valedictorian, but he envied me because I was a top athlete.

As I walked down the halls of the sanitarium, I heard people screaming in the rooms. The walls and floors reeked with disinfectant and urine. I felt like I was in the movie, *The Snake Pit.* I half-expected to see Olivia de Havilland come running down the hall with several tortured souls chasing her, tearing at her dress.

Finally, I decided to go to Iona College, which I had already turned down. I was worried they might not take me on the second application, so I called Marty Glickman, the famous sports announcer who had written about me, and asked if he would recommend me.

He eagerly complied and, due to him, I was able to resurrect my original application and they awarded me a four-year scholarship. I was given the choice of starting over as a freshman, or waiting a year. They wanted me on the freshman team, so I transferred and started over. A little extra education couldn't hurt.

I entered Iona in the fall of 1952. Right away, a conflict flared up between me and the coach, Jim McDermott. He looked like Humphrey Bogart did in *The Caine Mutiny Court Martial.*

He liked the way I played ball, but didn't like me personally. He had heard about a song I had written called

"How It Feels to Be Blue" and how popular it made me with the other students. The possibility the song could make me famous may have made him jealous.

He told me, "I don't want you to have a name, I want the school to have the name."

When we played against Connecticut University, he didn't start me. When he finally put me into the game, we won. Marty Glickman, the sportscaster, who had recommended me, got annoyed with McDermott. An all-out battle started between me and McDermott, so I started to spend more of my time at the movies. I also spent my free time writing songs. I sent one of them to the Arthur Godfrey show and it won an award.

In the meantime, my father and Uncle Nick's concession at 711 Fifth Avenue was doing well. They gave haircuts and shined shoes for some pretty famous people. The concession was across from the posh St. Regis Hotel. People from the hotel stopped by.

Pa continued working as a letter carrier by day. He told Joel Herron, the famous songwriter and an WMGM orchestra leader, who wrote such hits as "I'm a Fool to Want You," about my songs. When my father gave Joel one of my songs, he played it and loved it. He arranged a meeting to hear my other songs.

Joel lived in a beautiful apartment on Central Park West. It was immense. He sat down at the piano and started to play my songs. He particularly liked "How It Feels to Be Blue." At his suggestion, I sent it to Richard Hayden who wrote the hit song, "Ruby."

Hayden was the artists' representative at Mercury Records and was most complimentary after he listened to my song. I also showed it to Ernie Maresca, the writer of "Runaround Sue" and many Dion hits. Maresca told me I needed a special artist for this song.

With my permission, he sent it to a few recording artists, including Jimmy Dean, but nobody grabbed it. Joel suggested I change the name to "How I feel About You," which I did, but still, nobody bought it.

Joel took my song, "The Girl With the Raven Hair," and had it published with his name on it as co-writer. He played it on the George Skinner Show. It was exciting seeing my song performed on television, but I didn't receive any money for it.

My father gave me a copy of Norman Vincent Peale's The Power of Positive Thinking and said, "If you want to get ahead in life, you've got to think positively. Being negative gets you nowhere. Always look for the good in people. Never let anything get you down."

"Yes, Pa," I agreed. I wanted to be an actor and I wouldn't let anything discourage me.

My junior and senior years in college, I studied with a private voice coach, Elsie French. From her, I took elocution and drama lessons twice a week. To pay for it, I part-timed at a liquor store, making deliveries to people in the neighborhood.

The voice in my head told me Denver would become an important part of my life. I had no feelings for Denver and certainly no desire to live so far away from show business. Many years later, my son, Dale, went to work in a ski store and settled down in Denver.

Toward the end of my senior year, I was having trouble passing my French course. An administrator, Lloyd Smith, and some of the faculty were celebrating the end of classes in the cafeteria. I had a beer. The administrator went to his car.

The voice in my head told me "Go talk to him, tell him your problems. He'll help you."

So I followed him out and asked him if I could talk to him. Smith was very kind and stopped to listen to me. As we stepped away from the crowd, I said, "I'm having a lot of trouble with French. There's a big test coming up and I don't know what to do."

He asked, "What can I do to help?"

"Can you get the French test for me in advance?"

"I hardly know you." All he knew was that I was the kid who was always clowning around.

We went to a bar and downed a few drinks. Loosened by the liquor, he told me, "I'll call the French teacher in the morning and ask if he can do anything for you."

I was pretty high, and he seemed concerned I was going home in that condition. He suggested I sober up at his apartment, which was in the neighborhood. When we got there, I flung myself into a chair and threw my head back. The whole room was swimming.

Smith said "You'd better get some sleep." He patted the couch. "Come over here and lie down."

I hastily refused.

"Alright, then close your eyes," he continued, "and tell me what's going through your mind."

I told him I dreamed I was going to be a movie star. Suddenly I heard the voice in my head and I said, "I see a woman with dark hair and we have a baby. The first one is a boy."

"What else do you see?"

"I'm going out to Hollywood, but I can't see what I'm gonna do."

The voice in my head didn't tell me whether or not I'd be successful out there.

"You're talking too much. Come over and I'll rub your back."

Oh, no, I thought. What am I getting into here?

"I can't Mr. Smith, I know what you want, but I just can't do that."

"It'll be all right."

Sure, I thought. For you.

So I said, "I'll hug you, I'll even kiss you on the cheek. But that's all I'll do."

He laughed. "You're a nut, you know that?"

"All I want is some help with my French."

He sighed. "I'll speak to the French teacher. I'll tutor you for a test."

I got a D in French, but at least I passed. I graduated from Iona College with a B.A. I was 25.

In fall 1956, I decided it was time to start professional acting classes. I chose not to go to the American Academy of Dramatic Arts because I had been told their approach was too mechanical. I wanted to learn the Stanislavski method, which actors like John Garfield and Lee J. Cobb were successfully using.

To support my acting studies, I found a job teaching Physical Education at Regis High School on 81st Street and Madison Avenue. I coached the basketball team and discovered I was good at developing young athletes into good ball players. If someone stated a kid had no chance, I'd say, "Give me time. I can make anybody good."

And I did.

While working there, I enrolled in various classes at acting schools like the Herbert Berghof Studio and the Gene Frankel Workshop, and took classes with Michael Gazzo who wrote *Hatful of Rain.*

I chased all over Manhattan taking every course I could fit in. I was enthralled and thrilled with the art of acting. When an actor did a good scene in class, there would be applause and praise. Not only did you win approval from your teachers and peers, but you would feel an overwhelming sense of pride and accomplishment after a scene was done.

Not all scenes worked. You failed at many of them. That was part of the process and you got a lot of criticism. You were forced to develop introspection. My private paradox was, that while I was a student during the day, I coached and taught after school hours.

I was bewildered at first when I attended classes at the Herbert Berghof Studio because it seemed to conflict with the methods and terminology taught at Gene Frankel's school and the other classes I had been taking.

I called my mother between classes. She could tell immediately I had a problem.

"What's the matter, Ed?"

"I don't know what to do in these classes. I want to be an actor so bad."

"So? Why can't you just be yourself?"

That's the advice F. Scott Fitzgerald gave Sheila Graham, or so she stated in her book, *The Beloved Infidel*, later made into a movie.

Fitzgerald said to Graham something like, "Darling, you've lost that spontaneity, that's why your programs on radio aren't working. You lost that thing you started with. All the great poets and Greek philosophers do the one great thing: 'Be thyself.'"

Graham listened and got her career back on track.

I started to focus on the classes at the Berghof Studio. Former members included Rod Steiger, Jason Robards, Geraldine Page and Jack Lemmon. I took classes with Herbert Berghof himself, as well as with some outstanding instructors, including Irene Dailey, Aaron Frankel and Lee Grant, who was tops. She helped me tremendously.

I had Marian Rich for voice. Alice Hermes helped with my speech and I was able to lose a good deal of my New York accent. I took everything, including Anthony Mannino's class for "technique." I didn't have many classes with Bill Hickey, but we did have nice conversations.

Anthony Mannino's Technique classes helped enormously. I did a lot of improvisational work with him, taking five 15-week courses over a two-year period.

I opened up during the improvisations and improved. There were others in the classes who were better at improvisations because they were louder and bolder. But Mannino said, "Nobody stands out like you do."

After I had been taking advanced acting classes with Berghof for a while, he advised me to get together with a good female acting partner.

He kidded me in class, "Ed, what strong actress would you like to do a real good scene with?"

He had a thick accent. He didn't like me to call it German; he preferred "Viennese."

I knew it would get a laugh, so I answered with a Viennese accent, "How about Uta? She's as strong as a vooman can be."

Uta Hagen was not only his wife, but she was a famous actress. She had starred on Broadway as Blanche in *Streetcar Named Desire* and had won the Tony Award as Georgia in *The Country Girl.* Several years later she starred on Broadway in *Who's Afraid of Virginia Woolf*, originating the role of Martha, that Elizabeth Taylor played in the movie version.

Berghof roared with laughter and said, "When I go home tonight, I'm telling Uta what you said."

Whether this was the reason or not, Uta and I never hit it off. She was the only teacher with whom I ever had a problem. Berghof said it was because we had different styles or methods of acting.

Many students got along with Uta and loved her, but some got along better with Berghof. I got along better with Berghof. He thought it was because I was trained to work from the inside out, and Uta was from the other school, which started with the external, vocal, physical, then proceeded to inner work. Both are legitimate ways.

Berghof kidded us about it. "When Uta performs on Broadway," he said, "she starts vocally, but she gets to the inner before the play's over."

Berghof's approach was different from Uta's. He taught us to start slowly and get to know the character, "feel" the character. Then we got the relationship going by communicating, listening and reacting to each other. We were to play our "actions," our "objectives" in the scene.

Uta liked to work sensorially with physical objects, to "sensitize" the actor, which is also a great approach. She instructed actors to work with physical objects, like moving a refrigerator or carrying a heavy suitcase.

Lee Grant also believed in using physical action to get a handle on a role, to get into the character. An actor should give himself something physical to do. I loved the approach. It made sense to me. When I used it, I could relax. I didn't worry about anything other than being present in the scene. As long as I knew I was there physically, feelings and words came much easier to me.

Anne Bancroft was in my class with Herbert Berghof. She had been cast in William Gibson's *Two For the Seesaw* on Broadway but had yet to play on a New York stage.

Annie wanted to be great, so she continued studying and training during rehearsals and performances. The rumor was she was getting $550 a week, which to me was big money. To her, it was an opportunity and a labor of love.

In contrast, Henry Fonda was getting $2500 a week against 15 percent of the box-office gross. The author William Gibson had written the play in 1953, but it had been rejected time after time until Fred Coe bought the play and packaged it.

The play made Anne Bancroft an important star. Prior to that, she had been a minor motion picture and television actress. Lee Grant was one of the actresses being considered for the role of Gittel Mosca before Anne Bancroft. She played the role later with Dana Andrews.

Annie had to run from the 5:30 to 7:30 p.m. class to get to the theater. One of her memorable scenes in *Seesaw* was when she was throwing pillows, which was Herbert Berghof's advice to her — to use objects.

Sandy Dennis was in Lee Grant's class with me. I did an improvisation with her and two other actors. Lee criticized Sandy because she made one of us deaf, one of us dumb and the other one blind. Lee said it was unfair to the actors. How could we communicate?

Sandy went on to star on Broadway in the early 1960s in *A Thousand Clowns* and *Who's Afraid of Virginia Woolf?* with Uta. She repeated *Who's Afraid of Virginia Woolf?* in the movie with Elizabeth Taylor and became a film star.

Acting seemed to come easy to me. There was a moment at the Herbert Berghof Studio, when I said to myself, "Is this as easy to do as I think it is?"

By fall 1958, I had been at The Herbert Berghof Studio for two years. I was 27. I stopped taking classes elsewhere and did all my studying at Berghof's. I was accepted into Herbert's advanced class.

I needed a permanent job to pay for my increasing expenses, so I started working at Parkchester Recreation. It was a division of Parkchester, a residential community project for middle-income families. Owned by Metropolitan Life, it consisted of several tall buildings, each with four quadrants.

Because it was a day job, I had to switch to all night classes at the Berghof Studio.

In my advanced acting class with Berghof, I did a scene

from *Career* by James Lee, a play about an actor who gets drafted into the Army just before his big break. I played Tex, a drunken soldier coming home from the war.

After the class, one of the students, who had been at the studio longer than I, came over to compliment me. His name was Frank Laughton, but he called himself "Charlie" because he was an admirer of Charles Laughton, who had been in important movies like *Mutiny on the Bounty*, *The Hunchback of Notre Dame*, and *Witness for the Prosecution*.

He told me, "That was a very nice scene."

"But Herbert didn't like it," I said, unhappily.

"No," he said, "but you did some very nice things. Don't let him undermine you."

He had studied with Lee Strasberg. When Berghof yelled at me, Charlie encouraged me.

All the great actors, like Marlon Brando and Geraldine Page, were members of the famous Actors Studio and I yearned to get in. I auditioned for it and was thrilled when the people that auditioned me liked me and had me audition again.

I passed the second audition. When I went for my third audition, people told me I was lucky to have been called back even once. My final audition was a scene from *A Hatful of Rain*. I had just taken classes with the author, Michael Gazzo.

Just as I started the scene, I got distracted and annoyed by the sounds of lunch bags crackling and people whispering. It seriously disturbed my concentration. I decided to use the anger in the scene, and when it ended, I thought I had been pretty good. They turned me down.

I have to admit I was a little bitter. It may have been evident and hurt my chances of acceptance. I wrote a letter to Lee Strasberg complaining about the way I had been treated.

Strasberg wrote me back, "Your letter was probably motivated by the fact we didn't pick you a third time."

I showed the letter to Lee Grant who was sympathetic. A couple of other students and I shared a cab with her after classes. I lived further uptown than the others, so I had time to talk to her alone.

She said, "Oh, don't worry about Lee Strasberg. You don't need the Actors Studio. Just keep studying your hardest and you'll make it without him."

Strasberg was the most highly-regarded of acting teachers and mentors. I observed that it was his habit to choose people for the Studio after they were already stars or on their way up. It appeared to me that he used these name actors later, to make the public think he had taught them. They were members of the Actors Studio, but he rarely had trained them himself.

People talk so much about Marlon Brando being a product of the Actors Studio, but Lee Strasberg never worked with him. It was usually Sanford Meisner and Stella Adler who had trained them.

I soothed myself with the thought that the Actors Studio would embrace me after I became famous.

AL'S PROGRESS

AFTER HIS FIRST 15-week course at the Berghof Studio, Al decided to continue taking classes with Herbert. The studio was moving to a new location, on Bank Street in the Village, and thereafter was to be known as the HB Studio.

Al's mother was concerned about his studying with Berghof. She called me at home one day. I don't know how she got my number. I assumed Al had given it to her. She asked, "Do you think Al has any talent?"

I said, "Yes, but it's got to be developed. The basic talent is there, and I think he's got what it takes to make it big time."

But she had her doubts about "this Herbert Berghof." She sounded upset, fretting that Al might be wasting his time, spending all kinds of money for lessons.

I tried to reassure her. "He has a lot of potential, and he's definitely not wasting his time."

This seemed to calm her a bit.

"And he wants it so badly. I think he's going to hit it big time."

I honestly believed that.

She said, "I don't see how he can, coming from where he does. There are so many better things for him to do."

"Give him time," I said. "Don't worry, I'll make sure he's guided in the right direction. I promise you."

She said, "We really can't afford this much longer, but I'll give him a little more time."

"Great," I told her, "because I think Al can become a big star."

I later told Al she had called me. I asked him if he wanted me to go over and talk to her.

"No. She won't listen. She has to make up her own mind about it. She's a very strong person."

"What does she look like?" I asked.

"Oh, she's pretty. She's got red hair. She's a cross between Susan Hayward and Gwen Verdon."

"Wow," I said, "that's an interesting combination."

He obviously thought Rose was very beautiful. And he was proud of her.

I told him, "Al, you don't know me that well yet, but I'm very good at smoothing out relationships. I mean, maybe if I spoke to her, I could convince her you're good and she'd hang in there with you."

But he wouldn't allow it. He said, "Ed, no, I don't want you to get involved with her."

If there was a problem between them he didn't want me to know about it.

One day, I was alone, walking along Grand Concourse at about 187th Street, across the street from the Loew's Paradise, a tremendous theater. Out of the blue, my voice spoke to me. "This unknown kid, Al Pacino, is going to be a big movie star and it will be partly because of your efforts. You are inspiring him."

This voice was strong, beautiful and commanding. It sometimes came with waves of color, like a rainbow, and elated me. Other times it was soft and gentle, telling me I was its messenger.

The voice continued, "You'll remember this later. Look up at that theater marquee. One day it will announce Al Pacino in a major movie. I am not saying this to short-change you, because great things are going to happen to you, too. And forgive him if he should slight you. You have already fanned the spark in him and he is striving for fame and success. However, I want you to realize there are more important things than fame and success for you."

That stopped me in my tracks.

One time when I was with Al in the Bronx, I sang a song, "Out of Place" that I had written with Carmen "Cappy" Cappazolla.

Al remarked, "You're so talented and you're not doing anything with it. You can write songs, you can act, and you can sing."

My mother was always kind to Al, but she thought I was frittering away my time with him, that it would interfere with my own progress.

One day, when I brought Al to the apartment, she

whispered, sarcastically, "Keep teaching him the acting and he's gonna become rich and famous and you're gonna ask him to help you and he won't do it."

My mother kept prodding me to wake up. She was concerned and overly protective because she thought I was too open and generous, spreading myself too thin.

Over the years, she had watched people take advantage of me. When I was a kid, I would be appointed team captain and I'd have to do everybody else's work. Or I'd be asked to take care of the Special Ed kids when I should have taken time to relax on the playground.

When I was older, she worried people would hire me and not pay me what I was worth or they'd con me into taking care of their handicapped kids for free. She knew I had a generous spirit,was vulnerable and could get hurt easily. Why shouldn't I? I learned it from her.

I heard about a novel called *Tubie's Monument*, from a friend, Francine. She said it had good dialogue between an Italian boy from the Bronx and a theatrical manager. Shazam! I thought of Al.

I read it and knew it was perfect for us. In one of the scenes, Joe Lavingo, the young actor, meets Tubie, the manager, an older guy, in front of the CBS building in Manhattan. Al would be the fledgling actor and I'd be the seasoned manager.

I gave *Tubie* to Al to read. I told him I thought it was a good vehicle for us, that the character of Joe Lavingo was very likable and innocent.

"It's a natural for you," I told him.

Wouldn't it be ironic to do a scene about a manager who discovers an Italian kid from the Bronx?"

Lavingo had been doing commercials for television, and every time one aired, millions of women rushed out to buy the product. He was a big success in commercials, but he had grown tired of doing them. He had made millions for Tubie (me) and he had had enough.

We performed the scene for Berghof. Overall, it went very well. Al performed with down-to-earth honesty. I was a raving, ranting lunatic who, after making oceans of money with Lavingo, was furious he was leaving me.

I lashed into him, "I made you! I made you what you are! How can you leave me? I taught you how to eat, how to talk, how to walk. I did everything for you. Now you're gonna leave me to go into business with your brother... in a butcher shop? How can you?"

I was then supposed to grab him, sink to my knees and beg him to stay. "Don't, don't quit on me," I pled.

After the scene concluded, Berghof shouted, "Marvelous, marvelous!" He praised it to the skies. Then he said, "But, Ed, maybe you should have shaken Al harder at the end. It would have been even more powerful."

"Thanks, Herbert," I responded. "I'll remember that next time." But my voice was saying to me, "No, you wouldn't want to hurt Al."

He was so defensive in the scene. Shaking him harder might have spoiled his performance. I decided I had played it just right. But then I had second thoughts. Maybe I was wrong. Maybe I should have shaken him harder and it would've been a better scene. I got a thrill out of doing powerful scenes for Berghof, receiving the praise, and even taking the criticism.

When we finished, I handed the book to Al and got the strangest sensation. I said, "Al, if you ever make it big as an actor, this would be a great vehicle for you."

Al was criticized for his posture, and more than one teacher had suggested he take dance classes, or what they called "body movement." Al couldn't afford to pay for another class, so I went and talked to Berghof.

I told him I would pay for Al's movement class, but Al mustn't know about it. Berghof said I had already done enough, and that it wouldn't be necessary. He would himself give Al a scholarship to Anna Sokolow's Body Movement Class.

More and more, I was taking Al under my wing and I felt he appreciated it, because his confidence was growing with my help. He needed to get in touch with himself, and he was now allowing more of himself to emerge.

Bruce Cohen, Al's childhood friend from the Bronx, starting attending class with us. He was Al's age. When he saw me do a scene, he later commented, "Ed, do you realize what talent you have?"

"I think I'm pretty good," I said, "but I also know I've got a long way to go."

Not knowing if you're really good is almost as bad as not knowing you're really bad. Compliments can be very misleading. They can go to your head and stop you from learning if you're not careful.

Rose, Al's mother, called my mother, to find out how Al was doing. Two Italian women talking about their sons. Rose called my mom a few times. Rose was a friendly woman, but very concerned about Al. Of course, my mother was overly concerned about me.

She told Rose, "I hope they're not wasting their time." Rose agreed.

I've often thought how sad it was, Al's own mother withdrawing her support of Al and his desire to act professionally, and how she passed away before she saw him make it big. After she died, Al told me she had been ill for a long time. He thought maybe she had not taken her medicine. I never learned what really happened.

In Berghof's class one day, Al and I watched a young actress, Penny Allen, do a complicated scene in which she was totally immersed, totally living the character.

She became hysterical in the scene. Her face flushed red as a beet, charged with emotion, her eyes full of fire. Tears flooded down her cheeks. She went nuts — in character. She had the real stuff that make great actors.

Al and I were mesmerized by her performance.

"Boy, if only we could act like that," he said. Then he grinned. "Some of these gals here can really turn that emotion on."

I followed his gaze. He was eyeing Penny's scene partner, Kristen. He liked her looks.

"Kristen's pretty, isn't she?" I teased. "And all the guys are after her." I added in very bad, Berghof-like German accent, "Vot you vant? You vant Kristen? Kristen maybe vants you, Al. I tink she vants your body. She vants you maybe to go home mit her."

Al laughed and said, "We'll see about that."

But Penny had something special. She was the actress to watch, I thought.

"When I was a kid," I told Al, "I loved to watch the old character actors. They were great. Penny's got that quality, like Garbo, like Ethel Barrymore.

"Did you ever see Vivian Nathan?" Al asked. "She's a great character actress. I'm gonna be a great character actor some day."

Berghof praised Penny's performance that day. She deserved it. I was happy for her.

I approached her a few days later during our body movement class. "That was a great scene you did in Herbert's class," I whispered.

She thanked me, but concerned that I was flirting, told me right up front that she was married. Her husband was Charlie Laughton, who had been so complimentary to me in my acting class with Herbert. I had no idea.

"You're really good," I told her. "Who did you study with before you came here?"

"Charlie," she said. "I study with my husband. He learned a lot from Strasberg."

From Charlie she had learned Strasberg's technique of using the five senses and how to sensitize objects to release your emotions.

I told her, "Al Pacino was also impressed with what you did."

Penny soon informed me Charlie wanted to start a Sunday night class at Berghof's. He was adept at the techniques Strasberg taught, such as sensory work. She asked me if I'd be interested and assured me Charlie wouldn't charge much — I think it turned out to be $3 per session.

I thought, Why not? Sundays were quiet for me after church. I offered to help get a group together. Maybe Al, Joe, Bruce and I could be the nucleus of a small class.

"I'm always willing to learn," I said. "Let's do it."

I told Al about the class with Charlie.

"We're doing pretty good work now, but there's always room for improvement."

I wanted us to be the best. Whatever I could share with Al, I did. "Maybe we could learn that sensory work we're hearing so much about, the stuff that Strasberg teaches."

Al, as usual, was eager to try it. I then asked Joe and Bruce if they'd be interested. They were enthusiastic and wanted to join us. We started class with Charlie on Sunday nights at the Studio and it turned out to be an excellent workshop. Charlie taught us to endow objects with personalization. He gave us sensory exercises. I had taken a similar class before, but Charlie was able to explain it and get it across in a way that made beautiful sense. He was an excellent instructor.

He said, "Ed, you've been studying with Berghof for

three years. I've watched you work. Now let me see you not studying. Let me see Ed De Leo really let loose."

I said, "I'm ready. Just show me how."

He grinned. "Bring in a good scene next week and I'll show you how."

There were some perfect scenes in *Golden Boy*, by Clifford Odets, that had been produced as a movie starring William Holden. I picked an ideal scene for Joe and me. He was Joe Bonaparte, the fighter, and I was Moody, a fight manager. Joe bursts into Moody's office and begs Moody to help him be a better fighter.

Charlie wanted me to bring in some objects that meant something to me to work with. Before I did the scene I was nervous.

I told Charlie, "I promise, I'll give it a try," even though I didn't have much faith in the technique yet.

I brought in my little All City basketball trophy, the article from the New York World Telegram, and some photos of people who were very close to me. Charlie instructed me to put the objects on my desk, asked me to sit down, forget about lines, and just think about the people in the photos and the objects.

I obeyed, and man, did it open me up! I had never experienced anything like it before in a scene. My voice told me, "Charlie knows what he's doing."

Charlie raved about my work in the scene. He said, "Ed, you got the character perfectly. You not only used yourself, you were the character. You became Moody. Your voice became deep, very different. To be honest, I never realized you had that much in you to do so well. Your voice has great authority."

After class, Al sidled over. "Ed, your voice was great. It was exciting. You really became Moody."

That's all he said. I was afraid Joe might be upset or

critical because I had gotten so completely involved with my objects I hadn't communicated with him in the scene. I might have upstaged him without realizing it. On the ride to the Bronx, I was reassured when Al said what I had done in Charlie's class really impressed him. He said Joe had been too involved in himself and his objects to be aware of what I was doing; but I had done just what Charlie had directed me to do.

"You've got to be aware of everything," I said, "the interaction between the characters, everything that's going on."

He understood what I meant, but he said, "Charlie made an interesting statement to you. He said, 'You've studied acting for years, now show us the character.'"

"Yeah," I said, "Charlie shines a light right into your soul. He illuminates the dark places and doesn't let you get away with tricks. We should keep studying with him."

As actor-wannabes, we made the rounds together, checking into auditions, reading the notices on the bulletin board at Actor's Equity office, and reading every casting notice in Showbusiness and Backstage.

We couldn't get our feet inside a single door. Our careers were going nowhere fast. But we stayed positive and kept training. I kept up my classes with Herbert and the other teachers. Al continued with Charlie.

Charlie Laughton spotted and probed the contradictions in Al. He nicknamed him "the wild square," Bohemian on the outside, traditional on the inside.

Al once said, "I was sitting in a restaurant across the street from The New York Shakespeare Festival's Public Theater. The actors were sitting around a table, with a red-and-white checkered tablecloth and an umbrella, the sun was coming in from the shade — it looked like a Renoir painting.

"There were seven or eight of them, talking. I said to my friend, 'You see them? I can't get my eyes off that group.' It was as though they had existed hundreds of years. You could see their roots, their background, how much like a family they were, how that was something I always wanted... I was drawn to them. Maybe that is what I want... I don't know."

It appeared Uta didn't approve of Charlie's class. She may have been a bit jealous. She complained some stage props were missing from her classroom on Mondays. Charlie's class was conducted Sunday nights. The complaints escalated and gradually, Charlie's students started to wander away. It would not be long before he had to disband.

Al said, "Nothing's going to stop me from acting."

Charlie praised Al in many of his scenes. Al and Charlie were warming up to each other, growing closer daily. Al would pepper him with questions, anxious to learn more about acting.

Berghof, whom I still believe was an excellent and very human instructor, said to me one day in the class, "Ed, you give and give in your scenes, and you're marvelous. But there's one suggestion I want to make: Become a little bit more selfish. Be a 'selfish bastard.' You've got to be more like Uta. She takes and takes in a scene. She's what I call a selfish actress; and that's what you need, to be more selfish. You're too nice."

I hated hearing the advice because I was afraid it was true. I knew I gave myself away to everybody and didn't protect my own needs.

"Follow my advice," he urged, "and you will be a success."

I laughed. "When?"

He said, "Later. Your type always makes it later in life. You're going to have to do a lot of other things before you make it."

My heart sank. Obviously, from the very beginning, I had been a character actor. I was attractive, I thought, but I had to face it, I was "character" handsome, not "hunky leading man" handsome.

Over coffee after class one night, Berghof said, "Al will be all right. He's from the streets. He knows how to fend for himself. He knows how to survive."

After a while I felt I had grown stale. I had studied too much. I wanted to work. To do the real thing... on stage. I needed a break. For the time being, I had had all the training I could absorb. I began to think more and more of taking off for Hollywood.

Al didn't respect most of the Hollywood types and he expressed it vocally when we went to movies together. Acting was our life, whether we were doing it ourselves or watching actors on the stage or screen.

Forty-second Street was lined with theaters screening double features. We saw Paul Newman in *Cat On a Hot Tin Roof,* Ingrid Bergman in *Anastasia,* and Alec Guinness in *The Bridge on the River Kwai.* Susan Hayward, in *I Want To Live*, reminded Al of his mother, especially the red hair.

One day, up in the Bronx, Al, Bruce and I were shooting baskets in a schoolyard. There were only a few people in the yard, so we had the court pretty much to ourselves. Bruce had been sniping at Al all day, apparently wearing an envious chip on his shoulder.

He snarled at Al, "Everything goes your way, you know that? Everybody wants to do things for you."

Al was startled. "What do you mean? Who does things for me?"

Bruce nodded at me. "Ed, for instance. That guy'll do anything for you."

I was embarrassed. Al broke into one of his typical,

crazy, wide-eyed grins. He knew I believed in his talent. He also was aware of how much I was helping him. His expression told the story. But I was more than a teacher or coach. I was a true friend, and he knew it.

On the way home to the Bronx later, we were walking under the Third Avenue "El" (the elevated train) on Fordham Road. Al suddenly had an intuition he was going to be a big star.

He said, "I hope I don't have to experience all that hate and jealousy, that stuff that happens to people when they hit it big."

I said, "Well, it depends on whether they're really your friend or not. If they're your friend and you make it big, they'll be happy for you."

"Well, you're the type of person who'd help people anyway, aren't you?" Then he thought about himself. "I'm not. It's every man for himself in this world."

I wasn't sure how to react to that statement. I had a sinking feeling in the pit of my gut, a sense of futility.

I said to myself, "Why am I killing myself for this kid if he's going to drop me the second he makes it?"

But Al was intuitive. Almost as if he had read my mind, he said, "Don't worry, Ed." He gave me a friendly pat on the shoulder. "You, I'll never forget."

We hung around in my neighborhood in the Bronx before and after classes at Berghof's. Sometimes we went over to my cousin Sonny's house. One day, while we were waiting for a bus on East Tremont Avenue, the voice in my head instructed , "You must tell him."

Al stopped suddenly and stared at me as if he had heard the voice himself.

I felt stupid, but I blurted out, "Al... you know... you're going to be a big star... a very big star."

And he said, "I know." He said it very simply, not pretentiously, not egotistically, just... inevitably.

I didn't tell him I heard it from a voice in my mind. Instead, I said, "Something tells me so."

That's when he told me he had had his astrology chart done and the chart had predicted stardom for him.

Soon afterward, Al started having trouble with Berghof in class. After one session, I had a hard time keeping stride with him as he hurried up along Bank Street, away from the Studio. He was furious and told me he was through with Berghof and the Studio.

"They're not gonna stop me from acting," he said.

"Who?" I asked him. "Herbert and Uta?"

"No. People in this business. What I'm gonna do is act in lofts. I'll act anywhere, just to keep acting. Sooner or later somebody will discover me."

"Al," I said, "do you want to go through all that? Off-off-Broadway?"

"Yes. I'm gonna keep at it until somebody sees me."

"Me, too. But wherever we perform, let's make sure we get write-ups. We need good portfolios."

I knew nothing could stop Al. But what about my dream?

Through our mutual love of acting, Al and I had become almost inseparable. We would stand on street corners talking about Chekhov, Tennessee Williams, and Arthur Miller. We read plays out loud in Edgar Allen Poe Park in the Bronx. We rehearsed scenes with Joe and Bruce in coffee shops and ice cream parlors. We joked about our ambitions. We were all going to make it, but which one of us was going to make it first?

Al and I always went home on the train together.

Anyone watching Al or me perform would have predicted we both were going to make it. It was assumed if one of us got there first, it most likely would be me, since

I had more experience. But, wouldn't it be great, I thought, if we made it together, and soon?

Al stopped taking classes at the HB Studio and started to study solely with Charlie. Charlie quickly assumed my role, guiding and inspiring Al, teaching him privately.

Al's mother, Rose, completely stopped encouraging him. She warned him that acting was for rich people. It created a chasm between them. The breach between Rose and Al over his relentless determination to become an actor caused him great pain and confusion. Rose didn't want to hear about it anymore. She was certain it was an impossible dream because of his roots.

To Rose, Al insisted that soon something big was going to happen for him. In an attempt to placate her, he lied that he was going to take training to become a draftsman. Rose didn't believe him for a minute.

When I completed the 15-week-cycle with Uta Hagen, I wanted to continue studying with her, but she abruptly told me, "Ed, I can't teach you any more."

I didn't know what to think. Did she think I knew everything she had to teach, or was she trying to get rid of me? "You're from a different type of school."

"What do you mean?" I asked, still in shock.

"It's a personality thing. You're coming from one place and I'm coming from another, and I don't think we're ever going to get anywhere together."

I let that sink in and then admitted she was probably right. The voice in my head told me, "This is just what you needed to stop acting classes."

I already had all the technique I needed from Lee Grant, Herbert Berghof, and Charlie Laughton.

I blurted, "Then I guess I'll just go to California!"

Uta was my last teacher at the HB Studio. Someone told me a few years ago that she didn't like the loose way

I worked.

An older actor in Uta's class, told me, "I think Uta's threatened by you. You radiate out there on the stage. You're so alive. Uta doesn't teach actors how to do that. She teaches something else, a different technique, the mechanics. She can't teach radiation."

I almost laughed.

I was all fired up with my improvisational training, which I didn't want to lose. Good improvisational skills are difficult to learn. That training had made a difference in my acting. I had been wooden before I had taken Mannino's class. What I had learned there had freed me.

Al was quick to reassure me after Uta's dismissal. "You're good, Ed. You've been good from day one."

I said, "Well, I'm going to let you in on a secret. I was lost in these classes when I first started."

Al had never worked with Uta. I think Al didn't take her classes because some other students hadn't gotten along with her and it made him cautious.

Penny, meanwhile, was becoming a strong influence on Al. Charlie had taken over as his private coach, becoming more and more a father figure to Al, guiding him as I had previously done. Al was turning to him more and more because I was leaving for Los Angeles.

I did one last scene with Al for Charlie, another scene from *Crime in the Streets*, by Reginald Rose, the play we had done in Berghof's class the year before. Al played a juvenile delinquent and I was the social worker trying to reform him. Charlie was showing Al how to use objects, how to get into that "world."

In the scene, I went to his apartment and found him playing with his street toys. He had his own circle of objects. I tried to reach him and lift him up out of his world of selfishness.

After the scene was over, Charlie said, "See, Ed, Al was doing the right thing. He came off very well. But you were in a vacuum. You weren't using your objects. You weren't selfish enough."

I said, "My objective in the scene was to reach this boy, but I couldn't do it because Al was too much like the character with the selfishness."

He wasn't communicating with me in the scene. I was irked with Al. I thought Charlie was teaching him to be a selfish actor. I didn't believe in competing in a scene. I felt we should have interplay as the characters and relate to each other. I didn't like the idea of having to be selfish to be good, to ignore the other character. I must admit, though, it worked for Al in the scene, as it had done for me in the *Golden Boy* scene.

I felt we never really had rapport in the scene. Al was contained in his own tight little world and there was no give and take. But Charlie bought it. Al had the makings of a star and Charlie told him so.

I felt slighted and out of the loop. Al was turning to Charlie and leaving me out in the cold. I had no more influence on him. It hurt, but I never mentioned it to him.

Al could see I was irritated, and it appeared to bother him. He suggested we rent a place in Greenwich Village. It would be cheaper for us to pool the rent and we could work on our scenes with no time wasted traveling. It seemed like a good idea at first.

We trudged around looking for a place. There was a fifth-floor walk-up we liked and we met the landlady. But I was reluctant. Always living close to the edge financially, I worried if we took a place together and Al went on to fame and fortune, I'd be stuck with the apartment and the whole rent.

I told Al my father was pressuring me to give up acting and get a nine-to-five job. The truth of the matter was I wanted to go out to California to get away from my father's hassling.

"What I think I'm gonna do is go to California and look for work out there. Bruce is going, too. We have enough acting training. I think we're ready."

Al didn't like the idea. He thought I'd get lost in the Hollywood crush. He added, "Besides, who is going to coach me?"

"You're surrounded by teachers," I snapped, "And you've got Charlie." I meant it sincerely. "You'll be all right."

"Charlie's class doesn't have many students. Without you and Bruce there won't be anybody good to work with."

"Why don't you come with us? You're ready."

Al refused to consider it. He muttered his mother was giving him a hard time and still needed his help. She was very disparaging of his career at that point. He seemed on the verge of tears. "Who'll I do if you go?"

I realized at that moment just how dependent Al had become on me. "Don't worry, Al," I said. "I'll still help you. I'll be back. We'll only try it for a while."

"Please, don't go. I'll be lost without you here."

I told him, "I can probably scrape together enough money to bring you out if you need to get away from your mother."

He said, "No, I can't go. She's too sick. I can't leave her alone."

So I said, "Don't worry. I'm just gonna go out there and case the territory." I really didn't expect to stay long. "You watch," I said, "the minute I'm gone, you'll take off and become a big star. Technically, you're ready for it. But keep working with Charlie."

MY STAB AT HOLLYWOOD

I ARRIVED IN HOLLYWOOD with a letter of recommendation from Herbert Berghof. The only person I knew was my sister, Gloria, who lived in Tijunga.

Gloria's husband, Ben, worked for *TV Guide*, preparing the racing form. He was in the printers union. I stayed with them until I could locate a place of my own. I had no car, so traveling into Hollywood from Tijunga was complicated beyond imagination. I finally took a room at the Park Hotel on Hollywood Boulevard near Highland Avenue.

Hollywood of the 60s was not the glamorous land of make-believe I had seen in the movies. Television was taking over. The section of Hollywood, where the Paramount Pictures and Columbia Pictures studios were located, looked like a dreary factory town, as did the areas surrounding Warner Brothers in Burbank, MGM in Culver City, and Universal Pictures in North Hollywood. The only glitter and tinsel were the tourist attractions on Hollywood Boulevard.

Berghof had written the recommendation for me to show a couple of people he knew who were involved in the movie industry. One was Jess Carneol, a screenwriter who had been a musician in Gene Krupa's band.

I got in touch with Jess and, to my relief, he was cordial. He invited me to have a drink with him. I was sure this was going to be my big break. He would help get me into the movies. I knew I was ready.

I was in terrific physical condition. I was 5'11", weighed 170 pounds, and I was a good actor. I felt freer than I did in New York. I had a new-found confidence.

Jess was well-connected and agreed to arrange an audition for me at Twentieth Century Fox, possibly as a contract player. Most actors, however, were free-lancing through their agents, eager to be relieved of their studio contracts because the studio star system was fading fast. Sanford Meisner was in charge of talent at Fox. I met him in New York when he auditioned me for the Neighborhood Playhouse where he was artistic director. He had never really interested me as a teacher, but he had turned out some top notch actors, like Robert Duvall.

Jess recommended me highly to Meisner and was ready to arrange the audition when the Writers Guild went on strike. Jess had to hurry to New York with his wife, Kay Leonard, who was also a writer and an administrator in the Writer's Guild of America. The WGA was the union for screenwriters and television writers.

Not only did film and television production grind to a halt, but my opportunity to audition for Meisner was cancelled as well. So, there was no work for me either way. Bad timing.

When Jess returned, he gave me the bad news. "I'm sorry, Ed. My wife and I had dinner with Herbert and Uta and they had a fight over you. Herbert said, 'Ed De Leo is marvelous. He's a fine talent.' But Uta said 'No, he's not. He was in my class for 15 weeks and I don't like him.' She didn't recommend my helping you."

I figured it was because of the clash I had with her. As to why she didn't like me, I had no idea. Maybe Berghof was able to get more out of me than she could. Then I recalled the time she had asked for written critiques of the actors in her class. I had written, "Your students are too external." Too naive to have thought about repercussions, I had unwittingly personally attacked her. Too late for amends.

Jess reported that Herbert and Uta had quarreled about me in the restaurant, out loud, with everyone looking. "Why did you recommend him?" she yelled. "Why don't you recommend your other students?"

I had heard Uta could be vindictive. But if she liked you, there was nothing she wouldn't do for you. She preferred working with leading men, good-looking actors. She went for the physical attractiveness. Rock Hudson's looks were her ideal.

She had appeared to like me at the outset of class, but my criticism must have ruffled her feathers. From that moment on, I became persona non grata. I didn't meet Uta's high standards.

Her students catered to her as if she were the queen herself, running after her like pet puppies. Uta relished the fawning. I didn't fawn. I was more independent. Somebody once suggested I might have reminded her of her ex-husband, Jose Ferrer. He married Rosemary Clooney. I'm still guessing at the reason she turned on me. But at this stage of my life, I don't care.

I didn't drive, nor did I have a car, and I needed to sign up with an agent in L.A. Nobody would see me without an agent. Stuck in Los Angeles with no agent and no car proved to be a double handicap.

Bruce followed me to Hollywood two weeks later. He had changed his name from Bruce Cohen to Bruce Gregory. How could he be a movie star with a name like Cohen? Gregory sounded like he was somebody.

I had told Bruce to ask Herbert for a list of people to see on the West Coast and he arrived it in hand.

Back in New York, my father ran into Samuel Goldwyn Jr. at his concession and told him about my being in Hollywood. Goldwyn told him to have me look him up. He'd try to help me.

When he returned to the Coast, I contacted him and he was nice enough to see me. Unfortunately, he couldn't help me. "I can't even get a job for my wife, who's an actress," he said. "But, keep in touch."

Thanks, a lot.

AL IN NEW YORK - 1961

NOW 20 YEARS OLD, Al continued training with Charlie Laughton while he took odd jobs and auditioned for every role he heard about.

On the bus ride to an audition in Boston for a play about gangsters, he and Bruce Cohen (Gregory) stopped in Rhode Island to visit Bruce's friend Vincent Calcagni. Calcagni helped them act like gangsters.

Late at night, he drove them around town; all three wore black masks and gloves. Two policemen noticed them drive past a few times and stopped them. The three explained they were actors, but when the officers opened the trunk, they spotted a loaded gun. The boys explained it was just a prop.

Officer William J. O'Coin, Jr. and his partner took no chances. They drove them to the Woonsocket, Rhode Island police station where they were fingerprinted, photographed, and charged with carrying a concealed weapon. Bail was set for $2,000, which, of course, they were unable to pay. Because he was cooperative, Al spent only three days in jail. A small price to pay for a lesson in life.

Back in New York, Al had to portray a guy in a scene who confronts the law and talks back to a cop. Having just undergone a similar experience, the role was real to him, making him very believable. It made a big impression on Charlie.

MY STRUGGLE IN HOLLYWOOD

AFTER A YEAR or two of trying to support myself in Hollywood, I heard Dick Wilson was holding classes at a little theater on Sunset Boulevard. I thought this might be a good way to connect with other actors.

Wilson was famous in every household in the U.S. as Mr. Whipple of the Charmin tissue commercial. He was a terrific character actor. In his class, I met George Atkinson and other wonderful actors.

I discovered I was freer to be myself than I was in New York. In L.A., I was a clean slate. I didn't have to worry about what anybody thought. I could do whatever I wanted.

I started dating a lovely, high-spirited actress, Jeannie Poley, who was in the class. People compared her to Barbara Eden. We did a showcase together for Eddie Foy III, a prominent casting director. He liked me and Jeannie but the showcase turned out to be a dead end for both of us. However, Jeannie became the great love of my life. At the time, I even planned to marry her.

An actor, Eric Morris, liked my acting. He put a group of actors together for a production of *End As A Man* at the Store Theater just off Hollywood Boulevard, near Western Avenue. I formed a repertory company and we produced a series of plays including *Career*, by James Lee and *The Big Knife*, by Clifford Odets.

In *The Big Knife*, I played a character called Hobb. I was so nervous about it, I had to have a drink to do it, but people said I was a standout. Everything I had learned in New York was now paying off.

I played Perrin McKee, a character part, in *End As a Man*, by Calder Willingham. It was directed by Lincoln Damien. A tense and often amusing drama, it showed how military schools turn boys into men. It was made into a movie in 1957 called *The Strange One* starring Ben Gazzara, George Peppard and Pat Hingle.

I was finally on stage and people were paying to see me. I had not experienced that in New York. The audiences applauded my performance. Eric Morris was the star, but everyone told me I was the best actor in it. As a result, Eric and Lincoln took me for coffee and politely told me to cool it, I was stealing the show.

In Los Angeles, "little theater" had little relationship to the film industry. Hollywood was not a theater town. You couldn't make a living on the stage. It was next to impossible to get directors and agents out to see plays. They wanted to see something you had "in the can." If you had nothing on film to show them, they weren't interested. The days of the "screen test" were fading away. You only tested for movies when a director was interested in you.

Although I performed in a few plays, I wasn't earning enough to support myself. I couldn't ask for money from home, because my father was ill and my mother wasn't working. She was taking care of him. I needed money; I was desperate.

I had a brainstorm. If I couldn't get work in movies or television, perhaps I could make money acting on my own. There might be individuals who could use the services of a seasoned actor. I could act out roles for them.

I made up some fliers and put a classified ad in the Los Angeles Herald Examiner. I said I was available to play scenes with people in their home for a small fee, for food or even work.

The ad said, "Your fantasy fulfilled by skilled actor. I'm your best friend." I added "But please, no kinks or kooks." I had begun to perceive what Hollywood was like. It was a freewheeling place, sexually, and I really didn't want to get involved in a scene like that. I also feared catching some horrible disease.

My father had always warned, "Be careful. Don't get into trouble sexually. Don't get roped into marriage until you're sure it's the right girl."

I had no idea the ad would get such a response. I should have known. After all, this was Hollywood. I listed my phone number in the ad, but protected myself with an answering machine. Respondents left their names and numbers and I would call them back.

I got hundreds of calls, many of them weird beyond belief. People actually wanted to hire me! What a crazy turn of events. What a way to continue acting. I went out to Hollywood to become a movie star. Now I was placing classified ads to act out people's fantasies.

My first "job" came from an older woman, Doris Ridgewood, who asked me to pretend to be her three-year-old boy. She revealed she had lost a custody fight with her husband and it was driving her crazy. I was to pretend I was Dicky and talk to her in a baby voice.

She took me out to seashore in Santa Monica where she cooed maternally, "Dicky? Dicky-boy?"

I was supposed to answer, "Yes, Mommy! Oh, Mommy, Mommy, look at the boats!"

All day long I pretended to be her son, lisping baby-talk the entire time. It really did the trick for her, whatever that was. I was so convincing she wanted a return engagement.

She wormed out of me that I was a starving actor and thereafter she would say, "You're a marvelous actor, Dicky-boy. You'll be a big star, I'm sure."

Doris was extremely religious and she encouraged me to go to church. The next thing I knew, she wanted to take me on a cruise. When I hesitated, she pouted, "I'll pay you extra to go on the cruise."

"How can I pretend to be your little boy on a cruise in front of all those people?"

She said, "Oh, I don't want you to pretend to be my son. I want you to pretend you're my lover."

I blanched at the thought, but I needed the money. So I drove down to San Pedro with her and boarded the ship, one of the Princess Line. We cruised to Catalina and other islands off the coast of California and Mexico. She bought me special clothes for the trip and I wore a tux at night for dinner and dancing.

During the cruise she let it slip she was running away from her brother-in-law, who was stalking her. He was trying to make sure she wasn't getting involved with someone. When I got nervous, she assured me her baby was safe. It was only the child's custody everybody was fighting about.

The situation shifted swiftly. She became flirtatious and seductive. I tried to please her every way I could, but at sex I drew the line. I was not going to sell my body for money, not an inch of it.

She took it well, friendly even, and confided to me she had two other grown children, that Dicky was a change-of-life baby. She admitted she was no longer a doting mother, and wanted to be free of maternal duties now. She wanted to enjoy her life finally.

She dressed in beautiful gowns and hats and gloves. Though she was pushing 60, she was still fairly attractive, confessing that after she had lost a lot of weight, she'd had some nips and tucks done here and there .

Nightly I danced with her and once pretended I was a singer from New York. I got up and sang with the ship's orchestra. She seemed to get a thrill out of it.

Apparently because I pleased her, she introduced me to some friends whom she told what I did. I got hired to play roles with them. Word of mouth is even better than advertising, it seems.

One person she introduced me to was Morty Hoberman, a little man who worked in the downtown garment industry. He, too, wanted me to pretend to be his son. His natural son had refused to go into business with him, and went so far as to move to the East Coast to escape. Morty asked me to be present when he met buyers. My job was to pretend to be savvy and enthusiastic about Morty's business.

Whenever he'd talk about his company, I'd cheer him on. "Yeah, Pop, yeah, it's fantastic, etc." Or I'd assure him the clothing line was fabulous and was gonna sell like hot cakes. Blah, blah, blah. Half the time I didn't know what the hell I was saying, but, thanks to my training, I improvised and just glowed with the flow. He paid very well.

Back in New York, Al was doing great without me. He and Charlie were committed to prying open doors in the theater world. They had become drinking buddies. I was pulling in more money than either of them at the time, but they weren't compromising their talent.

Al sacrificed the temptation to try Hollywood. He was a true artist, persisting in trying out for plays in basements and warehouses and lofts, which is what he swore he would do until somebody saw him perform and hired him.

The jobs from the ads gave me money to take singing lessons and do a couple of demo records. I quickly discovered singing was not going to get me anywhere. So acting it would be. I continued the capers. My improvisation classes with Anthony Mannino were a boon, enabling me to play roles convincingly.

An ex-marine, Mickey Donovan, called me. He was a big drinker. Nobody would drink with him because he got smashed and went bonkers. Often he had to be carried home unconscious. He needed a drinking pal who would tolerate his insults and see he got home safely.

So, for a price, I became his drinking buddy. Mickey paid me very well. All I had to do was to pretend to be an old Marine buddy, have drinks with him, and listen to him talk about our war life. He'd get blasted, insult me, then pass out. I'd take him home.

I didn't completely throw myself into these roles. I was always aware, whether my clients knew it or not, that I was an actor. I was paid to be there for a specific purpose. I couldn't match drink for drink with Mickey, because we would both be drunk and stupid. I drank with him for several weeks, and the money supported me.

Offstage, I may have been the busiest actor in town. The capers permitted me to play many characters, use dialects, change wardrobe and makeup and go to many different and unusual locations. I met all kinds of characters, you name it — gays, lesbians, disillusioned tourists, former silent film stars. This was Hollywood. Occasionally my escapades turned out to be dangerous.

Howard Brayborne, a tough guy with a fake WASP name, wanted me to pretend I was Louie Chicanti, the head of a local syndicate.

Howard was attempting to buy a yacht and the owner,

Sam Biedermann, was reluctant to sell. Howard asked me to pretend to be his "banker." He ran me through a rehearsal. "Your voice is too high," he complained. "You gotta lower it a little... make it sound a little more Italiano."

He showed me a few tricks, and I added a few bits from movies I had seen. Finally, he said, "Now you got it. You're Louie Chicanti. I almost believe you myself!"

I was petrified the owner of the yacht might see through my act. But Howard reassured me, "If you can fool me, you can fool anybody! I'll buy you a blue suit, an expensive white shirt and tie and you'll be A-OK."

I was nervous. "What if I don't know what to say?"

He said, "Any time you're in doubt, just look mean and say, 'No, no, no!'"

So with my act polished, I accompanied Howard out to the yacht. When Sam showed up, I went into gear. I said to him, "Sam, my God, you-a got a good-a yacht here. Any amount you-a want. You-a make Howie a good deal and I take care of it."

Sam said, "For me to come out ahead, I need two and a half million. It's worth twice that."

"Do you realize who this is here?" Howard glared at him. "We'll give you two million cash. Take it or leave it."

I panicked, not knowing whether or not Sam Biedermann could be pressured into selling at that price. He was. I knew old Sam was expecting the money to come from me, but. I hoped when the time came to put up or shut up, Ed De Leo would be back in New York and Louie Chicanti would have disappeared. However, I quickly discovered Howard planned to skip with the boat. I was in deep dog puck. I hadn't agreed to be party to a con.

Lucky for me, Howard got cold feet the next day. "Sam wants us to finance a bunch of other things for him...a savings and loan, a hotel in Vegas. It's time to bail out, and quick."

He knew that since I was a "floater" there was no record of me in Los Angeles. "I'm gonna tell Sam you had a heart attack and died, so the deal's off."

Howard paid me well to keep my mouth shut, but I would've kept it shut for nothing.

Back in New York, my father was failing. My mother and Joan asked Gloria and me to fly home. He was in the French Hospital on 33rd Street, between 8th and 9th Avenues. Before we could make the travel arrangements, Pop rallied and seemed to be doing well.

To send money home to help out, I took a job at the Warner Theater on Hollywood Boulevard. Because of my academic credentials, I was able to work up to manager in a short period of time. I looked pretty spiffy in the new tuxedo I got to wear on the job.

Bruce Cohen, meanwhile, decided to go back to New York. Though he was auditioning for leading-men roles, he couldn't take the "Hollywood bullshit."

"Everybody in Hollywood talks nice to you, but nobody helps. In New York, they tell you up front they can't help you. Here, it's all bullshitting."

If he was going to be unemployed, he figured he might as well be unemployed where his friends were. Actually he spent more time weightlifting than networking with industry people. The female agents in Hollywood loved him, but he would never follow up with calls. I couldn't talk him into staying.

An actor can get rusty unless he keeps his instrument oiled, so I looked around for somebody to study with. There weren't trade papers for actors in L.A., such as *Showbusiness* and *Backstage* in New York. To find a teacher, you had to ask around.

I did, and decided to take classes with Martin Landau

in Hollywood. This was nearly 10 years before his success in *Mission Impossible.* Jack Nicholson attended that class with me. He was writing screenplays also and later had a couple of scripts produced.

In acting class, I noticed right away he had talent, but he struggled as an actor for seven more years until he "suddenly" became a star in *Easy Rider* in 1969.

BACK IN MANHATTAN

IN NEW YORK, Al continued to be coached by Charlie Laughton, but away from formal sessions like Berghof's. With Charlie's guidance, Al got cast in a few off-off-Broadway productions, doing classics, like Strindberg's The Father. Charlie criticized and critiqued Al's performances, cementing his relationship with Al.

Al leaped over to children's theater. He did The Adventures of High Jump at Theater East in Manhattan, and then Jack and the Beanstalk at Cafe Bizarre, which was directed by Matt Clark, a wonderful character actor who has worked a lot in features and on television.

In June 1962, Gloria called with the news our father had died. I felt as if I had been stabbed in the heart. I loved him and agonized that I hadn't done more for him. I regretted not having gone back to see him when he was sick. It was the saddest day of my life.

I called Joan and advised her I would come home as soon as I could get a flight. I promised to stay for a couple of weeks to help settle Father's affairs. I didn't want to move back to New York.

I called my mother. She was shattered. She wept, "Please come back. Gloria's married. She's got children, she can't come... and Joan's getting married soon. I have no money and I need you here."

What could I do? Things hadn't worked out in L.A., so I figured I might as well go back where I could at least be useful. "OK, Ma. I'll get on the next plane."

The good son. The nice Italian boy. Too generous, too unselfish for his own good.

There were thousands of would-be actors like me struggling in Los Angeles and New York City, and it didn't appear I was going to get the chance to entertain and inspire people the way I'd dreamed. So I returned to New York. I was 31 years old.

From Idlewild Airport, which is now JFK, I went right to the house on Valentine Avenue. Weeping and wailing, Aunt Lizzie, Aunt Lucy, and my cousins Frances, Grace, and Rose were hovering around Ma and Joan, who was still living at home.

I'm grateful my father lived long enough to see me graduate college and at least start my acting training. His last words to me were, "Pursue your dreams and be fair and square to everyone."

His loss really hurt me. I wanted to be like him.

Al, meanwhile, was living down in the Village. He rented rooms wherever he could and sometimes even slept in theaters. He was determined, no matter what he had to endure, to succeed.

I wanted to see him and my other friends again, but I kept putting it off. I told myself I couldn't get down to the Village because I was working day and night, or I was living up in the Bronx and it was too long a trip. In truth, I was afraid Al was mad at me for having split from the group. I figured he had a whole new life going and he didn't want to hear about my problems.

Sometime later, I got in touch with Bruce and met him at Nedicks on 57th Street near Central Park. He suggested we go down to the Village to see Al.

I said, "No, I'd feel out of place in the old circle, especially with Al hanging out with Charlie and Penny."

"What do you want to do, just forget him?"asked Bruce.

I thought about it. "No, and I really don't want to go home. All my mother's sisters are there tonight and they're still mourning my dad, crying and going on all the time. What the hell, let's go see Al."

Beneath my doubts, I knew Al was a true friend I could count on. That proved to be the case. It seemed like only yesterday since I'd seen him. He was genuinely happy to see me. I told him about my adventures in Tinseltown and, hearing about my outlandish escapades, he said he was glad he hadn't gone out with me.

Al's mother, Rose, died soon after my father. She was only 43. Al was 22. Maybe because they had drifted apart, it was more of a shock to Al. He was devastated. Now they could never resolve their differences.

Money was tighter than ever for me. My father had been a mail carrier for 35 years. His pension money and social security payments went to my mother. It was barely enough for her to scrape by. There was certainly nothing left over for vacations or luxuries.

Dad had willed me a tiny sum, which I used to pay off a few debts, but it didn't cover all of them. We had to sell his stamp collection. I wanted to give my mother some money to travel to see my sisters whenever she wanted. I also wanted to go back to Berghof for more classes. So, I decided to pursue work full time. I applied for and got back my old job at Parkchester Recreation.

Within a year, Al's grandfather, James, died. He had been the most important influence in Al's life. Al took his death badly. On top of that, he had no place to live, no money and no job. He couldn't sleep nights. Mentally, he was a wreck.

The country was at war in Vietnam. Al dreaded the possibility of getting drafted. He hated the idea of having to fight, but when he was graded four-F and turned down by the Army, he became even more depressed.

He took part-time work delivering Show Business, a newspaper for theater people. One day he started to have trouble seeing then he passed out. Refusing to go to the hospital, he started dosing himself with prescription tranquilizers. From time to time he would drown his troubles in booze.

Once he went to visit a friend in a mental institution. His emotions, as well as his clothing, were ragged.

"My coat was down to the floor and I was wandering in the hallways when I met this very nice woman. We sat down and began talking and after a half hour, she said, 'No hope for you; you have to be committed.' I got out of there real fast."

This is all he needed to hear. He knew he'd better pull himself together. But he carried a sense of morbidity around with him, sometimes imagining himself as a corpse being carried around in a casket.

He didn't have himself committed, but he did seek help. He went to a clinic a few times, until he found someone he could just sit and talk with. He finally got to the point where he could say the things really on his mind. To his amazement, he didn't disappear, nobody killed him or accused him of being guilty. It was a tremendous relief, but the pressures still built from time to time.

Al and another aspiring actor, Martin Sheen, took a room together. They worked at Julian Beck's Living Theater as stagehands. Julian Beck and his actress-wife, Judith Malina, developed a unique acting company doing classical theater as well as experimental theater and some neo-realism. Al and Marty hoped to get cast.

They watched rehearsals of *The Connection*, by Jack Gelber. Marty swore he'd play that role one day. And later on, he did — his first leading role.

When he went on to play in *The Wicked Cooks* in a little off-off-Broadway theater, he arranged for Al to be his understudy to save him from starvation.

ME

MEANWHILE, I had picked up classes with Lee Grant again to keep in shape. In one class, I did a scene from *Come Back Little Sheba* with fellow student, Maude Rowles, a cousin of the comedienne, Polly Rowles.

Polly saw me in the class and recommended me for the leading role in a play, *Outrageous Fortune* by Rose Franken. It was being staged in a little theater in the 50s. I memorized my lines riding back and forth on the subway to work and I had to take sick leave from my job to attend rehearsals.

I played a Jewish husband, and I was on stage in almost every scene. On opening night, I was so terrified they had to push me out on stage. I couldn't remember my first line. It came to me after I was out there, but I decided never again to learn lines the old way. I'd learn the action and character first.

Doris Ridgewood, a woman I had met in California, came to see me in the play. She found me backstage and said, "You were absolutely marvelous."

"I had good teachers," I replied.

"What you have, no teacher could give you."

The play ran for only a week, but we filled the house every night.

AL

IN 1963, Al got his first acting job in a stage play for an adult audience. It was in a production of *Hello, Out There*, by William Saroyan at the Cafe Cino.

Charlie had known Joe Cino and arranged for Al to get a part. Charlie directed it. He had done the play with Al in his workshop class.

Al had never before faced an adult audience. When Al said one of his lines, the audience laughed. They laughed because the play was funny, but he didn't know it. He was so unaware of what he was doing.

He thought, "Oh no, I don't know anything about this."

He went into the alley and cried. Charlie found him and said, "Al, you've got to play it two more times tonight and then 12 more times after that."

Al completed the run of the play. The experience, however, gave him such distress and insecurity he didn't perform publicly for over a year.

ME

WITH THE TASTE of Hollywood still in my mouth, I got together with Tony Andresakis, who had been in one of my acting classes at Berghof's and was my partner in the audition scene for the Actor's Studio. We decided to make a low-budget movie, which he could direct and I would star in.

We improvised a screenplay called *Wild Wild Walter*. I raised the money for it and Tony assembled a production team who would work for little money.

The story was about a mother and her 35-year-old son, Walter (me), who falls in love with a homely girl, played by an actress I really liked. She had a foreign accent and called herself Draga. The girl's mother was played by Dorothy Farrell, Draga's mother. I was in almost every scene.

I wanted Al in the movie. There was a part for a young cop. But Tony didn't know Al that well and didn't think he was right for it. We all worked without pay and we shot the film in black and white. The first cut of the picture was not very exciting, so we shot additional scenes, this time in color. The new sequences were Walter's daydreams.

We screened the picture at a screening room off Times Square. On my way to the car, I met Al and Charlie on the street. I was dressed up and wearing a homburg. After greeting each other, Charlie asked me what I was doing. I told him I was coming from the screening of a movie I was in. A movie?

"Yeah. *Wild Wild Walter*. I did the lead."

Al stared at me. Charley remarked at how great I looked. "Look how thin his face is!"

Al didn't say a word. It didn't dawn on me he was probably wondering why I didn't get him in the movie. But he was off doing the off-Broadway stuff with Charlie.

Nobody asked me to be in *Hello, Out There*.

I said to both of them, "It's so great to see you."

Al said, "Keep in touch."

AL

AL STRUGGLED, going from job to job. For awhile, he was an usher at a movie house. People would ask him all kinds of questions, "What time does the show start?" or "What is the last show that went on?" or even, "Is the movie any good?"

Finally, he figured out these people would listen to

anything he said. To test it, he bet another usher he could get the people to line up across the street. Then he told the people that because of the crowds, the line was forming across the street, in front of Bloomingdale's. The people lined up, but Al got fired.

Al got fired as an usher another time after he stopped in the lobby to look at himself in a three-sided mirror. He had never before seen his profile. He was about 24.

He couldn't believe it. Who was that strange-looking person? He had never seen the back of his clothes or the back of his head before. He couldn't stop staring at himself. The manager caught him in the act. He didn't like Al from the very start. Al thought the manager really just didn't like ushers.

He said, "Pacino, what are you looking at?"

Al mumbled something and the manager warned him not to do it again. But, a little later, Al couldn't resist another study of himself as he was walking down the stairs. The manager caught him a again and said, "You're fired!"

Al never stopped, never broke stride, just kept going downstairs. He felt a rush of happiness.

"I should have been very unhappy," Al said, "but I wasn't."

He went down to the locker room and began giggling. A couple of his friends asked, "What happened?"

Al said, "I've just been fired."

"Why?"

"Looking at myself too much."

He ushered at Carnegie Hall and frequently showed people to the wrong seats. Occasionally he would read books in the men's room and let the theatergoers fend for themselves.

Moving furniture was his next line of part-time work. He got the job by subbing for Charlie who was working as a mover between theatrical activities.

"The first thing you look at when you're a moving man is the books," Al has said. "Everybody has books, thousands of them. They put them in boxes. It's very deceptive. They have five thousand paperbacks in boxes."

Al is the only person in the world who would go to a moving job in a taxi. The other workers would say, "Al's a little late," and he would come flying out of a taxi to lug pianos up the stairs for $2.50 an hour. He and Charlie considered starting their own moving company called CHAL Movers (CHarlie and AL), but they never did it.

Al saw his actor-friend, Martin Sheen, play Hickey, the wife-killer/salesman, in a production of *The Iceman Cometh* by Eugene O'Neill.

Al thought, "I think I can do that."

He could relate to the character and he wanted to do the role himself. He'd practice it in alleys talking to pedestrians and pigeons. He had a favorite spot on Sixth Avenue where he always did his Hickey. He would start talking about his life. Then he would become Hickey. Some typical New York passersby didn't even notice. Others thought he was crazy.

One of the first things he discovered about acting was you've got to make it "personal" — no matter what it is. He had his own Hickey, not Martin Sheen's or even Jason Robards', who played it on Broadway. He also observed it is the role counts, not where it is being performed.

Al loved to audition. It was his only opportunity to act before an audience. He never expected to get the roles. He also started to play bits on stage between jobs — children's theater, revues, even stand-up comedy.

He had a comedy routine about an inmate in a mental institution who tried telling the other inmates and workers he didn't belong there. After finally convincing someone that he was sane, he would snap and bite the man's finger.

One of his favorite routines was *The Man With a Python*, which was based on a Sid Caesar joke he started acting out for his mother when he was 13 years old. He developed it into a 20-minute sketch and performed it at coffee houses in the Village.

The sketch was about a man who owned a huge python snake. The act consisted of the man getting the python, in pantomime, to slither up his body; and then, through vibrating, to send it back down and into the cage.

But the man was a complete fraud because he couldn't control the snake. Then he was invited to perform his act on live television. At first, he was able to coax the snake to climb his body. The man delivered a humorous running commentary as the python snaked its way up.

One of his lines was, "I'll just let it get up a little further." Finally, he started to gyrate and scream, "Get it off! Get it off!"

It was funnier than it sounds.

The comedy routines enabled him to survive. He apprenticed at avant-garde off-off-Broadway theaters performing at Elaine Stewart's Cafe La Mama and in coffee houses in Greenwich Village.

After his performance in *Jack and the Beanstalk* at Cafe Bizarre, one review said the play wasn't half bad, if you could find the theater in the first place.

Al's typical wardrobe was a pea jacket, baggy pants and a balaclava.

ME

MY SISTER, Joan, and Bill Dempsey got married in California. Since Gloria was living there, she made the arrangements. My mother flew out for the ceremony and the festivities, but I was unable to go because of my job.

While they were in California, I decided to find a new apartment, a place I could call my own. I was aware my mother was having a difficult time living in the same place, coping with all the old memories of life with my father.

Since Joan would no longer be living with us, we wouldn't need such a big place. Also, our neighborhood was changing for the worse, so my mother wasn't enjoying the atmosphere any more and, climbing the stairs of the fifth-floor walk-up was proving too difficult for her. So, I encouraged her to give up the apartment and stay with my sisters and me — a few months of the year with each of us.

I started scouting around for a place big enough for me and, at the same time, for my mother to have a little space of her own.

My boss at Parkchester Recreation located a nice two-bedroom apartmentfor us in the Bronx, at 1510 Union Port Road, Apt. 2G. We snapped it up and put the lease in my name.

There was a bedroom for my mother and privacy for us both. I paid the deposit and we moved in. Because she didn't have to pay rent anymore, my mother was able to save a few thousand dollars, which she gave to me to buy new furniture.

ME AND AL

AL CALLED ME. He was upset because he had to meet his father's new wife. The past couple of years had been bad for both of us. He had lost his mother and grandfather, and I had lost my father. Neither of us was working as actors, which is what we both really wanted to do.

I invited him over to see my new apartment and to say hello to my mother. When he got there, he seemed uncomfortable. Perhaps the warmth expressed by my mother made him miss his own mother, and grandfather. Perhaps it was because I had a steady job and he was just scraping by to survive, but it was obvious he felt alone and despondent.

My job at Parkchester Recreation was steady, but I was still hard up for money. I took a second job teaching Physical Education classes at Holy Family School on Castle Hill Avenue in the Bronx. The principal's name was Sister Madonna.

One day, while I was working with the kids in the playground at Parkchester, I was startled to see Al standing outside the gate. This was not a neighborhood he frequented. Charlie was with him, but waited outside the playground.

Al sauntered over to me. "Hi, Ed. How are ya?"

We hadn't seen each other for a while, so his sudden appearance was a surprise.

"Great," I said. "How are you?"

Al said, "Ed, I need money for rent. Can you do me a favor, lend me some money?"

I'm guessing Charlie stayed outside the gate because he thought I might resent him and his presence might intimidate Al.

I asked, "How much do you need?"

He said, "Well, rent every week costs me $15."

I had a little money in the bank, so I said I'd be happy to lend it. I didn't carry my wallet when I worked in the playground, so I told him, "I can't give it to you right now. Come back in an hour. I'll go the bank during my lunch hour. Be back here in an hour, OK?"

He said, "Great! Thanks!" Then he kind of shuffled and blurted out, "You got a quarter on you?"

He wanted to get a soda from the machine while he was waiting. I reached into my pocket. Empty.

I said, "I don't have a cent on me. If you don't mind taking a little walk, I have a friend, Geraldine, who works in Recreation over in the east quadrant. Tell her Ed said to lend you a quarter."

Al was reluctant. "Alright...thanks. I'll go look for her."

I said, "Don't worry. I'll give her the quarter back."

Years later Geri said to me, "Tell your friend Al Pacino he still owes me a quarter. You think I can get my quarter back after he's made millions of dollars in the movies?"

I said, "Geri, that's my fault. I promised him I'd give it back to you myself, but I completely forgot it. You sure I didn't give it back to you?"

She said, "I don't want it from you. I want it from Al."

So I said, "I think he's a little hard to reach now. I'll give it back to you with interest."

She laughed and said she preferred being owed the money by Al Pacino. More glamorous, I guess.

On my way to the bank I remembered a book I had been reading about tithing. It stated, "Always give a little bit more than you can." So I decided that's what I was going to do with Al.

I gave him not only one week's rent, but enough for three or four. I was so pleased to see his eyes light up. It was a joy to see his smile. When Al was happy, his smile was the greatest thing in the world to see, because he was depressed a lot. I figured if I could cheer up this good friend, what the hell. He'd do the same for me.

"Now, let's keep in touch," I said.

He said, "Definitely. Let's try to do some plays together off-Broadway."

ME

I WAS WORKING at Holy Family only two days a week, which left some time for teaching. I left Holy Family and joined the faculty at St. Raymond's High School For Boys, a Catholic school on St. Raymond's Avenue in the Bronx.

I was asked to teach an acting class. The experience of coaching Al and Joe made this a snap for me. One of the "brothers" asked me to direct the students in a production of *Abie's Irish Rose.*

The play is about a young Jewish man who wants to marry a young Irish woman and it starts a family feud. It had been the longest running play in the history of the American theater. I rehearsed the kids and mounted the show. It received critical acclaim by the students, the parents and the other teachers.

I then directed a production of *Brother Orchard* by Leo Brady, about a ruthless gangster who takes refuge in a community of monks. It was an all-male cast and perfect for a boys school. Edward. G. Robinson and Humphrey Bogart had done a movie of the play in 1940.

I enjoyed directing the kids, but it was also frustrating. I was helping others do what I wanted to do — act.

ME AND AL

AT LONG LAST, Al was moving up from off-off-Broadway. He was going to appear in a play by August Strindberg, *The Creditors*, at an off-Broadway theater, The Actors' Gallery.

It was a one-act play and it was being presented with a companion piece, *His Widow's Husband*, by a Spanish writer, Benvente. The producers were looking for an actor to play the male lead. Al told me to find a copy of the play and study it.

I located the play in the library and read it. I called Al and expressed how excited I was by it. He recommended me to the director, Frank Biancamano.

I went down to the theater, a converted warehouse on West Broadway, to read for it. To my astonishment, I got the part. It was the first off-Broadway production for both Al and me, and even though we were in separate plays, we were on the same bill.

Charlie took over the directing of *The Creditors*, sharing credit with Biancamano who was directing me in my play. *The Creditors* was a major event for Al and Charlie. Al really shone. He used his own street speech instead of stage speech and it worked. It loosened him up.

Charlie said, "It was momentous. In life, Al's speech wasn't that good, but when he acted Strindberg, it was like Frank Sinatra when he sang — like an angel!"

This was Al's first taste of acting as an art. Unfortunately, there were as few as eight people in the audience some nights and the show had a short run. Soon — too soon — we were out on the streets again, looking for new acting jobs.

AL

IT WAS 1966. Al was about 26. A friend told him about a job that was available as a building superintendent. The compensation was a rent-free apartment and $14 a week. He applied for a boiler's permit and got the job.

It was his first apartment on his own. He was no longer living in a rooming house or sharing a place with a girl. Now he had his own home. He had no money and hardly anything to eat, but he had a roof over his head.

Al anticipated the position might help him meet women. He taped his 8"x10" glossy on his door with the word "super" below it. It got him acquainted with all but one of the women in the building. He tried to charm her by offering to fix the lighting for her. The attempt failed. She slammed the door in his face.

Then an exquisite young woman moved into the building. He couldn't believe someone that beautiful existed. He was so anxious to meet her he couldn't wait for nature to take its course, so he decided to cause the lights in her apartment to go out. Surely that ought to get her downstairs to his place asking for help.

Al went down to the basement to locate the fuse box. He had been the super for six months, but still didn't know where the fuse box was. After some difficulty locating it, he loosened the fuse he thought controlled the electricity in her apartment.

He ran through the building and out into the yard, to check and see if he had loosened the right one. By the time he ran back to her apartment, he was exhausted. There she was at the door. Overanxious, Al blurted, "I can fix your lights and do you want to see the Village?"

She was fresh from the boonies and didn't have a clue what he was talking about. He silently chided himself, I came on a little too strong. I'm blowing this.

Of course he was blowing it. The lights in her apartment were still on. He had "blown" the lights in the wrong apartment. He hung on ineptly as the super for 11 months, his longest job.

Once, when he was unemployed, he accepted a woman's offer to move in with her. She gave him his meals but, to his dismay, he was expected to pay for them with his body. Feeling like a hooker, he split the next morning.

One dismal day, while making the rounds, he discovered the body of an actor friend in an alley. He reported it to the police and fled. He couldn't stay around to watch the body being carted off.

He had begun to drink excessively, but so far had managed to keep himself under control. It was a fruitful time for him, yet, it was also the lowest point in his life.

He had too much to drink one night and spent the night huddled up in a store front. While he was asleep, he got robbed. He borrowed subway fare from a friend and went to visit Charlie in Far Rockaway, NY. He walked across the sand to find Charlie on the beach. Even though he was nearly broke himself, Charlie lent him a few dollars.

Charlie maintained a powerful influence on Al as a teacher as well as a friend. It was a growing period for Al. Through Charlie's tutoring, he was learning to utilize himself and his life in his roles. Charlie awakened Al to the realization acting is poetry, an art that employs the voice, the body, and the spirit. He introduced Al to writers, to the "stuff" that surrounds acting. Charlie, Penny and their daughter, Deirdre, were quickly becoming Al's family.

Al told me Charlie was a great actor himself, but he wouldn't pursue roles. Charlie had completely usurped my role as a father figure or big brother. While I had been a significant influence on Al, inspiring him and getting him started, it was Charlie who took him to the next level.

Al tried directing and made friends with other struggling actors such as Susan Tyrrell and Sally Kirkland.

Tyrrell, who had been one of his lovers, said, "Al is like an animal, like a stallion with his reins pulled too tight. He needs to have his freedom more than most performers. And, when Al is free, he flies."

ME

I WAS GETTING frustrated. I felt if I didn't do some acting soon, I would lose my mind; so I started taking classes at The Irwin Piscator Dramatic Workshop.

I became friendly with an actress in my class, Dolores Hansen. We did scenes together and rehearsed them at her place on Francis Lewis Boulevard in Queens. We quickly became lovers and shared many wild, sleepless nights together.

I believed Lee Grant would be a better teacher for her than her instructor at Piscator, so I suggested she go audit Lee's class. When she decided to study with Lee, I joined her and stopped my classes at Piscator.

On my way home from spending the weekend with Dolores on Long Island, I spotted Al getting off a train. I was trying to make a connection at 42nd Street to transfer to the Bronx. It had been a couple of months since we last saw each other, so we walked over to Schraft's together to grab a cup of coffee and catch up.

He told me, angrily, he had been offered some unseemly opportunities that would have gotten him ahead in the business, but he refused them, unwilling to sacrifice his integrity as an artist.

I agreed, "I'd never do anything like that to advance my career. I don't want any kinks or kooks in my life." But I wondered if my adventures in Hollywood had been compromises.

Al insisted it was important to respect ourselves and draw the line if we wanted to succeed, no matter how long it took.

One day Dolores announced she was pregnant. With bravado, I said, "Good, I always wanted a son."

She saw through me, though, aware I didn't really want

to marry her, and she generously let me off the hook. I chose to believe she would have told me if the child was mine. Either that or it was her intention to have an abortion. We continued taking classes together, but it was awkward. She slowly drifted away from class, then me. I never knew if she had the child or an abortion.

As time went by, I became seriously depressed. Problems were compounding — no acting work, bad love affairs, and a sick mother to take care of — leaving me very unhappy.

When I realized I was seriously considering suicide, I had myself committed to Parkchester Hospital for therapy. Other than my teenage experience with therapy, I was green about the nature of this stuff, and didn't realize what I was getting into. I stayed in the hospital for three weeks.

The upshot was, Dr. Malvin Coren told me what I needed was a friend to talk to, to confide in, that I was bottling up all my troubles.

As soon as I was in the hospital, I wanted out. I had heard about people who had committed themselves, expecting to get well quickly, only to wind up locked away in mental institutions for the rest of their lives. I panicked and, in a sense, talked myself out of the despondency. I wanted to get on with my life.

I wrote a letter to Al, telling him my troubles, and received an answer from him in three days. His letter was uplifting and it pulled me the rest of the way out of the depression.

Joan and Bill took an apartment near us in Parkchester. It was great relief for my mother. She would not have to be so dependent on me. Unfortunately, there was no room for my mother at their place, so she was forced to stay with me.

I was stuck. A 35-year-old man, living with his mother.

But I loved her and accepted the obligation to take care of her. Her great sense of humor got both of us through those otherwise difficult times.

"Whaddaya wanna do tonight, Marty?"

AL

AS AL CAME TO the public's attention, he was compared to Dustin Hoffman, who was also just taking off as an actor. Al was offered a job understudying Hoffman in *Jimmy Shine*, by Murray Schisgal, on Broadway, but he turned it down. He wanted to act, not just stand around waiting.

His desire was fulfilled. He auditioned for director Alec Rubin at Alec Rubin's Theater of *Encounter on West 72nd Street.* He was cast in the leading role in *Why Is a Crooked Letter* by Fred Vassi. He was remarkable in the role and won an Obie nomination.

The Obies are like the Tonys, but for off-Broadway. Ironically, he was beat out by Dustin Hoffman who won for *The Journey of the Fifth Horse* by Ron Ribman. But for Al, even getting a nomination was a major achievement. It was the first public recognition he had received to date

I met with Al between shows and we walked over to one of those park-like islands located all over Manhattan. We sat down on a bench to talk. Suddenly, I became aware of my voice. I caught something about Al, who looked at me curiously, apparently wondering why I was suddenly so distracted.

I told him what my voice had said. "You're going to meet somebody special soon, and you're going to live with her."

Soon after that Al met Jill Clayburgh in Boston.

"You're gonna stay together a long time," I told him.

But my voice was telling me more and I repeated it to

him. "Then you're going to meet a manager."

This, later, turned out to be Marty Bregman, a prominent theatrical manager in New York, who also produced several of Al's pictures.

"But wait," I said, "There's somebody else...a redhead."

Al laughed. "A redhead? Who?"

"I don't know who she is, but a red-headed lady is coming into your life." I said, "The redheaded lady is gonna tell this manager about you. He's gonna sign you up and you're gonna take off from there."

The redhead later turned out to be Faye Dunaway.

I didn't tell Al about my voice. He'd have thought I was nuts. He thought I was just fooling around, pretending to be psychic.

Al auditioned for *The Indian Wants the Bronx*, by Israel Horovitz, a workshop production at the Eugene O'Neill Memorial Theater in Waterford, Connecticut. Director James Hammerstein gave him the role of a drug-crazed psychotic instead of the role he wanted.

He was a sadistic punk who savagely abuses an innocent intruder on his turf. The two hoodlums terrorize an aged Indian man. The Indian was played by John Cazale and the two became good friends.

Al was so believable it was frightening. He exploded with violence. Almost too much. It was his first real taste of applause.

Robert De Niro who had also walked the streets of New York looking for work as an actor, became a friend of Al's. They had similar backgrounds and both had studied at the HB Studio. De Niro, however, had nothing but praise for Uta Hagen.

Several months later, Al appeared in his third production that year: *The Peace Creeps*, by John Wolfson, at New Theater Workshop Company, directed by John Stix.

Al thought it was the right time to apply to the Actor's Studio again. This time, he was accepted. Dustin Hoffman was accepted the same year. Al had been rejected only once. Hoffman had been rejected four times. The talk at the Studio, though, was always about how great Dustin Hoffman was.

The Studio scared Al and he became despondent. He talked about having himself committed to Bellevue, a mental institution in Manhattan. Charlie persuaded him not to do it. It took Al six months to work up his nerve to perform a scene at the Studio. He did two monologues, one as Hickey, one as Hamlet.

Lee Strasberg looked at Al's card and said, "Al Pacino? Hickey and Hamlet? Where are you from?'"

Al told him. Strasberg shook his head. "We take all kinds here."

Al didn't attend the Studio a lot, but he became very friendly with Lee Strasberg. They would go to lunch together and listen to classical music in Lee's apartment. Lee even arranged for a loan from the James Dean Memorial Fund to help pay for Al's rent.

Doing three plays in one year and getting accepted into the Actor's Studio was a dream come true. Al stopped looking for odd jobs and stuck to acting for his livelihood.

During that first year at the Actors Studio, Dustin Hoffman got cast in The Graduate. Al was completely broke and had to move in with Charlie and Penny on Grand Street on Manhattan's lower East Side. Penny was then performing David Wheeler's Theater Company of Boston where she arranged an audition for Al.

He borrowed money for fare to get there. Hopeful he would get hired, Al carried all of his belongings with him in a paper bag. He lodged with Penny and slept on the floor. When he walked into the theater for the audition, he was handed a script of *The Caucasian Chalk Circle.*

He read for them and was offered a small part at $50 a week. He refused it, telling them he wouldn't do small parts. Since he had worked so often that year, he was confident he would get another good acting job soon.

ME

My voice told me I would be getting married and I would have two sons. I prayed this would come true. I wanted a family.

My mother said, "You'll meet the right girl and it will happen. My sister, Lucie, knows this girl in Brooklyn..."

"No, Ma, I'm 35 years old. No matchmaker stuff, no blind dates."

One day, on the playground where I was working, I saw an attractive young woman with chestnut-brown hair, pushing kids on a swing. Laughing, she seemed to be having as much fun as the kids.

The voice in my head declared, "You're going to marry that girl and have children with her."

I hadn't even met her yet. Twenty-six years old, she lived with her parents in the north quadrant and played with the kids simply because she loved children. I had noticed her there before, but had never really paid any special attention to her until that day.

One of the neighborhood fathers came charging up to me, stammering about his little girl who had gone to the ladies rest room and wouldn't come out. She had been in there too long.

I went over to the beauty at the swings and asked her if she'd go in and look for the little girl. She agreed, went in, and found the little girl angrily throwing cups of water all over the place. To the relief of the father, she brought out the little girl, who was now in good humor.

We introduced ourselves. Her name was Virginia Martinelli. I complimented her.

"You have a good way with children."

"I love kids," she told me. "Let me know if I can help you in any way. I live close by."

I had eaten a very little lunch that day and was still hungry, but I didn't want her to leave; so I asked her, "Could you get me a cup of tea and a container of rice pudding at the deli?"

She hurried off, brought it back, and it soon became a ritual with us. Later, we'd go to her parents' apartment and watch TV on my lunch break. She'd make me a sandwich and play records, like Sinatra's "That's Life," one of my favorite songs at the time.

"I'm going to marry you," she stated one day, not too long after we met.

"Says who?" I teased.

It became a frequent game between us, but as we got to know each other better, it didn't seem so impossible. Ginny was not the kind of girl I thought I would marry. She was not really my physical ideal. I liked cuddly blondes or brunettes, small, delicate, fetching creatures.

Ginny was none of these things. She was attractive but she was strong-willed and very assertive.

She'd say, "I want you and I'm gonna get you. I'm gonna have your kids."

She was convinced I was the perfect mate for her. How could I resist a woman who loved me so much and was unafraid to say so?

I insisted on dating other women and asked Ginny to date other men, but we were always drawn back to each other. She fulfilled some deep need in me and, obviously,

I fulfilled some deep need of hers. Though Ginny was assertive and strong, she also had a mysterious, secretive nature that intrigued me.

Sometimes very quiet, she'd keep to herself, unwilling to get involved with other people. But when we were together, she gave me her undivided attention. I had my audience! She made me feel important, and I certainly needed that.

AL

DAVID WHEELER in Boston remembered Al and hired him to play important roles in *Awake and Sing!* by Clifford Odets and *America, Hurrah*, by Jean-Claude Van Itallie. The pay was an attractive $125 a week.

At the Charles Playhouse, he met Jill Clayburgh, a complex woman and a talented actress, who had attended Sarah Lawrence College. She had done a student movie with Robert De Niro, *The Wedding Party*, directed by Brian De Palma. Jill co-starred with him in *America, Hurrah.*

A relationship bloomed between them during rehearsals and they soon became an inseparable pair. When they got back to New York, they took an apartment together downtown. They were both passionate about acting and had plenty in common to talk about. They respected each other's independence and single-minded pursuit of work.

Curious about how he would come across on screen, Al took a two-line role in a movie, Me, Natalie, starring Patty Duke. He played a junkie gigolo. The film was directed by Fred Coe and was shot in New York.

Meanwhile, Al stepped up his drinking to quiet his inner turmoil and psychic pain.

1968 proved to be a major year for Al. He played another hoodlum role in *The Indian Wants the Bronx*, but this time at the Astor Place Theater in New York. He got rave reviews and became an overnight sensation.

I attended the theater to see his performance. After the show, I sallied backstage to congratulate him. The place was jam-packed, so I waved to him across the room, too shy suddenly to approach him. I made up my mind to call him with my congratulations, and I started out.

Al raced over and caught up to me. "Hey, Ed, don't just wave and walk away."

I said, "Aw, Al, I figure I'm past tense with you."

He hugged me and said, "Don't ever feel that way. You'll always be my friend."

Jill Clayburgh was meeting Al after the show, and he invited me to join them for coffee. Al had told Jill he respected my opinion, so at the restaurant, she asked me what I thought about *The Indian Wants the Bronx*, and if I had liked it.

I said, "I couldn't watch anybody but Al."

She laughed. "My opinion, exactly."

Soon after that, Jill replaced Marsha Mason in the one-act play, It's Called The Sugar Plum, on the same bill with Indian Wants the Bronx. The double bill ran for 204 performances, and Al won an Obie for Best Actor in an Off-Broadway production. The author, Israel Horovitz, who won the award for Best New Play, asserted that Al Pacino was the best actor in New York City.

Unfortunately, *It's Called the Sugar Plum* didn't garner the best reviews. *The Indian Wants The Bronx* was invited to the Spoleto People's Theater Festival in Italy.

Al had risen so far from his impoverished roots, he was unable to manage success when it was upon him. As soon as he won the Obie, he began mysteriously to injure himself. First it was an injured knee, then his hip. He found himself frequently falling down or smashing into things. It was definitely the turning point for Al Pacino's career. Good reviews. Sudden success.

As my inner voice had predicted, Martin Bregman, an entertainment manager, saw the performance at the urging of Faye Dunaway, one of his clients, and a friend of Al's. Bregman went backstage and told Al he'd sponsor him in anything he wanted to do. He offered to be his manager — to handle his finances and his career. Al now had the support of Charlie, Strasberg and Bregman.

Al felt fulfilled and exhilarated while he was performing. When he wasn't, he felt empty and insecure. Jill was there to help, paying the rent on their apartment from an allowance she received from her parents.

She was cast in the soap "Search for Tomorrow" and some Off-Broadway productions. Al refused to do television. Their friend, Robert De Niro, also appeared on "Search for Tomorrow". They hung out together at the Ginger Man and Jimmy Ray's on Eighth Avenue with Charles Durning, Ralph Wait, Michael Hadge, Mitchell Ryan, and Joe McHarg.

In spite of his success, or perhaps because of it, Al was deeper than ever into alcohol. Though he was serious about Jill, he didn't feel ready for marriage. With two growing careers they'd have to be separated too often. They both wanted children but neither felt ready to get married.

ME

GINNY AND I were married in July, 1968, in the Actors Chapel at the Church of St. Malachy, with a beautiful candlelight service. At the reception at the New York

Hilton in Manhattan, Ginny's parents, her brother, my mother, and my Aunt Dolly celebrated. Since we all lived at Parkchester, Ginny was already well-acquainted with my mother and Joan.

Ginny's father had his own brokerage firm. He asked, "What would you two like for a wedding present?"

With a straight face, though I was joking, I said, "A town house."

My humor must have rubbed him the wrong way, for he hurried off and hired a lawyer. He mistakenly thought I was a hustler after his money. That got me off on the wrong foot with her family, and it never really got righted.

Ginny came to live with me in my apartment. She wasn't openly thrilled about sharing quarters with my mother, but she agreed to try it. My mother's room was set off from the rest of the apartment and pretty private.

To support my mother in another apartment would have been costly and she didn't feel well enough to travel to California to live with my sister, Gloria. Besides, all of her friends were in New York. Being cut off from them would have damaged her well-being.

To ease Ginny's fears, I promised her as soon as I made it, as soon as I had some spare cash, I'd set my mother up in her own place. Ginny was aware of my aspiration to become an actor and she encouraged me to pursue my career. I commenced classes again.

One day, Ginny secretly followed me to my class with Bill Hickey. She was curious about the actresses I worked with, what they looked like. She may have been jealous of the time I spent rehearsing with them.

Hickey spotted her at the back of his class and asked, "Who is that girl in the back?"

I turned to look and was shocked to see Ginny amid all the young, glamorous actresses.

After class, when I introduced her to him, Hickey wanted to know if she was "in the business."

Ginny shook her head, "I'm not an actress."

Hickey studied her, obviously impressed. "What charisma this woman has. That's what a great actress must have. That indefinable, mysterious something."

Ginny had a quality like Anna Magnani. It's what attracted me to her. How observant Hickey was. Ginny was all raw emotion, like Magnani, though she was only half Italian, her mother being English.

Ginny was not very social and didn't do much on her own. She stayed in the apartment most of the time. My mother, consequently, spent a lot of time with Joan, who lived close by in Parkchester. When she remained at home, she and Ginny got on each other's nerves.

Our marriage was taking a toll on us. Ginny became pregnant and I started to put on weight. I had lost my fitness when I stopped playing basketball.

AL

ON FEBRUARY 25, 1969, Al made his Broadway debut in *Does a Tiger Wear a Necktie*, by Don Petersen. Director Michael A. Schultz asked him to gain 25 pounds for the role. Al played a sadistic psychotic, Bickham, in a drug rehabilitation center.

The reviews were mild, but Al's performance got raves. The New York Times critic, Clive Barnes, called him an Italian Dustin Hoffman. Al detested the comparison. The show ran only 39 performances, but a Variety critics poll named him the most promising new Broadway actor. He won a Tony Award as Best Dramatic Actor, Supporting Role. A star was born!

Al injured himself again. This time it was a wrenched back. Thinking the accidents psychosomatic, he tried analysis. It didn't help and he drank himself almost insensible.

Al appeared on the "Merv Griffin Show." When he emerged on stage, the audience applauded as soon as his name was announced. He thought nobody knew who he was, so he was confused.

"What did I do?" he wondered.

So he bowed. It was a stage bow, the only bow he knew. He was practically parallel to the floor. As he was doing it, he realized it was the wrong thing to do, so he started to straighten up, very slowly.

Immediately, Griffin asked, "So how'd you get from the Bronx to Broadway?"

What a question! Al replied, "I walked — I didn't have the carfare."

Nobody laughed. Griffin then said, "*The Indian Wants the Bronx* and *Does a Tiger Wear a Necktie*. Aren't those funny names for shows?"

Al wondered how to answer that. He felt like saying, "No. Merv Griffin is a funny name for a show."

The interview was a disaster.

After *Me and Natalie* opened, Al asked me, "Do you think I'll be any good in movies?"

I reassured him. "With your talent and training you'll be great."

He accepted that.

ME

MY SISTER, JOAN, and her family moved out of Parkchester to Plattsburg. Now, as far as immediate family was concerned, I was all my mother had. She became friendly with Victor Beary, who lived upstairs.

A tall, aesthetic-looking man in his 50s, Victor taught voice lessons in his apartment. He visited with my mother frequently, helped her with her shopping, and joined us for dinner from time to time. Since I was out so much of the time either at my job or "making the rounds" looking for acting jobs, Vic helped relieve the tension between Ginny and my mother.

The Handicapped Association had been searching for a good recreation and social director and they approached Mike Doyle, an excellent teacher. He had more credentials than I, but turned down the job, saying he was too busy.

But he told them, "There's somebody better suited than me. There's a guy working at a private school teaching kids nobody else wants to teach."

He had heard about my work at the Holy Family School, and that I opened my heart to those poor kids. He told the president, "This guy has much more empathy with these children than I do."

They offered me the job. I thought, Why not? I could use the extra money to support mother so she could live by herself and be more comfortable.

I worked as the recreation director at night and on Saturday afternoons. I also served as recreation director for their summer camp. Soon I was making enough money to support both Ginny and my mother, and maybe look for a separate place for my mother.

New York is one of the biggest cities in the world, millions of people, yet it's amazing how frequently you bump into people you know. One day, I ran into Charlie Laughton on a West Side street. He asked me what I was doing.

"I've got a new teaching job. It doesn't pay much, but it's better than being not paid for not acting." Then, I thought, Go for it!, so I asked, "Why don't you direct me, Penny and Al in a play?"

"I'd like that," he said.

"Let's find a good three-character play."

I don't know if Charlie talked to Al about it, but they never responded to the idea. Perhaps it looked like I was trying to ride in on Al's coat tail.

Ginny gave birth to our son, Dale, on May 7, 1969, while I was chasing from teaching job to teaching job, and auditioning for roles as an actor. I wasn't home much regularly for dinner and I left early mornings to start classes at the school.

Ginny and I started to bicker. My mother always jumped in and took my side, which made matters worse with Ginny.

Something had to change. Ginny decided, now that Dale was born, she would get a job; so, she went to work for her father at his brokerage. My mother looked after little Dale while she was out.

Being a father made me realize I was a new person. I was not just a little speck in the overall scheme of things, I was the center of a whole new world. I had my own family! I was going to achieve great things.

ACT II

"The turning points of lives are not the great moments. The real crises are often concealed in occurrences so trivial in appearance that they pass unobserved."

— William E. Woodward
George Washington

MY LIFE BECOMES A CIRCUS

I WAS DETERMINED to concentrate more on acting, like Al did, even if it meant looking for jobs away from the mainstream. I methodically studied the casting notices in Backstage and Showbusiness and I checked the bulletin boards at the rehearsal studios.

I spotted an announcement that a dinner-theater on Long Island was searching for a versatile character actor who could play several challenging roles. They were doing Barefoot in the Park, Cabaret, Scuba Duba, and The Man of La Mancha. There were great parts for me in each of them.

I called to get an appointment and was told I had to audition out on the Island — at my own expense. The pay was only "scale plus 10 percent." The 10 percent was for the actor's agent, but since I didn't have an agent I could keep it myself. It sounded very appealing. I was sure they would like me and cast me. It would be worth investing in a trip out there to audition.

Playing several different roles over a two-month period would be a great showcase for my talent and I heard a lot of people were discovered in summer stock. I figured this could be an opportunity to be seen. It could land me a role on Broadway.

The producers wanted to see me the next day — at

10:00 in the morning! It would be a one-hour ride on the Long Island Railroad.

I raced out my apartment building, dressed in my best jacket and tie, carrying a briefcase full of pictures, resumes and a couple of scripts to read on the train. Mrs. Mershkowitz on the first floor wished me good luck. Word sure got around fast whenever I had an audition.

Our local mounted policeman waved at me, "Go get 'em today, Ed!"

I smiled and thanked him, but as he passed by, his horse let go with a steamy dump at my feet. Bad omen. To compound it, I bumped into a woman, knocking over her shopping cart. The cop laughed, but I didn't have time to enjoy the situation.

At the entrance to the subway, a ragged bum thrust out his open hand. "Spare any change?"

He looked like Boris Karloff in The Mummy. Our eyes held a second, then he abruptly turned his back. There was something familiar about him, but I couldn't put my finger on it. I raced down the stairs.

After an exhausting train ride that felt like I was being jostled inside a cement mixer, I got off at Speonk, Long Island. It was a sultry, hot day. I checked my watch and realized I was a half-hour late for my appointment.

A taxi dropped me off at the theater. It was a large, red barn. I spotted a sign that read Auditions and it had an arrow pointing to the side of the building.

As I approached the gate, a big rooster with sharp talons rushed me. I turned back and dashed into an enclosure, only to face a vicious-looking steer pawing the ground. Backing into a pile of cow dung, I leaped over the fence and bolted up the alleyway toward the stage entrance.

Breathing hard, I reached for the door handle, but the door burst open, smashing me in the face. An actor apologized, but it was too late. I clutched my mouth and a cap from one of my front teeth dropped into my hand. I jammed it back onto its post and went inside.

Smelling of cow dung, I introduced myself to an assistant who beckoned me toward the work light on the stage. I could see a skinny woman-producer and a fat director sitting in the front row.

The director honked, "Mr. De Leo, ready to start?

My God, I thought, they're not even going to talk to me.

"Which part?"I asked.

"Do you sing, Mr. De Leo?"

"Oh, yeah. Baritone. I've sung—"

The director interrupted, "Good. Start with "Man of La Mancha". Are you ready?"

With manufactured enthusiasm, I replied, "Yes, I am! Thank you!"

My tongue hit the back of my teeth and sent my front cap flying through the air. It landed in the producer's lap. She stared at it, disgusted.

Nervously, I proceeded to sing and read, trying to conceal the gap in my teeth. It distorted my pronunciation and I could see the director and producer watching me with complete disbelief.

"That will do, Mr. De Leo," the director finally said.

I asked, "You're not doing Dracula by any chance, are you?" I smiled broadly, showing off the missing tooth.

The producer handed back my tooth and said, "Thank you so much for coming, Mr. De Leo."

I arrived back in the city late in the afternoon. I was hot, exhausted and depressed, as I lumbered up the steps of the subway. Wet with sweat, I crossed the street and plodded toward a group of children struggling to open a fire hydrant. I stopped to watch.

The kids cursed and kicked the hydrant. I reached for

the wrench. "Let me do that."

I twisted the bolt, but it wouldn't budge. I twisted harder. Water abruptly gushed out and almost drowned me. The kids shrieked with delight. I sputtered, soaked to the skin.

I saw the mummy up ahead, thrusting his hand out at passersby. Soaked and weary, I came abreast of him and reached into my pocket. The bum saw me and scurried away. I stopped, puzzled. I shrugged it off, turned the corner, and went up the steps to my building.

As I entered the apartment, I pocketed my keys, put down my briefcase and sighed. I called out, "Ginny? Ma?" There was no answer.

"Anybody home?"

I spotted a note propped against a lamp on the cluttered hall table. Mail, magazines, a red sneaker, several hats and various theatrical mementos fought for space. The note was from Ginny. She was going to be back at midnight with the baby. My mother was at my sister's.

I waited up in the living room for Ginny. It was getting close to midnight and I sat in the dark room lit only by the street lights. I checked my tooth. It was holding.

I got restless, so I got up, turned on a lamp and looked at myself in the mirror. I struck a dramatic attitude, like James Cagney.

"You dirty rats!"

Then I did Bogart. I leaned in and tugged at a clump of hair. I took out a little case, extracted a pair of nail scissors and cut off an inch of hair. Satisfied, I put the scissors away.

I heard a key rattling the lock. The front door opened and Ginny came in. She saw me in the dark and was startled. "You're still up."

"I couldn't sleep. Too hot."

Baby Dale was asleep in her arms. She set him down in his crib. I leaned over and kissed him.

"Where were you?" I asked Ginny softly.

"Shhh!" She walked past me into the kitchen.

I followed her. Dressed in a chic, fitted suit, Ginny was in full bloom. Her job was changing her. Exuding from her pores was an uptown, successful aura. Her hair was expertly cut and fell into place however she moved her head. Her eye makeup and lipstick were a little smudged.

"So, how'd it go?" She opened the beat-up old fridge, studied the shelves, took out a chilly Perrier. She opened it and slugged it down, her legs planted apart.

"They said they'd call."

Ginny turned and saw my downcast expression. Her temper flared. "Don't tell me you can't get a half-season in some flea bitten dinner theater in the boon docks!"

"Well, my tooth—"

Ginny slumped down on a stool and stared at her feet.

"I just blew it off," I explained, "like the season, I guess."

Ginny got up abruptly and stalked out. I hurried after her into the bedroom. The bedroom, like the rest of the apartment, was claustrophobically small. And a mess.

Ginny was getting worse and worse at cleaning up, and she liked to accumulate things. The bed was unmade. Clothes were strewn everywhere, folded in stacks on the floor. The closet was open and shoes and paraphernalia spilled out of it into the room.

She shook her head. What was the use. She sat down and took off her shoes and pantyhose. That always turned me on. Ginny cast me a bored look and shucked out of her jacket. She hung it up in the closet.

"How long has it been since you had a job? Any kind of job?"

"Uh, two years. I don't know. The reviews I got for *The Widow's Husband*... I should've gotten a movie, a Broadway play, something."

Ginny looked around the room. "What a disgusting hole this is."

I felt guilty. "I should've made the bed, but I was already late."

She knew I was critical of the junk that she was accumulating. She never threw anything away. She gave me one of her looks and went into the bathroom.

"Should've, would've, could've."

While she brushed her teeth, I stood in the doorway and told her, "Ginny, why don't you quit work? Stay home with Dale. I'll get work. Something that pays.

She brushed past me, grabbed a T-shirt, and slipped it on. "How many times have I heard that?"

"I'll do it this time," I answered.

"Yeah, and droop around like an old basset hound. Then you'll call in sick and they'll fire you. Like always. You don't try, Ed. You say you will, but you know damn well I can't quit until I'm sure you... Oh, damn it! I don't want to quit. My parents want me to work for them, but I want to do it on my own. Larry told me... "

"Larry?"

"Larry Greenawalt."

"Oh, it's Larry now, not Mr. Greenawalt?

"At dinner he told me I could become a broker."

"At dinner? You had dinner with Larry Greenawalt?"

"So? It was work. Strictly business."

"Ginny, I trust you. I'd trust anything you tell me."

"Well, maybe you shouldn't."

She fell back on the bed and began to sob. The sound scared me and I went over to comfort her. She knocked me away, sat up, and said, "I want a divorce."

I was stunned. “Don’t joke with me, Ginny.”

“I’m at the end of my rope — with you, with the baby. I’ve got to get him out of here, out of the city.”

“We will. I promise. I’ll make the money.

“With what? Your next acting job at some God forsaken off-off-off-off Broadway church in Brooklyn?”

“You’ve got to believe in me, Ginny.”

“What do you think I’ve been doing all year? Even a season at some dinky dinner theater would’ve given me hope, but you blew that. And my being cooped up with your mother. I can’t take it any more. I want out.”

I was in despair. “Ginny, I can’t make it without you.”

“Well, you’re going to have to.quit show business and get a real job, Ed!”

“I’m an actor. If I give up acting I might as well quit breathing.”

“Well, I’m suffocating under the load I’m carrying. I’ve waited as long as I’m going to wait. I’m getting old! I’m 27 years old. Look how we live. We’re not moving. We’re just rotting here in this... this compost heap.”

“I’ll clean it up,” I said, knowing damned well most of the mess was hers.

“I’m talking about a clean sweep, cutting my losses.”

“You think I’m a loser.”

Ginny eyed me, teary-eyed. “I want a house, a real house, some privacy. A place away from the violence. I’m sick of bums pissing on my front door, holding out their hands every time I walk outside. I want some sunshine and fresh air, a place where Dale can grow up like a normal child, have normal friends and play sports...”

“It’s all about my mother, isn’t it? Let’s talk about this, please Ginny.”

“I’m tired of talking about it. I’m going to bed. You can sleep on the sofa.” She blurted out, “I want you out of here in the morning."

I was adamant. "I'm not leaving, Ginny!"

She quickly flopped on the bed. Seeing that familiar look on her face, I backed off and went to sleep in the living room

Come morning, I ran downstairs to look at the trade papers. There was a newsstand near the subway stop. The mummy was there, panhandling on the steps.

I bought a copy of *Weekly Variety* and started to read it as I walked back to the apartment. As I got into the creaky elevator, I heard the familiar soprano voice soaring up the scale, hitting an E flat, then trilling back down. I could hear sounds of hammering and debris hitting the floor. As I walked down the hall, I saw the door to the apartment open and a shopping bag in the doorway.

My mother had come home, but she wasn't there. I could hear her laughing next door at Connie's. There was a note by the telephone. It was from Ginny. She had packed all her things and taken the baby with her to Connecticut.

Her parents had bought a house in Brookfield and she was moving in with them. Obviously, this had been planned. Her parents had conspired with her. Ginny had waited for me to go out so she could sneak off with Dale. I was crushed.

In the note, she said that she wanted me to give up acting and live with her in Connecticut. I wadded up the paper and threw it against the wall. Giving up acting was not an option for me any more. It was now. Do or die.

My mother appeared in the doorway. "Look at you! Good morning!" She met me with a hug and pinched my cheeks. "I could eat you up. Those cheeks, like little crab apples. Honey, what's wrong?"

I felt ashamed. "It's Ginny. She took off with Dale."

"She walked out on you? Well, what'd I tell you? Didn't

I always say she was wrong for you? Ginny? I ask you, is that a name for an Italian girl? Threw you out? You shoulda junked her years ago. That phony, highfalutin'— What'd I tell you, huh? Didn't I warn you?"

"Mom, let it alone. I still love her. I'm gonna get that big role."

"Yes, you are, my sweet. You're gonna be a star. Why, you haven't even started yet."

"Ma, I'm 40 years old."

"A mere child. Character actors don't come into their own until they're 40. Come here! Get a look at that face." She led me to a mirror. "Look at yourself. You just started lookin' interesting. Gettin' a few lines, a little gray at the temples... added a little ring at the waist. That's good, real good, honey. Oh, want some Danish? Victor bought some over at the Hungarian bakery yesterday. It's yummy. I'll go make coffee."

"Don't trouble yourself, Ma."

But she was already hustling at the sink, drawing water for the pot, panting and gasping heavily as she worked.

The doorbell rang. I opened the door. It was Victor Beary, a long-time friend of ours. He was a tall, thin, aesthetic looking man, a voice teacher who lived and worked upstairs.

Always positive, he sang out, "Isn't it a great day? Hello everybody."

I greeted him, "Hi, Vic."

Victor walked in and kissed my mother on the cheek. She waved him off.

"I'm going to the market," he said. "Can I bring you back some veggies, Mrs. D?"

Ma smiled. It was a routine. "Yeah, but no cabbage. Could you stop at Luigi's? My tongue's flappin' for some good Italian salami."

Victor scolded her. "Now, love, you know what that stuff does to you. I'll make you a nice bean casserole instead."

"Victor, I appreciate your concern, but I'm bloated out to here with your bean casseroles. Red meat's good for the blood. You know how tired I've been lately."

"It's your body." He looked at me. "So, when do you leave for Long Island?"

I hesitated. "They didn't call."

"Well, loss is gain, Ed. God's got something better in store for you."

He always turned the bad around, something that was getting harder and harder for me to do.

"I sure hope so."

Victor looked at his watch. "Shopping can wait. I'll stay for some Danish."

My mother carried the coffee pot to the table by the window. "Come and get it. Oh, Vic, there's hot water. You know where that herb stuff is."

Victor made himself a cup of tea.

My mother turned to me. "Guess who I saw on TV."

"Who?"

"Al Pacino."

"What was the occasion? You know how he hates interviews."

"He's starring in a new project. He said it wasn't all cast yet. Ed, here's your chance. Call him up. He owes you big time."

Victor sat down. "That might be a very appropriate move, Ed."

I waved them off. "You know how many times I've called him? How many times I've gone up for roles in his pictures? He tries to help, but something goes wrong every time. I'm not going to call him again. Ever."

My mother would not give up. "Persistence pays, sweetie."

Victor added, "Pride goeth before the fall."

"Pride has nothing to do with it."

I got up abruptly. My mother and Victor exchanged a worried look.

"Where you going, Ed?"

"Out. Just out."

And I left. I don't think my mother had ever seen me like this before.

Outside the apartment building, an old blind woman, Jossie Sitacaro, was hawking newspapers. She thrust a paper at me as I passed. I reached into my pocket and handed her a quarter. She fingered it and scoffed. "Hey, it's a dollar, Sad Sack!"

I slapped the newspaper. "This is yesterday's news, Jossie."

"So, did you read it yesterday?"

"No..."

"Then, for you, it's still news! Dollar!"

I hastily handed her a dollar. I tucked the paper under my arm and continued on. All around me, as I ambled along, the street teemed with activity.

A violinist played a romantic tune, a hat at his feet. A dancer was spinning around, performing a routine. A juggler was juggling. A mime was miming. Laughter and shrieks melded with the intense noise of the traffic. A pair of lovers strolled arm in arm, kissing and cooing at each other.

I felt depressed, alone and out of it. I tossed the day-old newspaper away.

I crossed through the arches of the park. Children ran and played. Nurses and mothers chided them. People were warming the benches, eating lunch. Two old men were arguing over a chessboard. I spotted a bench with a bum sitting on it. I went over and sat on the other end, with my head down.

After a moment, I glanced over at the bum. He was muttering, "Life is a tale... told by an idiot... full of sound and fury... signifying nothing."

I eyed him intently. It was the mummy. I moved over, closer to him. It was then I recognized him.

"Rich? Rich Jaynes?"

The bum stopped muttering and looked at me. He jumped back, panicking.

"Why, uh, Ed? Er... how've you been?"

I smiled broadly. "Oh, great, just great. I thought I recognized you. I haven't seen you since... Hey, how long's it been?"

"That audition for *The Master Builder*. Five years ago, right?" He looked terrible.

"Five years? Where does the time go?" I asked him cautiously, "You been... busy?"

He sat back and crossed his legs like a corporate executive. "Oh, yeah. I got all kinds of irons in the fire. You?"

How could I tell him? I replied, "Oh, yeah. Things are really looking good for me."

"Anything special?"

"Yeah. Several things. Can't talk about 'em. You know... Don't want to jinx 'em."

"Know what you mean. It's like if you talk, you set off all these jealous vibes in the universe."

"Right, right. So when was your last good role?"

He hesitated. "Ah, well, that part in Scorsese's picture, uh, *Mean Streets*. Then there was... Well, it's been a while."

"Once an actor, always an actor, right?"

"Yeah, but sometimes it gets to you... not working."

"You just have to keep slugging away.

"That's what they say. Tell me, Ed, how do you get out of this business?"

I stared at him. Dirty, unshaven, in tatters, Rich was utterly sincere and frightened. So was I.

"So, Rich, how about lunch? My treat."

Rich leaped to his feet, dusted himself off, lifted his head and mustered all his dignity. "Sorry, but, I've got an appointment... er, an audition. Take a rain check, OK?"

"Sure thing, old buddy. Break a leg, OK?"

Rich hurried away, limping a little. I could picture him dragging his mummy wrappings.

On impulse, I got up and followed him, keeping safely out of sight. I saw him turn down a side street. As I quickened my pace to keep up, he looked back. I ducked out of sight. Rich limped on. As I got closer, he sneaked a look back, then ducked into an alley. I waited a few seconds, then followed.

I looked down the dark cavern between two buildings, littered with garbage cans and crates. I saw Rich limp over to a small hut made of a packing crate and corrugated cardboard. He kneeled down and crawled inside. My heart sank. There but for the grace of God went I.

I dashed out of the alley and plastered myself against the building around the corner, panting with fear.

Later that day, I went upstairs to Victor's apartment for a voice lesson. He didn't charge me. In return, we would share meals with him. In his monk-Spartan studio, a grand piano dominated the very clean and neat space. I struggled with a song from *The Man of La Mancha* while Vic accompanied me on the piano.

Victor grimaced. "Open your throat, Ed. You're way too tense."

"Tense is not the word, Vic. I've got knotted rope stuck in my craw."

"I'll make some tea. It's a nerve relaxant."

"I'll take some valium if you have it."

Vic cast me a warning glance and proceeded over to the stove to make tea. I began pacing the floor, unable to stand still.

Victor was worried about me. "Why don't you try meditation? It worked for me."

"I can't sit still long enough to meditate."

"That's precisely why you need it. When you quiet your mind, it's amazing what you can learn about yourself. All your problems can be solved if—"

I cut him off. "Vic, I appreciate the advice, but I really don't want to look at my problems right now. They're too... raw."

"You and your mother. You resist every attempt to help you. If she'd stay on a diet— Frankly, I'm worried about her."

"My mother? What about?"

"Have you noticed how confused she acts lately?"

"Confused? No."

"Like she's not getting enough oxygen or something."

I didn't buy it. "Mom's strong as a horse, Vic. Look how she took care of dad his last years."

"That's what just about killed her."

"She's never had a life of her own. When my father died, she went down with him."

"You're angry, you know."

"I'm not angry, Vic, I'm scared."

"You want to talk about it?"

"I saw myself today — on the streets, homeless, sleeping in a packing crate. That's the next stop for me."

"It'll only happen if you let it."

"Man, I'm an actor. I'm helpless unless somebody hires me. Vic, nobody'll hire me! Ginny left me. She's got my son. I can't support them or myself. I have no home. It's the packing crate for me."

"You've got to do something, Ed. Stop playing the victim. Get on top of things. There must be something you can do. If there's one thing you can do, do it. And pride be damned."

I shook my head. "There's nothing."

"I don't believe that."

Then I thought about it. "Well, there is one thing."

We said it together. "Al."

But I added, "I can't. His career is just taking off. I can't take advantage!"

"What's the alternative?"

I stared at him, frightened out of my skull. We went back to the lesson.

In order to see Dale and spend time with him, I had to go up to Connecticut every weekend; but I loved him and it was worth it.

Ginny's parents tried to convince her to divorce me, but she didn't want to divorce me. She wanted to be married to me. She just wanted us to live together, without my mother.

We finally agreed on an official separation. I had to fight in court to keep custody of Dale. Even though I didn't have a regular job and income, we were awarded joint custody and I had the right to continue seeing him whenever I wanted.

AL

IN NOVEMBER, Al was cast in *The Local Stigmatic* at the Actor's Playhouse, one of eight one-act plays by Harold Pinter. Critics were not kind to him and the show ran only eight performances. It was a flop and Al felt his career was over. He said it was the last play he'd do.

To add to his depression, Cliffy, one of Al's pals when he was a pre-teen, died of a drug overdose at the age of 30. Cliffy was the one who had been wild and got into a lot of trouble.

ME

ONE MORNING, while I was making up my bed, I looked down over the railing and saw my mother, lying on her side on the couch, near the window. She was breathing heavily, a little whine coming from her.

I was suddenly concerned, especially after what Victor had told me. Then she laughed and waved off an imaginary admirer. I picked up the phone and called Ginny at her office. A receptionist answered.

"May I speak to Mrs. De Leo please?"

There was a click, and Ginny got on the line. "How may I help you?"

"Ginny, I want you to come home. Please."

She tried to restrain her anger. "I'm sorry. No."

"Can I come out and see Dale today?"

"No. It's his first day at the nursery."

"I thought you didn't have the money."

"Daddy paid for it, which is more than you can do."

"That hurts, Ginny. It really hurts. You know, when you started working, I never asked you for anything. Not clothes, or new head shots, or hair stylists or even the dentist... All the things I needed to pursue acting full time."

"That was your choice. If you'll excuse me, I have an investor on the other line." She hung up abruptly, leaving me dangling.

I put the phone down and sank back on the bed. Another nail in my packing crate. I studied the watch.

Later, at dinner, my mother chattered away, oblivious I was not really listening to her.

"After they made love, John realized she wasn't real! She was an angel. They got to spend one last night together. I've never seen anything so touching, have you?"

I could hardly look at her, I was so depressed.

"What?"

She continued, "The soap. Those writers are really clever. The priest, when he told John what was happening, he was so tender, so gentle with him. Ed, that part coulda been played by you. He was so... so nondescript. Anybody could've played the part."

I seethed and muttered under my breath. Damnable praise from my mother.

"Speak up, doll. I can't hear you."

I muttered a silent hex. My mother peered at me.

"I see your lips movin', but I don't hear nothin.' You a ventriloquist now?"

"I might as well be. Maybe I could make some money at it."

"Eat your mashed potatoes. Isn't that gravy to die for?

"I'm not hungry, ma."

"You better eat it. Vic'll throw it out. You know what a militant he is. He irks the hell outta me."

"Ma, you need Victor. He helps you, out of the goodness of his heart, and he asks for nothing."

"Can I help that? He can help, but he can also keep his damn trap shut." Her eyes lit up. "Hey, y'know while you were upstairs, Al was on TV, talkin' his fool head off. Don't cha think that's kinda odd?"

"It's not like him, for sure."

"Did you call him yet?"

"No. And I'm not going to."

I got up and stalked into my room.

AL

MILTON KATSELAS, a director from the Actors Studio, offered Al the role of Kilroy in a revival of Tennessee Williams' *Camino Real* at Lincoln Center Repertory Theater. When a fellow actor smacked him in the play, it loosened two of Al's capped teeth, inhibiting his performance. The restraint, however, only intensified his performance. He learned something from this. When it happened to me, it made me lose the job.

ME

I STARTED having an identity problem and went to see a therapist. I wasn't happy with myself. I was turning into a bum instead of an actor. I couldn't dig my way out of a deepening depression.

Why couldn't I make it as an actor? I was making the rounds, I had the training, I had pictures and resumes, I went to auditions. But nothing was happening. Was it my looks? I needed to find out who I was.

I met an attractive woman at one of the social recreational programs. She looked like Lauren Bacall. She was the mother of one of the brain-injured children I was working with and she worked as a waitress.

I went to California with her, to get away from my problems for a couple of weeks. My sister lived in Glendale. I thought I'd visit her and see what the job scene looked like in Hollywood. Lorraine and I stayed at the

Roosevelt Hotel. The kid was with her. She found work in L.A. as a waitress right away. We had an affair, but she started to drink heavily.

I went to a fortune teller in Hollywood. She said, "Go home darling, there's nothing for you in Hollywood."

I also went to see a psychic who was giving readings before an audience. When I walked in, a woman at the door handed me a card to fill out. Suddenly, I felt a warm presence over my head. I went into the auditorium and forgot about it.

The woman on stage pulled my card and called my name. When I was on stage, she said to me, "Oh my God, this is a very special card." She gestured with her hand. "I see tremendous success. Are you in motion pictures?"

"No," I told her. "Not yet."

"I see Warner Brothers."

She was probably reading Al's future. Maybe I was thinking about him. There's a name for that sort of thing.

The woman who had been standing at the door said, "When this man walked in, there was a halo around his head." You will do something big one day. I see a hand microphone."

"Thank you," I said, totally disappointed.

Did she think I was going to be a singer?

I had a nice visit with Gloria and her family, and I looked up some old friends, but I felt out of place in L.A. I didn't have an agent, I was not a member of the Screen Actor's Guild, and my resume said New York. Even to get a bit part they needed to know you lived in the Los Angeles area.

When Lorraine and I returned to New York, she continued to get drunk. I couldn't deal with that, so I broke it off. Reconciling with Ginny would be easier than that.

I called Al, but he was in Boston directing a production of *Rats*, a play by Israel Horovitz's at the Charles Playhouse, David Wheeler's Theater Company.

I started working again with the handicapped, but I thought I might be able to make more money by also teaching in the public schools instead of the private schools. I wanted to teach Special Education.

I had the required B.A. but I needed to pass a test to get my license to teach for the New York City Board of Education. I had to prepare an essay and then demonstrate my teaching method in front of a group of administrators.

"How would you do *Hamlet* with a bunch of city kids?"

I replied, "I'd bring it to their understanding."

"'To Be or Not to Be.' What does Shakespeare mean by that?"

I explained it in a very simple way so that kids could understand it. They liked it and I got my license to teach English and Special Education.

At the request of the Board of Education, I took English teaching classes at Yeshiva evenings, a course I couldn't get elsewhere. It was necessary for me to teach English in the high schools.

My first job was as a sub at P.S. 116 in the Bronx. Morris Avenue was a rough neighborhood, but I did my job without getting hurt. My next job was at P.S. 126. Because my name was Ed and I was teaching Special Ed, the Assistant Principal called me "Special Ed." He would say, "Hi, Special Ed!"

The regulations for teaching Special Ed were getting stricter. You needed special courses to teach the mentally and physically handicapped in the public schools, or lose your license; so I enrolled at Herbert Lehman College, also in the Bronx. I studied at night for two years, graduating in 1972 with master's degree in Special Education.

My mother had a terrific sense of humor. One day, I

brought a severely brain-injured teenager home.

"Mom, this is Robert. It's part of my job to take care of him."

He was assigned to me by the NYABIC (the New York Association for Brain Injured Children). My mother smiled at him and gave him a big hug.

"Nice to meet you, Robert. Come on in."

Brain-injured kids usually have a short attention span and get distracted easily. Robert was trying to get rid of me and said, "Take your son. He did his job, now he can come home."

My mother and I laughed because I was supposed to be watching him, and he was reversing the situation. After that incident, anytime I was helping her with the dishes or doing some other chore, she would say, "You did your job, Ed. Now go home."

She and I had an act we did together, especially when Victor, the voice teacher who lived upstairs, came down. I imitated Ted Lewis, whom she loved. Dad had bought a high hat just for these occasions, the kind Ted Lewis had worn.

I'd say, "Is evvverybody happy?"

And she'd do Mae West and say, "Come up and see me some time."

Any time she felt bad, I'd tell her, "Go into your act, right away!"

Vic would sit there and laugh his head off.

I was in great shape. I had lost about 80 pounds and I felt good. I started to take singing lessons at the Fred Steel Studio and I went to the Weist-Barron Workshop for training in doing commercials. They told me I would never be accepted on soaps, that I was more likely to find work in the movies.

A teacher at school, Nona Grayson, a redhead with a

weight problem, confided to me one day, "Oh, Ed, I'm so depressed. My husband and I can't have a baby."

The voice in my head came on very strong. "Tell her, next year she'll have a baby and she'll name her Anne."

I told her and she responded, "I wish."

A year later, she rang my mother's doorbell and asked for me. She told my mother the story.

"Your son not only predicted I'd have a little girl, but he had no way of knowing my husband's mother is Anne and Bill wanted to name the first girl after her."

I never saw her again.

My mother said, "This woman came around with a baby carriage, and she wanted to thank you."

I figured it had been a voice from God and I was honored. Could this have been my purpose in life? To make predictions? Did I blow it? I don't really know. I want people to listen to this inner voice. I think it talks to all of us, but we have to listen for it. I wish I would have developed this sense. It doesn't come when I want it, only comes when it wants to.

AL

AL AND MARTY BREGMAN were looking for a movie for Al to star in. They sorted through a number of offers, such as *Tell Me That You Love Me, Junie Moon* and *Catch-22*. Producer Dominick Dunne, meanwhile, was casting for *Panic in Needle Park*, a movie based on a book by James Mills. The screenplay was by Joan Didion and John Gregory Dunne.

Faye Dunaway recommended Al to Jerry Schatzberg, her boyfriend, who was selected to direct. Schatzberg, also a Bregman client, had done *Puzzle of a Downfall Child*, in which Faye had starred. They had seen Al in *Indian Wants the Bronx* and decided to offer him the leading role, co-starring with Kitty Wynn. Kitty had distinguished herself as *Saint Joan* in San Francisco.

Al accepted and I was thrilled for him. The lead in a motion picture for Twentieth Century-Fox!

To prepare for the role, Al met addicts at Phoenix House and Reality House treatment centers and sat in on a methadone session where he learned the mechanics of using narcotics.

He was drunk when he saw the first screening, but he was surprised at his bounciness. He was all over the place in the role.

He said, "That's a talented actor, but he needs work. Help. And he needs to work. And learn. But there's definitely talent there."

Some critics described it as a painful picture to watch, but hailed Al's performance. Kitty Winn won the Best Actress award at the Cannes Film Festival. Comparisons with Dustin Hoffman still plagued Al, as Hoffman's Ratso Rizzo came to mind.

ME

MY MOTHER had to have one of her legs amputated. The doctor said her condition started years earlier when the shock of my father's death aggravated her diabetes.

I was devastated. The first time I went into the hospital room after the operation, she was having a ball with her nurse, who could have given Whoopi Goldberg a run for her money.

Acutely aware of the burden she would be to me now, she said, "Do you want to be free? Maybe I should die."

"Mom, it doesn't matter about the leg. How can I go on living without seeing (imitating her) that cute little face of yours? The only thing I care about is to see you happy. The hell with the leg. Let your fingers do the walking."

She laughed. I realized I was more upset than she was. She was brave about it and more concerned about me. She was aware my personal life was a mess and I wasn't doing what I wanted with my life. She told me to wake up.

Saying this to me in spite of her condition had a profound effect on me. It struck me as prophetic and made me want to change.

I needed money for nursing care for my mother. The extras because of the operation had drained me and my mother did not have enough insurance. Ginny, meanwhile, was living high on the hog in Connecticut, while I was working in New York. If I wanted to see Dale, I had to keep sending her money.

So, I stopped taking acting classes. I kept teaching, but was determined to somehow earn my living from my acting, instead of paying for it. There's more to acting than Broadway and the movies. I tried summer stock. I tried dinner theater. Maybe there'd be other outlets. I was open to anything.

One night in my mother's apartment, I was having dinner with her and Victor. You could hear the usual sounds of singing, hammering, dancing, and laughing reverberating through the building. It was Victor's turn to cook and he made a curry with mung beans.

"Ed, how about some more mung bean curry?"

I was almost sick to my stomach. "No, thanks."

My mother looked at her plate and sniffed the air. "I'll be up all night fumigating this place."

Victor smiled and joked with her, "What you believe is what you see, Mrs. D."

"Well, I don't see gas, but I smell it anyway."

She wheeled over to the sink with her plate and dumped the casserole in it. The food hit a glass and made a ringing sound. She put her hand on her chest and looked up, a little bewildered.

"What? Did someone ring the doorbell?"

Victor and I said simultaneously, "Was that the front door or the back?"

We laughed. My mother was even more confused.

"It's an old joke, Ma. Don't you remember?"

She asked, "What did I do with your father's dinner?"

Vic, concerned, hurried over and wheeled her back to the table. He cast me an I-told-you-so look.

My mother came out of it. "So, your pal, Al's becoming a movie star?"

"He's doing great," I said.

"What'd I tell you? Persistence is the name of the game. Maybe you should learn from him. Wait'll what's-her-name hears."

"I told her."

"She'll figure if Al Pacino can make it, so can you."

"I doubt it. Not Ginny."

"Fellahs, if you'll pardon me, I need my privacy. Take your fun and games outside for awhile."

Victor and I took a bus down to Times Square. The usual hordes were out in full force — the hawkers, the pimps, the tarts, the starers and the gapers. Theatergoers hurried toward the movie theater. We ambled along, elbowing through the crowds.

Victor said, "Maybe you oughta get her in for another check-up."

"I've tried. She doesn't have insurance, and well, like me, she's always broke."

"My guru is a healer. Take her to see him."

"She would never go see him. She believes in God, but for healing and stuff, she relies only on doctors."

We crossed Eighth Avenue and walked up the street to Joe Allen's, a hangout for actors. We went in and sat at the bar. Victor studied me over his ginger ale.

"So level with me, Ed. Are you ready to give it up?"

I nursed my beer. "No. I believe it's gonna happen. I gotta believe it, Vic. Does that make me a hopeless nut case?"

"No, you've got to believe. Belief makes it happen."

"What about you?"

"Me?"

"Yeah, you wanted to sing at the Met. Why didn't you?"

This was a sore spot for Victor.

"That was before I woke up. Every time I auditioned, I got tensed up, couldn't sing a free note. When I took up self-enlightenment — Don't laugh now..."

"Hey, how long we know each other?"

"Ten years? First time I meditated, I had a vision. God told me my mission was to teach, not to strive for self-aggrandizement."

"Them's pretty big words, brother."

He continued. "So I'm happy doing what I'm doing — giving, teaching. It makes me feel contented to be sure of my mission. You know, Ed, maybe acting is not what you're supposed to do. Satisfying the little human ego is not where it's at.

"It's all I know. It's what makes me happy, even if I'm not making big money. It's what I live for. How can I give it up?"

"You're broke and you're living with your mother. You've lost your family, all to gratify your ego."

That hurt. "Don't remind me. What else can I do? Besides, how much further down can I go? I gotta start back up the hill sometime."

"In the meantime, how're you gonna make ends meet? You don't have Ginny to prop you up now."

We walked along 42nd Street, passing dozens of brightly-lit movie theaters flanked by electronics stores and beer joints. We went back to Victor's studio and I listened to more of Vic's advice. It made him feel good.

"So, act!"

"Where?"

"Advertise. I do. In *Showbusiness*, *Backstage*, the *Voice*. A lot of my students come from those ads."

I thought about it. Not a bad idea. "Yeah! I could take an ad, like I did in California."

He asked, "For acting students?"

"Nah. I've done that. Actors! They're the worst. They never pay. Everybody wants a scholarship."

"Tell me about it."

"Bette Davis took an ad once, too. She got work."

"She was a star."

"Yeah. Still, it might work for me here, too."

"How so?"

"You know, you see classified ads for all kinds of things. Fantasies, furniture, fun..."

Victor looked shocked. "Act out fantasies?"

"Why not?" When I was in L.A. I fulfilled some people's fantasies and they paid me for it."

"That can be pretty dicey. People in California are pretty health-conscious. Here in Sin City it's a different race track."

"Hey, I'm a grownup. I know how to take care of myself. And it might put bread on the table until Al comes through for me."

He studied me, concerned. I was grinning from ear to ear. I knew what I had to do.

The next day, I visited the office of *The Village Voice*

and told the receptionist I wanted to place an ad. She directed buzzed me through to Miranda Abbott's office.

The advertising rep was not what I had expected. She was 30, small and vibrant, with a flowing mane of pre-Raphaelite curls. She wore a 40s granny dress and shoes that looked like they were purchased at a thrift shop, all very loose and figure-concealing.

"Randa," who was used to taking most of her ads over the phone, looked up at me with curiosity. "Hi, what can I do for you?"

I almost forgot what I had come for. "Uh, you take personal ads, right?"

"Yup. Have a seat. I'm Miranda Abbott."

"Ed De Leo."

"Great name."

She got to me. I sat, perspiring. I was very edgy and uncomfortable, but as I focused on Randa, I liked what I saw. Randa sensed it and flashed me a brilliant smile.

She broke the ice with, "So, Ed, what is it, a one-inch or a three-inch?

She caught me off guard. I blushed.

"Huh?"

"The ad. One inch is the regular. I can give you a special price if you do a four-week run. Three issues for the price of four."

I only wanted to try a test ad. I said, "I don't know."

She was used to this. "OK," she said. "The copy? Have you already composed it?"

Again I realized I was not prepared. "I'm not a writer. I'm an actor."

"Well, I am. A writer. I can help you compose it."

"OK. Do you call writing ads writing?"

"No way. But since I'm a writer, I'm pretty good at coining catchy phrases, things like that."

I felt relaxed with her and interested. "What do you like to write?

"Books."

"Have you published anything?"

"Yes, but not under my own name. I mostly ghost."

"Ghost?"

"You know. Say some celebrity wants to do his bio but he can't write, so I write it, pretending to be him. Books like that."

It occurred to me maybe Al would like somebody to write his story. "Could you write Al Pacino's story?"

"That's one actor who really fascinates me. I'd love to do his story.

"He happens to be a friend of mine."

She was impressed. "No kidding!"

"His full name is Alfredo James Pacino."

"I knew that. I've read everything anyone's ever written about him. He's the greatest actor in the world, in my opinion."

"He's great now, but you should've seen him when he started. He was all over the place, chewing up the scenery. We studied acting together. I coached him a lot."

Randa was mesmerized. "Really? Where was this?"

"We both went to the HB Studio. Herbert Berghof."

"Good school, I hear. Uta Hagen, Bill Hickey..."

"Right. I'm impressed."

"You meet a lot of actors in my line of work." Then she teased me with, "So, if it wasn't for you he wouldn't be what he is today?"

"Oh, I don't know about that, but I did encourage him. All he needed was some individual guidance and confidence."

"And you're still friends?"

"Sure. Why shouldn't we be?" Yeah.

She looked at me, hesitated, then said, "Maybe I'm being a little pushy, tell me if I am, but I'm dying to meet him. Could you arrange it?"

"Well, he's awfully busy. He researches every part he plays and he gets involved in every aspect."

I guess she realized she might be overstepping. "I understand. Say no more. Now, about this ad. Hey, what do you need an ad for? Surely you meet women all the time."

"It's not personal."

"No?"

"To level with you, I need to make some money, to pay for stuff — like child support — until I get a good acting job. I've got a lot of irons in the fire."

"You divorced?"

"Separated."

"Good. Oops, sorry, I didn't mean that."

"I'm flattered. How can I say it?"

"Say what?"

We both cracked up laughing. She snorted, "Oh, the ad. I'd better get on the dime here. I work on commission, so I'm wasting my time, not to speak of yours."

"You're not wasting my time. I'm having more fun than—"

"I read you. I've not been exactly setting the world on fire myself lately. In the personal arena."

"Are you married?"

"No, I'm not. But I've decided to—" Then she remembered again. "The ad."

"The ad, right. Could I take one that says "I fulfill all your fantasies. You furnish the situation, I act it out?"

"I couldn't have phrased it better myself. How many runs did you say?"

"Let's try it for one issue."

"Right, OK. I assume you want to run it with a box

number and have us forward the letters."

"OK, I guess that'll do for now."

"Fair enough. Will that be cash or charge?"

I handed her a credit card. She ran it through her little credit card gismo and handed it back to me. "Let me know how your response is." Then she handed me her personal card. "Here's my card. The top number is the office here, the other's my home."

I tried to hide my grin, also my cap. How humiliating it would be if it came loose again. I got up.

"I'll talk to you soon."

She smiled. "I'm looking forward to it."

I shook her hand and left.

A few days later, as I was walking up the street, I saw the mummy leaning against a building with his hand out.

He spotted me through the corner of his eye and, unaware of my seeing him, he turned and ran. I continued on.

When I got home, my mother was watching one of her soaps. Without looking up, she asked, "Where you been all day, doll?"

"Down at Actors Equity," I told her, "reading the bulletin board. They post shows that are casting."

"You were there all day? Anything going on?"

"Everybody wants work. Nobody's casting. All the shows are imports from England."

"You couldn't take anything, anyhow. Not with Al's movie shootin' right away."

"Right, right."

The doorbell rang. I let Victor in. He chirped, "Isn't it a wonderful day?"

I shrugged and my mother glared at him. Victor handed her a pile of mail. She began to sort it. Victor announced, "Market day. Anything special, Mrs. D?"

She gave him one of her Garbo looks. "Why do you ask? You'll buy what you think I need and not what I want. Besides, I'm flat broke. End of the month."

"Doesn't matter. Wong Lo has the incredible extra firm tofu—"

"You'd better eat by yourself tonight, Vic. These lips ain't never touched tofu and they ain't startin' tonight."

"The sauce I make for it, you'd swear it was chicken."

"Pick up some chicken, Vic. I'll pay you... later."

My mother held out a letter. "One for you, darlin'."

She sailed it to me and I caught it. One of our routines. I took a bow and looked at it. It was from the *Village Voice*. Vic noticed and looked at me. I tried to remain impassive as I tucked it into my back pocket.

Up in my room I read the response to my ad. "Interested in your service. Call 547-7989." I thought about it, then picked up the phone and dialed.

I swallowed hard when the woman answered. I assumed a new voice. "Miss Mandel, I just got your letter. You know, from the *Village Voice*? What is it you would like me to do?"

She suggested that we meet first and talk. I agreed. That way, we'd both be more comfortable. She wanted to know my name.

"My name? It's, er. Brown. Leo Brown."

She suggested we meet at the Cafe Figaro at 3:00.

"I'll be there. How will I recognize you?"

She told me she would be wearing a red beret and a black jacket.

"OK, see you then."

I hung up and was suddenly very nervous.

The sidewalk was teeming with strollers. I approached the Cafe Figaro and eyed it apprehensively. I straightened myself up and went inside.

The place was pretty calm. It was mostly filled with idle coffee drinkers, some late lunchers. I noticed an anxious-looking, haggard, 30-something woman eyeing me as I scanned the room. She yanked a red beret out of her tote and jammed it on her head. I walked over to her table. "Miss Mandel?"

She spoke in a very sweet and timid voice. "Oh. Hi. Are you Leo?"

I tried to play it cool. "Yeah."

"You don't look like a Leo."

"No? What do I look like?"

"An Arthur or something. You look like a banker or a—"

"I'm not. I'm an— I'm in communications."

"Oh?"

"I've disappointed you."

"Oh, no, not at all. You look nice. Much kinder and nicer than I expected. I was afraid you'd be—"

"I like to think I am. Nice. May I sit down?"

"Oh, please do. "

I sat down. She stared at me shyly, then said, "I'm not used to this sort of thing. Should we talk money now?"

"Uh, fine, if you'd like."

"Two hundred dollars. At the end of the evening. If that's all right with you?"

"Depends on what you want me to do."

"If the arrangement doesn't please you, just say so, because—"

"I'm sure it will be fine, just fine."

"I think so. Here's what I'd like."

And she proceeded to tell me. When I agreed, she was pleased and anxious.

I watched her leave, wondering what I was getting myself into. I took a buck out of my wallet and left it under my coffee cup. I noticed a door key by Miss Mandel's cup. I hesitated, then picked it up and put it in my pocket. I strolled out of the cafe.

That night, outside an upscale apartment building, a man in dark clothes lurked in a doorway, smoking a cigarette.

An innocent-looking couple walked arm-in-arm, leaning on each other, laughing. The man scanned a lighted window in the building on the opposite side of the street.

The man entered the lobby of the building and got into the elevator. He got off at the fourth floor and walked stealthily down the corridor, looking at numbers on the doors. He paused at 406.

Inside the apartment, the entry was pitch black. A key rattled in the door. The door slowly opened and the man slipped in. He quietly closed the door behind him.

In a room at the end of the hall, the man observed vertical bars of light where the shades were too narrow for the windows. He moved toward that room. His trouser legs made ominous swishing sounds as they brushed against each other.

A frightened female voice cried, out "Who's there!?" There was no answer. Just footsteps in the dark. The voice called out again, "Anyone there?"

No answer. The floor creaked.

In the dim light of her room, Sonya Mandel sat up in bed, clutching the covers protectively against her breasts, which were heaving violently. She screeched, "What do you want?"

No response. She trembled. "Just take whatever you want, but please don't hurt me, please!"

She listened. The footsteps approached her door. She stared at the door. The door squeaked.

She cried out, "Oh, God! Save me! Save me!"

Her eyes were wide-open and riveted on the door. She started to whimper and shiver. "Oh, please, please."

The man, in silhouette, loomed in the doorway. He started toward her.

She screamed.

I acted menacing. "Get out of bed!"

She cowered. "I... I can't. I'm... paralyzed... with fear."

I stopped, a little stumped. Suddenly she leaped out of bed and zoomed past me. I hesitated, then ran after her, growling.

She ran around the living room insanely, darting in and out of furniture, her flimsy, see-through gown flying every which way. She ducked behind a chair.

I stopped in the doorway, looked around, and then got into gear again.

"I know you're here. It's only a matter of time until I find you. And when I do, I'll make you pay!"

I rushed the chair and pulled her out. She bellowed hysterically.

I let go of her abruptly. "Sshhh! The neighbors—"

She gave me a deprecating look. "Fuck the neighbors! Keep it up! Keep it up!"

"What?"

"Let's wind it up!"

She skedaddled toward the bedroom. I stood, dazed. She peeped back around the doorway and bellowed raucously, "What're you waitin' for? The 1045 to Newark? Get your friggin' ass in here!"

Shocked to the bones for a moment, I drew a deep breath, bared my teeth in a growl and stormed after her.

In the bedroom she leaped into the bed and dove under the covers. I dashed after her and, with a flying leap, threw myself on top of her. She let out a yell that terrified me. At the same time, she raked her talons down my cheek. I rolled off, clutching myself in pain.

She lay there looking at me with hard, cruel eyes. Finally, she sat up, turned on a flattening white light, and turned to sneer at me. "Jesus! What a dud you turned out to be!"

"But... I thought I was just supposed to scare you. Just give you a thrill or two."

She took off her teddy. "Well, you scared me, but I'm still waitin' for the thrill!"

I stared at her stupidly then sagged with realization. "Miss Mandel, uh, ma'am. I'm no gigolo."

She was furious. "What the hell did you think I was paying you for? A diddle with a dead dildo?"

"I... I don't know. I guess I didn't think."

"Man, are you a dud!" She sighed, reached for her purse and took out her wallet.

I felt bad, as if I had misled her.

"If you're not satisfied, you don't have to pay."

She stared at me, narrow-eyed, then handed me a hundred dollar bill.

"Here's a hundred. For half a job."

I stared at the bill, humiliated, but I meekly took it and got off the bed.

"Next time," she said, "make it clear what your service is. I'm not used to throwing away good cash on Eunuchs."

I made a quick escape.

The next day, I went back to Randa's office at *The Village Voice*. She was so busy at her computer, she didn't see me standing in the doorway. I cleared my throat. She turned around and smiled.

"Well, hi. How's it going?"

I told her, "I got a response to the ad."

"And?"

"I think I'd better change the words or add something... to clarify the conditions."

She knew something had gone wrong. "We can do that. You didn't get hurt or anything, did you?"

"No, no, nothing like that. But it was a bit dicey. Maybe we could add the line 'no kinks, no kooks,' like I did in Hollywood."

"Fine. How about four more? At a special discount?"

I shrugged. "What the heck. Let's go for broke."

She was pleased. "I like a man who goes right out there on the edge. I'll write it up."

She took my credit card, ran it through her gismo, and handed it back to me.

"And put my phone number. It'll be quicker all around."

She typed it in, her back to me.

I wasn't sure whether to leave or stay. "That's all?"

She turned and smiled. "Oh, yes. Thank you. So, are you up for roles in any movies?"

"Soon I hope."

"Hey, I was about to go out for lunch. Would you—"

"Yes!"

We stared at each other, then broke up laughing.

We had lunch at a West Village cafe, sitting at an outdoor table under an umbrella. Randa wore a sweater over her flowered granny dress, a crocheted cap pulled down low over her forehead. I studied her as she ate her pasta.

Randa felt uncomfortable. "Don't watch me eat."

"I wasn't. I mean, I was just wondering if you weren't... too warm... in all those clothes."

She stared at me a little hostilely, then almost blushed. "I'm fine. I'm never too warm. I'm cold-natured."

"Then I guess what I'm seeing on your forehead is cold sweat."

She laughed nervously. "Probably. I haven't been out

with anybody... even to lunch... in a long time."

"That makes two of us. The last date I had was 14 years ago. I feel like an old rusty hinge. I don't know what's expected of men these days."

"I guess we have to just let happen, you know, whatever happens."

"A few days ago I would've agreed. But now, I've been thinking that may not be the best thing. Letting things just... happen."

"My friend Merrill is always talking about setting goals and going for them. She's so pushy it turns me off. But she does create a lot of action for herself. I guess I've been coasting too long myself."

"If you had a goal, what would it be?"

"To write. Write. Write."

"What's stopping you from doing it?"

"Look, my friend Merrill wants to meet you. She works upstairs at the Entertainment desk. Ever since I told her about you knowing Al Pacino, she's been nudging me, bugging me to introduce you. She'd like to interview Al."

I swallowed hard. "Aren't the *Voice's* credentials enough to get her through to him?"

"She's tried many times. He doesn't give a lot of interviews. Maybe you could put in a word for her. She's particularly interested in his early years."

What a coincidence. "I knew him then."

"Ed, could you and I meet sometime after work? I'd like to talk to you about Al. I could tape it for Merrill."

"Would she go for that?"

"I'll tell her that's the best I could do."

"But you'd be doing all the work for her."

"OK, I confess. I have an ulterior motive."

"Which is?"

"I really want to get to know you better. I guess I was

too nervous to just come out and say it before."

I studied her, then grinned. "Why not?"

We didn't follow up on it, however, because she didn't want to take advantage of me, and I didn't want my friendship with Al to be the reason for us getting together.

The new ad worked better and started to get a different type of response. I was somebody, and people were calling me. I was Ed De Leo — of New York and Hollywood!

My mother thought I was doing private coaching with actors. I would go Downtown at night and play out my scenes.

My next client was a wealthy woman, Sarah, who lived in a fashionable apartment in Manhattan on Fifth Avenue off Central Park East. She was blonde and very beautiful, a former show girl. Her husband was an owner of a Greek line and had many real estate investments.

I met her through a woman who had managed her theatrically and who had heard about my "service." Sarah called and asked me to come over. Her home was very cozy. She ran me all around New York City. We'd dance and dine, but that's as far as it went.

She'd laugh and chatter loudly to me and the cab driver when I dropped her off in front of her building. She wanted her husband to think she was having an affair. Sadly, he couldn't have cared less. He was having an active sex life elsewhere.

All kinds of nuts were answering my ads, even though I was clearly stating "no kinks, no kooks." I found myself in a few dangerous situations, as well, including entrapment. Somebody, for example, wanted to tie me up. There were many requests like that, so I had to be selective.

I tried to call Al at his Greenwich Village apartment. Charlie answered the phone. Al wasn't there, but Charlie was very cordial. I told him I was doing a lot of acting, but all little stuff. "I'm still waiting for my break."

He told me he never wanted to break up any friendship between me and Al.

I said, "Don't worry about it, Charlie. Al and I will always be friends."

I asked him if he was still teaching.

"Maybe I ought to take a few classes with you."

He declined. I got the impression he wasn't conducting classes any more.

On one of my train rides to Connecticut to see Dale, I was reading the novel, *The Godfather.* I had heard it was going to be made into a movie. I saw a dark, handsome guy playing Michael Corleone. The voice in my head told me Al would get the part. I had no doubt about it.

AL

SURE ENOUGH, Francis Ford Coppola wanted Al to play the role. But Al couldn't picture himself in the part. He saw Michael Corleone as someone more glamorous, more self-contained, somebody more like the actor, Alain Delon. But he went for it.

He kept blowing his screen tests by not knowing the character or his lines. He improvised the dialogue. Coppola urged Al Ruddy and Bob Evans to see Al in *Panic In Needle Park*. They did and Al was given the role.

Al, meanwhile, was being courted by MGM for *The Gang That Couldn't Shoot Straight* and finally signed for it. When he got cast in *The Godfather*, Bregman got him out of the other movie and Robert De Niro replaced him.

Al was nervous about working with Marlon Brando, who was a god to him. But Brando took an interest in him and his acceptance relaxed him. Brando suggested Al's brooding intensity would be right for the role.

Al knew many people hadn't wanted him for the role. He thought, I'll never make it through this picture; it's going to kill me.

He'd wake up at four in the morning worrying about the character, the transitions, and how believable he'd be. Then about a month later, when they began to piece together his scenes and liked how he was coming off, things got better.

Playing Michael was a hellish experience for Al. In movies, scenes are not shot in the same order they appear in the script. They are shot "out of sequence" because of locations and scheduling. Consequently, when it's time to do a scene you have to be aware of where the scene falls in the story.

The first scene they shot was when Michael kills two men in a restaurant. Then they went back to the scenes where he was just a sensitive kid out of college, in love, and never expecting to be drawn into the family "business." Then he had to change into an amoral, cold-blooded leader of killers. He learned a hell of a lot, even though he floundered.

Al liked to search and work, and it took him a lot of time to catch the right note in a role. He insisted on doing the transition slowly. He wanted to establish Michael as "a guy who didn't know quite where he was at."

He wanted the audience to see his ambiguity. When Michael did emerge as a powerful man, Al felt it would have enormous dramatic impact. He admitted he used to be lazy but *The Godfather* knocked the laziness out of him.

Al and Jill moved from 14th Street to the upper Sixties. Candice Bergen had lived there and moved to Hollywood. Al would rather have moved to a loft, but Jill wanted to live uptown. They left the "C. Bergen" on the door to give them some anonymity.

Though he had to shoot in L.A., Al swore he'd always live in New York. He missed the traffic, the walking from uptown to downtown, the bums, the street people, the favorite bars.

In *Godfather*, as the youngest son of Don Corleone, he changed from a bright young Ivy League University graduate into a ruthless killer.

Al felt like an outsider during *Godfather*. He underplayed the role and retreated when he was off-camera. He thought Francis Coppola was constantly worried about his job. Al felt like quitting and going home. He wasn't comfortable doing film acting. He wasn't used to it. Maybe he didn't belong in the medium.

He was in awe of working with Marlon Brando. In an interview, Al said, "You can't imagine my feelings during the first rehearsal with Brando. It was Jimmy Caan and Bobby Duvall and me, all sitting around, and there's Brando going on about the Indians. Francis is saying to himself, 'This is the first rehearsal, what's going to happen tomorrow? We have two more weeks of this.' And Duvall was making these faces. I had to leave and sit on the bed, because I was laughing and I didn't want to have Brando think we were laughing at him. Duvall finally said, 'Keep talking, Marlon, none of us want to work, just keep talking.' With that, Marlon laughed."

Al remembered, "I'll never forget Brando the first time I did a scene with Keaton. He came and stood right in front of the camera and watched. During the scene at the table, a leaf fell off the tree onto my shoulder. I took off the leaf and tossed it and later Brando said, 'I like what you did with the leaf.'Afterward, Diane and I just got drunk.

"But Brando was wonderful to me. He made me laugh, the things he'd do. I'd be playing a scene, and he'd show up off-camera, straight-faced, with a silly fake bird in his pocket. His support was so powerful, it helped me a great deal. What can you say about someone that gracious? He made it so easy."

Al had to go to Sicily for some location work and it made him feel more connected to his roots. The entire experience liberated him.

Al decided to track down his father. He took Jill to see him while they were shooting *The Godfather* in California. His father seemed "OK" to him. Al wasn't disillusioned.

He felt his father was a feeling person, that he felt a great deal for Al. It was hard, though, for him to say 'Pop' to somebody he had never said it to before. He had an urge to call him by his first name, but he figured, "What the hell, why not call him Pop?"

Al said his father looked at him like he was his son, not like he was Al Pacino the movie star. This is what Al had longed for a long time. The thing he missed the most was having people look him in the eye in a certain way, the way a mother looks at her son, no matter what he's done.

Al could tell when people weren't really seeing him, when they were just seeing the image. Many times at parties he would be sitting in the dark talking to somebody and it was wonderful. Then, when the lights went on, they would see it was Al Pacino and a new look would appear in their eyes. Suddenly everything was different.

When he was with his father, Al could feel the family. He felt the blood tie, "the bond that all of us have — the reason we all identify so strongly with *The Godfather*."

He wrote to his father later and told him how he felt about him. When he was with his father, it brought his mother back to him. Al also met his three half-sisters with Diane Keaton.

In working on the character of Michael Corleone,

what he wanted to create was "some kind of enigma, an enigmatic-type person." He wanted the audience to feel they saw Michael, but didn't quite know him. He wanted Michael to look wrapped up in something, like in a trance, as if his mind was overflowing with thoughts.

To achieve this, he listened to some Stravinsky music on the set, to give him that look. He felt that was the drama in the character, that was the only thing that was going to make him dramatic. Otherwise, he was afraid it could be dull. He had never worked on a role like that. It was the most difficult part he ever played.

When he saw a rough cut of the picture, without music and effects, he was very affected by it. Some of the violence scared him. He found it to be an emotional film. It was a picture in which you get caught up in the people, the family. The frightening thing to Al was these people you've gotten to know are doing violent things. You see them as real people, kissing each other, and you laugh with them. That makes the violence so much more frightening.

The restaurant scene, in which Michael assassinated the police captain and Sollozzo, depressed and scared the hell out of Al. Going through the experience of having to shoot two guys, took a lot out of him. After Al did two takes, he said to Coppola, "Don't let me do it anymore."

When he went back to sit at that table, his eyes lost their focus.

The crux of the role of Michael Corleone was the character change. The key to it was the credibility of Michael's metamorphosis from an Ivy League war hero, ambivalent about the family business, into his father's ruthless successor.

Al knew the change was the only thing to go for. In preparing for the role, he tried to figure out where to start. He did a lot of this homework himself. What was most difficult about it was doing a scene from the middle of the film during the first week of shooting or vice versa. He had to think about where he was in the "change" at any given point.

He broke the growth of the character into three stages. The first stage was the ambivalence. The second was having to cope with his doing the killings in the restaurant. And the third was, having made that move, to decide that that's the way he was going to be. He broke it up and tried to work within that framework.

I read the reviews. Pauline Kael wrote in the *New Yorker*, "Pacino creates a quiet space around himself. His acting, which is marvelous, big without ostentation, complements Brando's. Like Brando, Pacino is simple; you don't catch him acting, yet he manages to change from a small, fresh-faced, darkly handsome college boy into an underworld lord, becoming more intense, smaller and more isolated at every step."

Marlon Brando said in an interview, "I didn't say much to Pacino when we were making *The Godfather*, but I not only consider him one of the best actors in America, but in the world. The picture just reinforced my opinion. That sounds like a put-on? Well, I never meant anything more in my life. I don't go around touting other actors. The profession means too much to me."

At the premiere Al dodged photographers and refused interviews. He was not doing a Brando, as he was accused. Actually he was drunk.

Al went to a party thrown by his old friends Susan Tyrrell, Sally Kirkland and Candy Darling.

Sally said, "There were 500 people at the party and every girl there came to look at Al Pacino to try and get a shot at him. Let me tell you, women find Al fantastically sexy. It's sort of incredible when you think about it, that this little guy should be so sexy. But, believe me, it's true."

When *Godfather* opened, I called Al to congratulate him. He thanked me and told me it would be great if we could be in the same movie one day. Wouldn't that be marvelous? Of course it would, I told him, if somebody would only cast me. He told me not to give up.

I told him I was having trouble with Ginny, that she had emotional problems, and it was a hardship for me to go to Connecticut every weekend to be with my son. Maybe I should have her committed for therapy.

Al said, "Be careful about that. Don't do anything that'll make you feel guilty for the rest of your life."

In the spring of 1973, at the Academy Awards, Al got nominated as Best Supporting Actor. I was thrilled for him. But the nomination made him angry because Marlon Brando was nominated as Best Actor and was not on screen as much as he was.

He watched the awards on television.

Al's compensation was $35,000, which wasn't much for a year of work. It got spent quickly. MGM sued him for $2,000,000 because they claimed he had committed to do *The Gang That Couldn't Shoot Straight* but did *The Godfather* instead.

So Al had to pay for lawyers. He even had to pay the expenses. He was broke after that, and in debt. But he didn't care. He had been broke many times before, from the very beginning. He knew he would sooner or later have more money than he would ever need.

The Godfather made a million dollars a day for the first month of its release and outgrossed *Gone With The Wind.* The largest money-making film in the history of the motion picture industry, worldwide, it won the Academy Award as Best Film.

Fame was hard for Al to adjust to. He was still shy. New situations, relationships, women, and suggestions came his way. He was suspicious about everything. He was also fighting internal demons such as loneliness, depression, isolation. He felt like the character in *Dr. Strangelove* who rode the bomb.

Jill once bought him a plastic tub tray because he loved to spend hours soaking in the tub with a drink and a phone.

To soothe his soul, Al decided to return to the theater. He liked doing both plays and movies, but he was not as crazy about making movies. He was aware that many other actors, really fine actors, preferred film. But it was a personal thing with Al.

He didn't necessarily think the theater was better than film, he just hadn't found his real "raison" for doing film. He learned things from it, but when he walked across the street and the camera followed him, it seemed silly. He couldn't explain why.

Films are fragmented, he figured, they didn't challenge the actor the way the stage did. He intended to keep on making them, though, because he knew they helped him.

His fame as a movie star didn't give him what he wanted. It cut him off from what he really wanted to do — return to the stage. It also got in the way of how people perceived him when he did return to the theater.

He re-joined the David Wheeler's Theater Company in Boston for a revival of David Rabe's *The Basic Training of Pavlo Hummel.* It was the story of a young man maturing during his tour of duty in the army. He did it not because of his feelings about Vietnam, but because he thought it was a great play and a challenging character.

Hummel was not a loser. He had an incredible will to live. He had courage. Al was very positive about him. He was a character he would like to be around.

"Hummel keeps them laughing."

While they were rehearsing, director David Rabe was amazed when Al searched for a way to play a certain scene. He suddenly played it 20 different ways — whimsically, passionately, angrily, grievously, childlike, befuddled — hardly taking a breath between them. It was like putting on many different suits.

Al compared acting on the stage to swimming — to taking the first stroke, and then another and another. One day while waiting in the wings to make his entrance, he thought about how making that first stroke was his life. He stood there and he said to himself, "I'm gonna do this. I've done this so many times before and I'm doing it again."

And he thought that you have to go on, and maybe you don't feel like it. Or you're this, or you're that. But you go on. That's what he liked about a play. You get on and ride. There's a rhythm to it. And he believed in rhythms.

When Al was interviewed by the press in Boston, he took a call from Martin Bregman.

"Yah, Marty. Say, they want me to stay for another week. 'S that OK? Yah, good. Hey, has Gene read the script? Yah? He likes it? Yah, I'll be in touch. OK, s'long."

For the interview he wore a baggy pullover, a dark-colored T-shirt, jeans and boots. He ate his lunch out of a sauce pan. Same old Al.

He knew what he wanted as an actor, but he didn't know what a career was all about yet. He had never gone about building one. He didn't know what he was supposed to do. Everything was so relative.

When he first got into a limousine, he thought, "Wow, is this me?" Then it wore off. He went through a tie period, then the T-shirt period. The glamour part of the business had no appeal to him.

He couldn't even sit through the premiere of *The Godfather*. He was drunk. The lights went down and he had to go out. Seeing the rough cut was easy, but seeing himself on screen with a lot of other people was tough for him. He imagined watching himself on screen in a sensitive moment, and seeing somebody getting up and walking out in middle of it.

ME

I WAS DEEP into my own acting: doing the capers to support myself, to keep "performing" any way I could.

Sadie Projansky, a woman in her 70s, had bad eyesight, but one of her friends told her about my ads. Her husband, Abe, had worked for Federal Express but evidently fell in love with overseas shipping. He left for work one day and never came home. She had a nice place, but she played it down.

I had to dress up in one of his suits, that reeked of camphor, and wear a yarmulke. She dressed up in a beaded evening gown and we had a candlelight supper. She had prepared one of her husband's favorite meals, stuffed cabbage; but it was so rich, I almost choked on it.

I had to humor her with lines like, "Sadie, Sadie, married lady."

She started to cry and said, "Sadie, Sadie, is no longer married!" Mascara mud was running down her face. "Her husband had passed away."

My mother never knew I was doing the capers. I sometimes played my characters to cheer her up. I pretended they were for auditions. I came to see her as different people, in various costumes and disguises.

The capers paid the bills, but I wanted to act. I kept

making the rounds, but couldn't get auditions. I thought I might be able to get a foot in the door if I had a letter of recommendation from Al. I could show it to agents, directors and casting directors.

I called Al's office and spoke about it to his secretary. She obviously asked Al if he would write a letter for me and he agreed without hesitation.

His secretary asked, "Who are you? Al said, 'Whatever Ed wants, give him.' Boy you must have a good relationship with him. He told me the only two people he would do anything for like are his grandfather and Ed."

She wrote a nice letter of recommendation for me and Al signed it.

AL

IN 1973, Marty Bregman arranged for Al to star in a new movie, *Scarecrow*, based on a screenplay by Garry Michael White. He was to co-star with Gene Hackman as Lion, a wandering self-styled philosopher-comic who has serious yearnings for his own place in the sun, away from the jails and skid rows of his past.

There were constant "altercations" between Al, Hackman and the director, Jerry Schatzberg, who had directed Al in *Panic In Needle Park*. To Al's delight, the scenes were filmed in chronological sequence and Penny Allen, Charlie's wife, was in the cast.

True to what he had learned from working on *The Godfather*, he tried to live the part, absorbing as much as he could, and always thinking in terms of the character. That approach made acting exciting for him.

Scarecrow was about people he did not understand. It was about two guys who were like nomads. They came from different places and they met on a country road. The story was about their relationship, how they affected each other, and what eventually happened to them.

Al played a guy from the Midwest who was going back to see his kid whom he had never seen. He had left before the kid was born, and he didn't know if it was a boy or a girl. He was going back to resolve it for himself. That was a life Al didn't know, so he had to find out about it through playing it.

Many critics didn't like the movie, finding it pretentious and heavy-handed. In *New York* magazine, Judith Crist said, "This crow ain't for eatin'." She found Al to be more Dustin Hoffmanish than ever before, but she said he was "completely endearing." She also thought that Penny was "superb."

In the *Los Angeles Times*, Charles Champlin called the film "one of the new year's best movies." He called Al's and Hackman's performances "astonishing." The movie was generally thought of by the public as an art film.

Al respected Gene Hackman's acting, but didn't feel connected to him personally. They didn't hate each other, but Al had felt closer to Brando. He was sure they could never be friends because they were from different worlds.

Ironically, Hackman said of Al, "Some actors scare you by their genius. No matter how good you think you are, you get the uneasy feeling that somehow, by something too mysterious to explain, they get deeper into humanity than you could ever do it yourself."

With comments like that from Hackman and the earlier one from Brando, how could Al not become a superstar?

At the peak of his fame, turning down hundreds of offers, he returned to the Theater Company of Boston (at $200 a week scale) to play Shakespeare's Richard III, one of the most difficult roles in Shakespeare, if not the entire dramatic world.

He felt the need to do something classical. It was time. He had never tried Shakespeare. He had learned his craft in the theater, and decided he would always go back to refresh himself. Films didn't challenge him the way the stage did. He had to do it. He had no choice.

The press and the public were leery of Al's doing Shakespeare. They thought it was too risky for him. But, he felt it was a risk not to take risks. Without it an actor can go stale and repeat himself.

He didn't feel like a person who took risks. No matter what Al did he seemed to provoke controversy. It was not intentional.

Another reason he went to Boston was to help him avoid the impact of the film. It would give him something to concentrate on. He hadn't worked on the stage for a couple of years. Again, Penny was in the cast.

Al did a lot of experimenting with the role of Richard. New things kept coming out of him. He took his hump on and off at will. He put a little stuffing on his back.

He did Richard as a turkey. He tried playing it standing up straight. He changed his accent from English to Japanese. He used a very high-pitched voice. He did Richard as many different people — Lee Strasberg, George C. Scott, even his grandmother.

He joked that he might try doing it in a barrel. His philosophy was that it was a matter of "trial and error" — making allowances for failure or taking a chance on being absurd. You experiment, then you distill. He didn't think there was such a thing as an ideal Richard.

"It's always yourself. Who else is it? We're so many people."

Richard was performed at the Loeb Theater in Boston, but it wasn't very good there. They moved to a church and the production came to life. Something happened. The audience grew. Al came out of the pulpit and put his head out and talked through a microphone. The concept had continuity and consistency.

The *New York Times* and *Time Magazine* attended and the reviews were encouraging.

Al and Jill split up after living together for five years. Neither wanted to get married, both wanted children, but they couldn't make it work.

Al didn't relish doing sex scenes, especially the kind with lots of huffing and puffing. He had not yet done any intimate movies, so he wasn't sure how he would handle one. He didn't think that kind of "stuff" mattered to a movie.

In *Panic in Needle Park*, he had a love scene with Kitty Wynn and it was very difficult. What helped him was having a structure, a form, and a meaning.

"If it's going someplace, if it's moving the story, if it's pertinent, then you can do it easier. But with some of these things, they're just indulging in a lot of sloppy kissing and humping."

When he had to watch lovemaking in other movies he would say, "They're doing this now just to show you that they're making love."

And nine out of 10 times, it would come off flat. It didn't have to be there. Meaning had to be there.

Al figured out why he liked to act.

It was a great thing to suddenly be in 1850, 1790, or 1930. Or even 1972, the present, where he could suddenly be somebody else — a murderer or a priest. Actors, he felt, were fantastic people. He couldn't think of any other thing to possibly be. He thought people who weren't actors were really missing something.

"It's really a lot of fun."

Al arranged for his grandmother, Kate, to see all of his plays.

She said, "We meet him afterward in his dressing room, and we go to a restaurant and have a good time."

When she saw the premier of The Godfather, Paramount sent a limousine to pick her up. She got to mingle with many celebrities. She commented to an interviewer, "I thought Sonny was wonderful, but all the others in the picture were very good, too."

Kate was a celebrity in her neighborhood because of Al's fame. Her grocer asked her to get him a signed picture of Sonny. When Al visited her once he brought some friends from the play in Boston. Kate made supper for them. Her only regret was Al criticized his old neighborhood. She thought he said too many bad things about it, as if it were the slums. In her mind, it was a nice area.

Al started seeing Tuesday Weld. Tuesday had been a sexy teen star in the 50s and had a reputation for brawling and drinking. She distinguished herself in the movie, *Pretty Poison*, in 1968 and then in *Play it As It Lays*, in 1972. Al was in love!

Al drove out to Montauk during the summer where he rented a cottage for the summer. Most celebrities who vacationed on Long Island stayed in the Hamptons, which was one reason why Al picked Montauk. He didn't go to places like Elaine's, a restaurant in Manhattan where the "sort of people" who summered in the Hamptons frequently met to make sure they were seen by each another.

He liked to go to Downey's on Eighth Avenue where actors who dressed in jeans and didn't like the glitz of Broadway's Sardi's went. Al frequently wore a wide-brimmed beach hat, sandals and a muted print shirt. He frequently went out unshaven, with his hair ruffled.

ME AND AL

MARTY BREGMAN, by this time, had been a manager for Barbra Streisand, Raquel Welch, Diahann Carroll, Sandy Dennis, Bernadette Peters, Faye Dunaway, Liza Minnelli, Woody Allen, Michael Douglas and Alan Alda. He was now the head of a company called Artists Entertainment Complex, which financed and produced movies such as *Kansas City Bomber*, starring Raquel Welch.

I called Al to see if he could give me a letter of introduction to Bregman. Maybe he could promote my career the way he did Al's.

When he asked me how things were, I told him I was living my own Scarecrow.

"The character you played, with the troubled wife, was me in real life."

The wife, played by Penny, who told Al's character there was no child, she had an abortion, was like Ginny. She had Dale and didn't want to share him with me. "You're acting those things, Al. I'm living them."

Without hesitating, Al wrote me a letter of recommendation.

Unfortunately, TWM Management Company was not interested in taking on any new clients. They said it wouldn't be fair to their current clients to represent additional clients.

Marty Bregman, however, promised to keep me in mind if any roles come along that might be right for me.

AL

ALSO IN 1973, Bregman wanted to produce a movie of *Serpico*, based on Peter Maas's book, with Al starring in the title role.

Serpico was about the real-life New York City Detective Frank Serpico, whose expose of the corruption rampant among his fellow cops led to the formation of the Knapp Commission. Bregman pitched it to every studio but nobody wanted it. Finally, Dino de Laurentiis went for it. Dino, who was in financial trouble, took it to Paramount and was able to make a deal.

When Al read the treatment, he thought, "Oh no, another cop picture."

But after he read Waldo Salt's screenplay, he started to change his mind. He found he related to it. To talk Al into doing it, Bregman had Al meet the real Frank Serpico. When Al shook Serpico's hand and looked into his eyes, he understood what the movie could be. He realized there was something there he could play.

Bregman negotiated a profit participation for Al in the picture. Al began to spend time with Frank Serpico on Long Island. John Avildsen was supposed to direct, but quit because of differences with Bregman. Sidney Lumet was then brought in. Al got totally absorbed in the role. He played a hippie cop.

To prepare for the part, he went out with a couple of cops one night. After just five minutes in the car out on patrol, he discovered he couldn't do that. Instead, he opted to hang around Frank Serpico, long enough to get to feel like him.

One time Serpico was out at Al's rented beach house in Montauk. As they were sitting, looking at the water, Al decided to ask what he thought might be a silly question. "Why, Frank? Why did you do it?"

Serpico's response was, "I don't know... if I didn't, who would I be when I listened to a piece of music?"

Al was impressed with the way he put it. He suddenly

understood the kind of guy Frank Serpico was and he enjoyed being with him. He saw mischief in his eyes.

Al got carried away with the role and stayed in character after hours of filming. One time, while he was sitting in a hot taxi with the window open, a truck spewed heavy fumes in his face.

He yelled out at the driverS, "Why are you putting that crap in the street?"

The driver asked him who he was. Al yelled back, "I'm a cop and you're under arrest. Pull over!"

He pulled out his Serpico badge and told the driver he would put him under citizen's arrest. Then he realized what he was doing.

ME

I WAS PAID by Herman Blender to attend a wild party with many famous people present. I wore a black tie and had to pretend I was a big film producer from the Coast. There were people there whom I would normally have hit for acting jobs, but instead they were soliciting me to finance them.

Herman said, "Pretend you have money."

Before I could get a drink, I was surrounded by a bevy of beautiful young actresses. Several of them started to play up to me. I drank with them, danced with them, and shot pool with them.

I started to follow one named Katherine into the bedroom, but was grabbed by Herman. He was putting together a group of investors for a film and was told if I was "in," so were they.

I knew something about movies and was able to drop a lot of names. Except for a waiter almost recognizing me from my acting classes, it was a successful evening for everybody.

AL

IN LESS THAN A YEAR, it was over between Al and Tuesday Weld. Whenever anybody asked him about Tuesday Weld, he would tell them it his "favorite drink."

A drink?

He would explain that when he walks into a bar, he really throws the bartender by ordering a Tuesday Weld. It was something he had invented — a Brandy Alexander poured over an Oreo cookie. Tuesday and Al used to laugh together about that.

During the filming of *Serpico* he fell in love with Cornelia Sharpe, who was in the picture with him. Sharpe, however, became interested in Marty Bregman and subsequently married him.

Al had a love affair with Diane Keaton that, over a period of time, was on one minute and off the next. He had known her when they were both younger, before either of them had made a movie. She was very young at the time. She then got involved with Woody Allen, and later, Warren Beatty. Now, years later, she picked up again with Al.

When Al was younger, if he saw an attractive young woman while he was walking down the street, he would start to follow her. Sometimes he would catch up to her, they would look at each other, and before long they would be "making out."

He hadn't done that for a few years, because anyone of celebrity who did that would have to be nuts. It would be in the tabloids. But one day, he happened to spot a real beauty and, out of curiosity, decided to see how far he could get with her. As they reached a stop light together, Al looked over at her, gave her a big smile and said hello.

"Hiya, Michael," she said.

It was then he knew it was all over for him. He slunk off and tried to hide behind a building but she followed him anyway.

"Come on out, Michael," she said.

"No," Al answered, "it's all over."

"What do you mean, it's all over? It's just beginning!"

"No, you're making a big mistake. I'm not Michael Corleone — I'm Fritz Weaver."

She looked confused and it obviously did the trick.

Al was living a pretty cloistered life. He didn't go to many parties, and when he was working, the only women he met were actresses. He had lived with women since he was 16 and all seemed to be actresses.

Every time he got started with an actress, he would hesitate about going very far. Sometimes they would say the classic line, "I'll give up acting." It would anger him and he would tell them not to give up anything for him. He wished he could meet women who were not actresses, somebody like a sculptress.

When *Serpico* opened, the reviews were terrific and so was the box-office response. William Wolff in the *Cue* magazine said, "There is electricity in virtually everything Pacino does, from the smallest gesture to the big emotional moments... [It is] tour de force acting."

Al attended the opening at a theater in New York — incognito in a pea-coat and a pair of glasses. As he left the theater with a stocking cap pulled down over his ears for warmth, a swarm of photographers surrounded him and a crowd quickly closed in for the kill.

A bouncer from the bar next door came to his aid.

"How am I gonna get out of here?" Al asked.

The bouncer led him down a path he had led other celebrities many times before — through the storeroom and out to the alley.

For his performance in *Serpico,* Al was nominated for Best Actor, against Jack Lemmon for *Save the Tiger*, Robert Redford for *The Sting* and Marlon Brando for *Last Tango in Paris.* Jack Lemmon won.

Al, Bregman, and Lumet had to sue De Laurentiis for their share of the profits. De Laurentiis had inflated the cost of the picture in the reports. It was settled out of court.

Al didn't like to talk about his private life to anybody other than his close friends. No longer the scrawny kid walking the streets looking for work, Al was changing. He was a success and had things he had never had before.

Even in some of the good articles written about him, the writers distorted his relationships and it was upsetting. It wasn't because the public was told about his personal feelings, it was because the airing of it would affect the relationships. He valued his relationships too much to have them spoiled by probing reporters. It may have hurt his relationship with Jill Clayburgh.

He felt that the only way to keep from being overwhelmed by material possessions was to concentrate on the things in which he was really interested, things that were more personal. Work was one.

This was just the beginning for Al as a man of means and he didn't know what the future was going to hold for him. He had a lot of money, and he knew more was going to come. It enabled him to help his friends and his relatives. It made him feel good. One of the good things about being famous was it made him feel accepted.

He liked women, but he didn't like to boast about his exploits. He has said, "I've always been partial to girls. Women brought me up. And when I was younger, I had fantasies of being sought after by the world's most glamorous women."

He was aware there were women who liked to suck up to stars. He knew he could take advantage of them if he wanted to. It could be very tempting. It was sometimes very difficult.

Women would come up to him and say, "I want to go to bed with you."

He never had that sort of thing happen before. He would respond to them by saying something like, "I'm very flattered, you're very nice yourself."

He thought he might be paranoid about it, but he found something very hostile when women did that. By going along with it he would be deceitful and he didn't want to be party to it.

He was a romantic and took his relationships seriously.

In 1974, Al was asked to do *The Godfather, Part II*, but he was reluctant. He figured he would be repeating himself. The producers thought he was holding out for more money and kept increasing their offers.

First they doubled the $35,000 he had received for the first *Godfather*, then they offered him $100,000.

Next they said, "How about $150,000?"

Al said, "I don't think so."

"How about if Puzzo writes the screenplay?"

He said sure, he'd read it. So Puzzo wrote a screenplay. Al found it to be "OK," but he still said no. The producers went up to $200,000.

Al said no.

They went to $250,000 and $300,000 and $350,000. Then they made a big jump and went to $450,000. But Al said no.

They called him into their offices in New York. There

was a bottle of J&B on the table. They began drinking, talking, laughing. The producer opened his drawer and pulled out a tin box. Al was sitting on the other side of the table.

The producer pushed it over in his direction. He asked, "What if I were to tell you there was a million dollars in cash in there?"

Al replied, "It doesn't mean anything — it's an abstraction."

He found it to be the damnedest thing. He ended up apologizing to the guy for not taking the million.

Meanwhile, Francis Coppola convinced him by talking to him about the script and inspiring him. He told Al he could age in the picture, and the movie was going to show the changing nature of the Mafia. That was a challenge Al couldn't resist. This time they wanted him.

He made them pay up front — a half a million dollars — but no matter how much they had offered him, he wouldn't have done it just for the money. He had to like the script. Anyone who acts for money is crazy, he felt. He had never done it before and he was not going to start.

Playing Michael Corleone changed his image. Everything he had done previously suggested he was a brutal and violent person. Michael had more subtlety. Because of it he was cast in Scarecrow as, in his own words, "as a kind of schnook."

For *Godfather, Part II*, Al's final deal was $600,000, plus 10 percent of the profits. This was after long negotiations. Filming was hard work because of the downbeat nature of the role.

With him in the cast were his friends Robert De Niro, as young Vito Corleone, and John Cazale as his brother Fredo. Lee Strasberg played the young Godfather's business associate, Hyman Roth. Robert Duvall, Talia Shire and Diane Keaton resumed their former roles.

The first part of the movie was filmed in Lake Tahoe on a baronial estate surrounded by an eight-foot stone wall. A lakeside manor was the new Corleone family compound. The Cuban sequences, however, were filmed in the Dominican Republic, with Santo Domingo doubling as Havana.

In the story, Michael Corleone was heavily involved in the casino business in Vegas and had extended the family investments to the casinos of Havana.

Al had difficulty communicating because he had trouble with Spanish. His difficulty with the language dated back to high school. He had been failing every academic subject at Performing Arts, but language was the worst. His Spanish teacher told him she wanted to talk to him about his "problem."

He told her, "I don't have any problem. I just don't speak Spanish and you do."

Al used the unfamiliarity with Spanish to his advantage. As an actor he used everything in his experience he could apply. The character, Michael Corleone, was visiting a foreign city, Havana, for the first time. He was in unfamiliar territory and couldn't even understand what people in the streets were saying. Something seemed to be going on and he was suspicious. Al could understand that completely.

The locals in Cuba called him "Al Pa-see-no" and the movie was referred to as El Pa-dree-no. The words almost rhymed and they were synonymous.

During the filming, Al came down with a siege of bronchitis on top of exhaustion. He was hospitalized and flown back to New York to recuperate for 10 days. He said he felt like Elizabeth Taylor. Back on his feet, he returned to Santo Domingo and resumed shooting.

Al was nominated as Best Actor but lost to Art Carney

for Harry and Tonto. De Niro was nominated as Best Supporting actor — and won.

Another major role under his belt, Al was still troubled inside and didn't know why. He started seeing everything in monochrome. Doctors couldn't help him so he decided to try psychoanalysis.

As Al has said himself, "When the panic button is pushed, when your nose suddenly looks like a banana and you start peeling it, then you go for help."

He went to several analysts once or twice, embarrassed to return to the same one for subsequent visits. He made appointments and just never showed up.

At the same time his drinking got worse. Charlie made him face it. He said to him, "You're drinking. Look at it and recognize it!"

Al hadn't known how serious it was and, even more important, he didn't know other people knew. It was a powerful moment in his life. Charlie made him face his demon. It was a struggle, but he started to cut down.

ME

ONE OF THE FRINGE BENEFITS of advertising in the *Village Voice* was talking to Randa. We had become good friends over the phone. After a while, I stopped by personally to renew the ads rather than do it by phone.

She always gave me a lift and I fantasized what it would be like to be married to her. Because of my off-and-on relationship with Ginny, I didn't make any moves. I still thought it could work between me and Ginny.

I really wanted her to move back to New York with me. She was still living with her parents in Connecticut and, even though she did not get along with them, she preferred it to living with me. I kept telling her I would find my mother a place of her own, but she wouldn't believe me. If I only had enough money, I would show her!

I heard Al had given Charlie a percentage of his compensation for *Godfather II.* I speculated whether or not he would have given that to me if I had stayed behind to coach and guide him.

While Al went on to do movie after movie, I acted, too; but it was in another world of acting, with my "clients." I loved to make people happy. I wanted to be loved by everyone. That's one of the reasons I was so good at the capers. I made the clients happy.

AL

IN 1975, Joseph Papp, head of the New York Public Theater, gave Al $40,000 to get Bertolt Brecht's *The Resistible Rise of Arturo Ui* staged at David Wheeler's Theater Company of Boston. It was a play that parodied Hitler's rise to power in Germany.

Papp wanted a quick production, but Al wanted an ensemble, workshop production with a long rehearsal period. His friends, Penny Allen and John Cazale were also in the cast.

Meanwhile, Al had been the first choice for *Dog Day Afternoon*, but he backed out of it. The role was that of a bisexual. He was concerned about the script, the director and the role. He had just done *Godfather II* and was tired of films. He didn't feel like making another movie. He found it "a hassle."

Having done so many years of stage, he thought he was one of those actors who couldn't adjust to film, because it was too laborious. He was aware that he was, perhaps, being too tough on himself. He was simply working in a medium he didn't know too well, and he felt unsure of himself. The role in *Dog Day* was offered to Dustin Hoffman.

When Al was asked to reconsider, he was given Frank Pierson's script to read. He thought it was terrific. Pierson had structured it beautifully and really made it sing. Al thought it was "alive." He had strong feelings for the character as he was written.

At this stage of his career, there were three reasons why Al would accept a role in a movie: the director, the text and the character. If he could relate greatly to the director, if the text was "pretty good," and he thought he could do something with the character, he might take it. Or if he could relate greatly to the character, and the text and director are "OK," he would also take it.

There had to be one really strong, positive element involved. That's how he chose things from then on. Prior to that, all three had to be great. In this case, Sidney Lumet was to direct, so it was two out of three.

In middle of rehearsals for *Arturo Ui*, Al had to leave to shoot *Dog Day Afternoon*. Cazale was cast in the second lead and Penny Allen was one of the cashiers, so they, too, left Boston to accompany him. Al also got Judith Malina (Julian Beck's wife) cast in the picture.

Sidney Lumet, according to Al, was a genius at staging. He never told you a word. Just by the way he has you move, the scene came alive. He pointed Al in a direction and said go here and go there. Al found it extraordinary.

One of Al's best scenes in the picture was when he came running out of the bank shouting "Attica! Attica!" It was an emotional rush. Lumet helped him with it.

He said to Al, "It's his day in the sun, with all those people out there." It was like charging at windmills.

Another favorite moment of Al's, which made it a

"universal" kind of film, was when the delivery boy delivered a pizza and then turned around to the crowd and said, in effect, "I'm a star!"

According to Al, "It hit right where we're at — the kind of energy wrapped up in the media and with imagery and fantasy and film."

He felt we didn't know enough about media yet, it's effect on us. It was new and it had to do something to us.

Charlie Laughton knew *Dog Day* would be an explosive picture. He said, "Al, do you know what it is like? It's like pulling a pin out of a hand grenade and waiting for it to explode."

After his last scene was in the can, Al returned to Boston with Cazale and Penny to complete the rehearsals for Arturo and it finally opened.

ME

I WANTED TO GO to Boston to see Al in the play, so I called Marty Bregman's secretary, Jenny, to see if I could get tickets. They couldn't arrange it because it was out of town. She told me the theater was not a big operation and Al was only being paid "scale" for performing in the play.

I took an actress friend, Barbara Soffer, on a bus with me to see him.

When I tried to contact Al, his secretary said, "Oh, Ed, it's great that you came. Al is broken up about a friend who just died."

I didn't know who she was talking about and I was afraid to ask. I assumed it Bruce Gregory. She informed me he had died of a drug overdose. Al had known Bruce since they were kids. Bruce was my friend, too. We had studied together and went out to Hollywood together.

Al was excellent in the play. He played an Italian gangster. It was very comical and wow, what a performance he gave! I was making an effort to stay in touch. He was happy to see me and told me to join him at the restaurant after the show.

It was a release for both of us, talking about old times, even though we never discussed who had died. If it was Bruce, it was such a waste. He had so much talent, but hated the business.

He had been married to a young woman whom I had never met. She had been a dancer and they had a child. He loved her. His career had been going nowhere, though he was very handsome and athletic — a good type. When he was in Hollywood, they really wanted him, but he didn't like the Hollywood scene. He couldn't connect there, so he returned to New York.

Faye Dunaway also came to see Al. She met Al after the show at the restaurant too. She was wearing a farmer's daughter-type shirt, and her beautiful red hair was tied in the back. Al introduced me.

"This is the man I told you about."

I don't know if it was Faye's attractive face, or Al saying what he said, but I was completely tongue-tied. Faye looked at me stunned, with her sloe eyes. I just looked back into hers and we couldn't talk to each other. It was as if I met my soul mate. It was an awkward moment frozen in time. She walked away to the table.

Al said, "Oh, come on, Ed. Join us."

But I said, "That's all right," and left them alone.

I felt more insecure than I ever had before in my life. I couldn't take it. I don't know whether or not Al had said good things about me or bad. I chose to think they were favorable.

I saw the play again, paying for another ticket. Barbara

waited at the hotel. After the play was over, I went over to the coffee shop to talk to Al. He was surprised I was still there and thanked me for coming.

I said, "Al, I want you to do something for me. I didn't come all these miles just to see the play. I'd be so grateful to you if you could help me get my career going."

I hated to ask, but if Al couldn't help me, who could? I was very blunt and I think he liked that. I was sitting down, eating a steak, and I added jokingly, "I'll even buy you a steak."

He said, "I'll do what I can, you know that." During the meal, he became evasive. Finally, he got up and said, "Gotta go. See you later."

I saw the show a third time, but I didn't wait to see Al again. I didn't want to be too pushy. I took Barbara back to New York.

Al may have tried to recommend me for parts, but didn't tell me about it. Maybe nobody cared, but I thought people who are being acclaimed would have some kind of power, some kind of control. I saw new people breaking in all the time, people of all ages. Why not me?

Arturo Ui ran for eight weeks. The production was full of problems. Critics came down hard on Al for his diction and his coming off as a neurotic in the role.

AL

DOG DAY AFTERNOON was edited and released to good reviews. It earned Al his fourth Academy Award nomination. Jack Nicholson won that year for *One Flew Over the Cuckoo's Nest.* It was stiff competition.

"I think I'm rich now," Al said, humbly.

With his agent and manager getting 25 percent, however, and the government getting 50 percent, he netted only 25 percent himself. When you are wealthy, everyone hits on you for money.

He didn't mind lending money to friends, but he would warn them by saying, "Look, if this affects the relationship in any way, forget it."

Invariably, it did, though. Al was always generous with me and I tried never to abuse our friendship. Once when I was in a bind, I asked him for help. I told him I was afraid to borrow money because it might hurt the friendship.

His response was, "With you, Ed, never!"

It was hard for Al to adjust to more fame. He said, "You know, fame is like candy, you want to keep it and you can't."

He had some bad times with it, so many changes to go through to get himself acclimated. One day he was a struggling actor, the next a rich success. The changes really shook him, mostly because of his early life. He had started out being alienated from the world, from society, and that alienation gave him the juice to go on, to be the person he was — the outsider.

The more Al saw of success and celebrity, the sillier it all seemed to him. It had nothing to do with life. He felt that in this life you shouldn't think about success. That's not where the focus should be. There are no rewards, Al said, except in what you're doing— unless you consider money a reward. He didn't. Success and "triumph" to him were all bull. Just to endure it was enough.

Jill Clayburgh was quoted as saying, "I'm speaking as an actress, not Al's former lover. I think he projects such power because of his total lack of egocentricity. A lot of actors want to be sexy, cute, adorable... do anything to win an audience to their side... cater to every cheap, trendy, obvious appeal that will make them loved. Al couldn't care less. He's too honest, and he loves the characters he plays too deeply to go in for that sort of thing. That's why he can turn acting into poetry.

"In that generation of actors working around New York in the 1960s, it was always Al and maybe one or two others they spoke about when they dared talk of genius... the kind of actors who might make it big."

Michelangelo said, "God free me of myself so that I can please you." It's the same way Al felt. He had to get away from the things that weren't important, even though at some moments they seemed to have importance. If he was a painter, he said, he'd have to get rid of everything in a room — the books, the radio, the phonograph, the bed, the refrigerator — everything — so he could just paint.

Al said there was a time when you didn't become an actor unless you loved to act. Now, in 1975, actors got to a point where they were affluent and cavorted with kings, queens, oil barons, and all the fashionable people. They were political spokesmen or politicians, investors, businessmen, sportsmen. They hunted elephants in Africa, they owned farms and built lakes and mountains. But they didn't act. And if they did, they did the same damned thing over and over again.

"Shoot the elephant! You know what I mean?"

Al didn't "cavort." He led a simple, humble life. His lifestyle was pretty much the same as it had always been. He was an actor. He was afraid if he enhanced his lifestyle it would all deflate like a balloon or disappear, and all the good things that had happened to him would vanish, like an illusion.

Al was depressed when he finished a project. All actors experience this. They're alive when they're working.

After only five years of making movies, Al had been nominated four times for an Academy Award. He refused to campaign for it personally like other actors did. He couldn't understand why other actors did.

He believed there were certain "manipulations" that went on, certain favoritisms and partialities. He didn't know where, specifically, but he could can sense them. He experienced losing the award four years in a row. It was so strange to him. You feel good about being nominated, then you get turned into a loser when you don't win it. You've been feeling terrific and suddenly everybody starts consoling you.

Whenever Al had to be in California he stayed in Malibu. He drove a motorcycle with such abandoned speed it scared even Steve McQueen. He was a major movie star, and he still had never been to a Hollywood party... or even one in Beverly Hills.

Not to let a year go by without doing something on the stage, he did *The Local Stigmatic* again, this time in New York at Joe Papp's Public Theater. It was directed, of course, by David Wheeler, with John Cazale in the cast, for a limited run.

Al was out of work for a year. Many movie offers came in, but he turned them down. He was facing his drinking demon. He analyzed the success that almost killed him. He remembered being so far down that at any time he could have caught pneumonia because he didn't have a warm place to sleep.

Success threw him. He had been down and out for so long he began to wonder how much further he could slip. Then, all of a sudden, he was the co-star in the biggest movie of all time, acting alongside Marlon Brando, one of the worlds' biggest actors. He couldn't adjust to it.

Al was familiar with a term in the drinking world called "reaching one's bottom." He didn't know if he had ever gotten to his bottom. He felt deprived of it. He struggled to quit before he hit it. He became conscious of a certain pattern in drinking, that it could lead to other things, a downward spiral. He tried A.A. for a while; and, while he didn't follow the program, he found it very supportive and meaningful.

But he was still belting the booze. He agreed with Laurence Olivier who had said a drink after the show is the best thing about the theater. Whiskey is very underrated. Al knew because he had been to psychiatrists and they didn't calm him down as much as a good belt. It made him socialize better, talk better with it. It helped him to be open.

What is amazing is that he never touched a drop while he was working. His efforts to cut down were working and by this time he had given up his three-day binges. Coming out of them left him too depressed.

He hoped that eventually, as he straightened out personally, he could deal with the pain of it all. He admitted his personal life was in trouble. It had been in trouble for a long time. He was aware that if he could align himself personally, it would be better for his work. Having more of a foundation in life would better fortify him to face the chaos of work.

ME

THELMA HOCHSTADTLER was obese. Her son, Nicholas, who had also been obese, passed on recently. She had wanted to get them both on a talk show. When she called me, in answer to my ad, I lied and told her my mother had also just passed on and I could sympathize with the way she felt.

She wanted me to come over and entertain her and Nicholas. It was one of the most depressing days of my life. Her apartment looked like a funeral parlor. She wanted me to sing some popular songs to her and to Nicholas. Her first request was "You'll Never Know," which was a hit in the 40s. I sang song after song to her and to the imaginary Nicholas, who had his own oversized chair.

It turned out to be a hoot and she paid me a little extra for my encore, Spike Jones' "Der Fuehrer's Face." In a weird way, it lifted me out of my depression. I couldn't wait to tell Randa about it.

I couldn't escape the capers, even when I was asleep.

I had a dream that a strange-looking character answered one of my ads and hired me to help him get a role in a movie. I, of course, got him the role. It was Al, in disguise. I told him he was no kink, but he sure was a kook. Another time I dreamed I had Al kidnapped so that I could play all his roles.

It turned into a nightmare, because every time the camera rolled, I either forgot my lines or I didn't know which movie I was in.

AL ... AND ME

IN 1977, MARTY Bregman's secretary, Jenny, called me and asked me if I had a copy of *Tubie's Monument.* Al had told Marty about the scene we had done years earlier in one of our acting classes. Marty wanted to read the book, but it was out of print. I told her I would look for it.

I had saved my copy, anticipating somebody would want it like this, but I didn't want to give him my last copy. So I called and visited every bookstore in the Village and finally found a paperback.

Marty Bregman's offices were luxurious. His room had blue stucco walls. On top of the wall-to-wall olive carpeting, there was a blue, gold and white oriental rug. From his window there was a great view of the East River. Everything from the molding to the wastebaskets was elegant. Marty thanked me.

"Where did you get this? We looked all over for a copy."

As I was leaving, Jenny stopped me. "What can we give you to thank you? I couldn't find the book anywhere."

I asked, "What did Al say to give me?"

"Oh, Al said, you won't want anything. He said Ed just wants to make people happy. He's that kind of guy. He won't want a thing."

Al was happy about it and called me. "How did you ever find that book?"

"I was determined to find it. I didn't want to give away my only copy. It's a hardcover."

He told me he wanted to get Carl Reiner to write a screenplay on it, and hopefully make it as a movie.

I said, "That would be great," thinking that this would be my big opportunity to act in a movie. "Who's going to play Tubie if you do it?"

He said, "They want Walter Mathau."

"What about me?"

"Ed, you know the studio's going to want a name. But, we'll save something good for you, don't worry."

I said, "I'd appreciate that."

Marty and his people looked through *Tubie's Monument* and couldn't find the scene Al and I had done. So I went over to their office to show them. I asked Marty's secretary, Jenny, if I could meet him.

I wasn't trying to go over Al's head or anything, but I figured this was a good opportunity for me. After all, I was helping them. Jenny checked with Marty and came back out, saying, "Yeah, he'll meet you."

He came out and thanked me for finding the book. I said

to him, "Marty, I can act too." I was a little brash. "Can you help me as an actor? Like getting me a part in a movie?"

Marty said, "Sure, see my secretary. We'll give you some extra work."

I said, "No, thank you."

I wasn't going to do extra work after all the training and experience I had. I had a lot more to offer that to just be a guy with no lines standing in the background.

Al must have spoken to him afterwards, because Marty wrote me a nice letter. He told me to find him a good script and he'd produce it, even if it was a one-act play from an acting workshop. Something with a lot of substance.

I sent him a script called *Leviathan* by a young writer, Thomas James Nesi. It was being developed by two Hollywood producers I had just met, David Sheldon and Harvey Flaxman.

It was a disaster movie, like *Towering Inferno*, about a seaside community that gets hit by an electrical storm and a tidal wave. Sheldon and Flaxman had Cliff Robertson, Orson Welles, and O.J. Simpson interested in appearing in it and were looking for financing and production. Sheldon was also the director.

Marty didn't want to do this type of picture, so I started to look further.

The next thing I heard, Carl Reiner had finished the screenplay for *Tubie's Monument*, and the production was put on the "Pictures to Do" list for Columbia Pictures.

Months later, I met Al on Madison Avenue, which was an amazing coincidence because that is where Tubie always used to meet Joe in the book. I asked him,

"Al, what ever happened to *Tubie's Monument*?"

"They think I'm too old for it now."

He had gained a little weight, but still looked youthful. But the kid in the script was supposed to be 23.

In the evening, my mother was roosting in front of the TV, watching *Jeopardy*. I was doing supper dishes.

My mother screamed out, "It's Ulysses S. Grant, Stupid! I could do better than that myself."

I challenged her, "Why don't you get on the show, Ma?"

"That'd be the day I'd turn stupid."

"No way. By the way, Ma, Dale's coming in from camp to see us Saturday afternoon."

"Oh, Goodie. Pick up some Gummy Bears at the Super, will ya?"

The phone rang up in the loft. I hurried up the stairs, calling back, "Will do, ma."

"You're getting a lot of calls today."

"Yeah."

I picked up the phone. My mother continued talking. "Calls for work?"

I listened to my calls. One of them sounded interesting. I called the number. 555-6262. Herbie Conklin answered. He sounded like a little guy, ordinary. He talked with a chip-on-the-shoulder attitude.

"I saw your ad. I have a little scenario I'd like played out. If you're interested."

"I'm all ears. When?"

"Saturday afternoon in Central Park by the boat basin. Something to entertain my kid. Four p.m. Do you take checks?"

"No, I don't. Strictly cash."

"Oh. You furnish the costume?"

"Absolutely. What would you like?"

"A caped superhero. Something like that. It's my kid's birthday. Something special for him."

"That's nice. What would you like me to do?"

He sounded like an agent. "You just show up. We'll take it from there, OK?"

"OK. Boat basin in Central Park. I'll be there."

I hung up, went back downstairs, lingered near Tillie who was once again absorbed in *Jeopardy*.

"Ma, could I go through your closet?"

She turned around and looked me up and down.

"Ed, is there something you're not telling me? I'd love you no matter what?"

"It's for my acting class. We're using costumes."

"I'm relieved to hear it, doll. Take whatever you need."

I went to her closet and started going through her things. I pulled out a long black cape and tried it on. I pulled down a flowing turban from the upper shelf and jammed it on my head. I turned to look at myself in the mirror. Not bad.

I went back to the loft and went through my make-up case. I tried on a handlebar moustache then an "Errol Flynn" one. I took off the turban, picked up a long, black, curly wig and put it on. I put the turban back on over the wig. I eyed myself in the mirror. Great!

I then sat down and painted a green mask around my eyes. I was completely unrecognizable now. Valentino.

I took a bus to Central Park on Saturday, dressed in my now-refined costume. I wore the cape and long flowing turban, the green painted mask, and the Errol Flynn moustache. Under it all, I wore black leotards, boots and turtle neck.

I descended the stone steps into the park and took a shortcut across the meadow. People stared at me in amazement as I cut through the boat basin. Several little kids started to tag after me, but I growled at them and scared them off.

At the picnic area, near the carousel, Herbie was serving birthday cake to a small group of children about eight years old. He saw me approaching. Suddenly, he picked up a cane and waved it in the air. He shouted to his son, "Brian? Hey, look! We're being attacked!"

As I walked toward the small group, I called to Herbie in my most macho voice, "Mr. Conklin?"

Herbie struck me on the shoulder and shrieked a war yell. I jumped back, confused. He shouted, "En garde!"

"What? What is this?" I didn't know what the hell was going on.

Herbie swiftly hit me on each side with the cane.

I bellowed in pain, "Wait! I've got to do my monologue..."

Herbie lunged at me and struck me several times. I tried to dodge his blows. The kids were shouting excitedly.

"Wait a minute!" I shouted.

But Herbie kept pummeling me. He glanced at the kids and slammed away.

"Who's the hero now, Brian? Who, huh?"

His little son shouted, "You are! You are, Dad!"

"Who's a loser now, huh? Who?"

"The Caped loser! That's who!"

The kids shouted and screamed. I tried to fend off the sharp blows, but I couldn't find a way out. I sank to the ground and covered my head with the cape. Herbie was everywhere at once.

Suddenly a mounted policeman galloped up and rode between me and Herbie. He grabbed Herbie's cane and said, "You're under arrest, mister."

He leaped off the horse, handcuffed Herbie and turned to address me, the caped lump on the ground. "You al-right, Lady?"

Brian corrected him. "That's no lady, officer, that's the masked avenger!

I turned over, showing my mustached face. The police-man pulled me to my feet. "You all right?"

"I'm fine..."

The policeman placed a call on his radio. He turned to Herbie. "I'm runnin' you in for Assault and Battery." He jerked Herbie forward, had him put his hands against the horse, and frisked him.

The little birthday group was thoroughly entertained when the policeman's backup arrived to take Herbie away. They screamed with delight and ran after the policeman with the horse. He was obviously their hero. I was upstaged.

Realizing Herbie was being taken away, I started after them and shouted, "Wait a minute! What about my fee?"

No one seemed to hear me. I was stiffed.

I arrived back home, my head bleeding from a cut. It looked worse than it was, but when my mother saw the blood, she crumpled up in her chair, in a dead faint.

"Mom!"

I kneeled at her feet and slapped her gently. She didn't respond. Victor came running in.

Seeing me in my outrageous costume, he asked, "What's with you?"

I moaned, "I killed her! I killed her!"

Victor stooped down. "No, I think she's breathing. Stay with her. I'll call an ambulance."

In less than a half hour, two orderlies were putting her onto a stretcher, attaching an oxygen mask to her face. One was taking her blood pressure. Victor hovered near them, his face pale with concern.

I asked one of the orderlies, "Is she still..."

He quickly responded, "She's alive, sir. Just barely."

I was devastated. "Oh, God! Don't die, Mom, don't die."

In the hospital, Vic and I waited in the observation station, just outside my mother's glass cubicle.

She lay there comatose, attached to all sorts of life-supporting machines.

When the nursing director came out, I asked her, "What's her condition?"

She looked at me sternly, "No change. The next 24 hours are critical. Who's your carrier?"

Victor chimed in, "Your insurer, Ed."

"She has no insurance. She's too young for Medicare."

"You should be prepared to pay up front then. This is not a charity hospital."

"How much?"

"See the business office. They'll let you know. But I'd guess you'd need at least $3,000 as a deposit before they let you even leave here."

I looked at Victor, frightened.

I didn't want to stay in the apartment that night, so I went up to Victor's. They had his telephone number at the hospital in case they needed me. Victor sat on a cushion in the center of the floor in the lotus position, deep in meditation. I tried to pick a tune on the piano, but couldn't get anything to sound right.

Victor suddenly looked up and said, "My guide says you should call Al."

"Your guide? Is it a voice? I hear voices sometimes."

"An inner voice, maybe. It's more like an intuition. Ed should call Al."

"I can't do that."

"This is no time for pride, Ed. Al will be glad to lend you the money. It'd be just an advance against your salary... from the movie.

"No. I'll get the money some way."

Still worried, I went back downstairs to our apartment and called Ginny.

"Ginny? It's me."

"Who?"

"How soon we forget. It's Ed."

"Oh. You just sounded so different. I'm sorry about Tillie. I was about to call you. Is she gonna be alright?"

"We'll know more tomorrow."

"Well, give her my... regards. While we're at it, Ed, I'm very upset with you. I heard about you running around Central Park in a cape and a wig. Dale found out from his friends who told him his father is a transvestite. What the hell were you doing? He's so upset with you, he won't talk to me about it."

"It was supposed to be a kid's party— I was hired to do a monologue."

"In Central Park? I've heard of Shakespeare In The Park, but you were doing Liberace as Superman!" Do what you want in the bathroom, but don't do your stupid antics out in public and give Dale a problem, do you hear me?

"I promise. Look, Ginny, you know I never asked you for anything, but I need some immediate cash."

"How much?"

"Three thousand by in the morning. It's for my mother—"

Ginny laughed. "Hah! I have $600 to do me until next month and I have a $1,000 worth of bills to pay."

"I guess I knew that. Thanks anyway. I know you'd help me if you could."

I went to see Freddie Coyle, a barber on the East Side, who was a private "lender." He had access to money and said he'd give me any amount I wanted as long as I paid it back in a week. I borrowed $10,000 at one percent — a week! I was sure I could scrape enough together to repay it and get my mother through this ordeal.

I went back to the hospital to see my mother. On the third floor, I stopped at the desk where the special care nurses were monitoring the critically ill patients. I spotted the head nurse and asked her, "My mother, Mrs. De Leo? How's she doing?"

Leonore Epstein, that's what her badge said, looked at me as if I was a defendant in a murder trial. "Mr. De Leo, Dr. Greinder says we can't keep her here unless you make a full estimated payment."

"What's that mean?"

"It means we project the cost and you pay up front. If a sum isn't used, you get it back." She arched her brows as if to say, "Why don't you try that and see how far it gets you?"

"How much would that be?"

"You'll have to talk to billing."

"Can I visit my mother first?"

Mrs. Epstein shrugged, and gestured for me to go on in.

Inside the cubicle, my mother lay gray and comatose, the machines breathing for her. I kneeled next to the bed and laid my head close to hers. "Ma?"

There was no sound but the force of air, in and out, in and out.

"Ma, you gotta fight. You're all I got left. Fight. For me, OK? I'll take care of you. I won't let you down. You've always been there for me. I'm here for you."

I kissed her. There was no response.

I went down to the billing office and they showed me the statement. Twelve thousand dollars! I couldn't believe it. After gaping at it, I sank down in the chair. I asked if they would accept ten, that I would give them the balance as soon as possible. They told me they would give me a cash price of $10,000 since this was not covered by insurance. Feeling like I was getting a discount at Sears, I got out my checkbook and wrote a check.

I strolled with Victor round the edges of Gramercy Park. Inside the iron-fenced enclosure, people sat on benches, reading, romancing, lolling. Children were running around, playing and shouting.

Victor tried to comfort me. "I'm doing healing meditations for her, Ed."

"Thanks, Vic. I hope it does some good."

"You gotta believe. I know you think I'm a weirdo, but God told me she's gonna pull through. She's going to be all right."

"I'll take that as gospel. What about me?"

"I didn't ask about you. What's the matter?"

"I'm in deep, deep dung if things don't come together this time. I'm stone broke and now I'm in debt big time."

"Any more action from the ads?"

"There was a call when I got home. Some little old lady. I hope this one doesn't stiff me."

We continued walking.

At the end of the week I gave Freddie, the loan shark, $500. I figured it would take me about 20 weeks to pay off the loan.

He looked at me in amazement. "Where's the other $9,500?"

He expected the entire $10,000 back in a week. I turned beet red and told him I would get it.

"You better," he said. "You better."

I was desperate again to get cast in something and called Al for help. I read in the trades he was going to do another picture, *Bobby Deerfield.*

"You sound great," he said.

"Then I must be," I told him. "Yeah, I'm... I'm feelin' just... great."

He asked how long it had been since we saw each other.

"Too long, Al," I said, "too long."

We all get busy, he explained. He wanted to know how Ginny was, and "the kid."

"Dale," I said. "Nice of you to remember. They're both

fine, but they're better off without me, I guess."

Al sounded surprised by that comment, and wanted to know what happened.

I explained, "My career kinda got in the way—." He knew what that meant.

I said, "I hear you're doing a new picture. I read the book. The role's perfect for you."

"I think I can do something with it."

"Who's playing your brother?"

He told me that the producers had their feelers out. The big stars were reluctant to play second fiddle to him. Egos, I guess.

I drew a deep breath and summoned all the courage I had. "What about me?"

He went silent for a moment, but I could sense him thinking about it. He told me I'd be perfect. I was a fantastic actor. He's wanted to do something for me for a long time and this may be the chance.

"I don't want you to think you owe me anything," I said. "Not at all."

If it didn't work on this one, then maybe the next one, he said. After all, I had been so helpful to him when he was struggling.

"That's too generous of you," I told him. "You did it yourself. I knew you had it in you, and I told you so."

He reminded me I had believed in him when nobody else did.

"When can I read for it," I asked?

He told me he was penciling me in and he would go to bat for me to play the role.

I was almost in tears. "You mean that? You really do mean that?"

He told me he wouldn't let me down.

Al's secretary called me and said, "Al penciled you in to

play his brother in *Bobby Deerfield.* I asked her what the role was about. She told me it was a movie about a superstar racing driver, directed by Sydney Pollack.

Like Al, the role he was going to play, *Bobby Deerfield*, came from the streets. Marty Bregman was not producing, but was still Al's manager. She told me the brother tries to get Bobby to leave the racing world and come back home with Mom and all that. The role was mine and I would be doing my scenes in Europe. Sydney Pollack was producing and directing. Sydney Pollack! One of the greats.

I was elated. Finally, a role in a movie. And with Al. I couldn't wait to sign my contract, to get fitted for wardrobe, to start rehearsals. I found out *Bobby Deerfield* was based on a novel, *Heaven Has No Favorites* by Erich Maria Remarque. I bought the book to get familiar with the character.

After talking to Al, I walked out into the sunshine. I stood still for a moment, then leaped into the air and clicked my heels together. "Yes!"

I waited for Ginny outside the tall glass-front building where she was working. I paced just outside the entrance. Ginny came out, wearing a tomato red suit, swinging her briefcase jauntily. She looked successful and, for once, very carefree. She spotted me and her expression soured.

She glared at me, "Well. Fancy meeting you here."

I tried to charm her. "Let me take you to dinner."

She shook her head. "Can't. Got a meeting. In East Hampton. So I've got a train to catch. What is it, Ed? Make it snappy!"

"Well, I... I just came from talking to Al—"

"Al Pacino! How is he?"

"Great, just great. And guess what?"

"I don't have time for games, Ed."

"He promised me a role in Bobby Deerfield."

Ginny stared at me with wonder. With skepticism, she

said, "I'll bet."

"He said he'd go to bat for me."

"You actually went to see him."

I had to say something fast, otherwise she'd think this was another dream. "Of course," I said. "He's got this great apartment on the East Side. One of those renovated art deco buildings that are very chic in the City now."

She looked at me suspiciously.

I continued, "The lobby was real chic, done in a hi-tech style with one of those caged elevators? His place is very plush... shiny hardwood floors… soft leathers. Al was on the phone when I walked in, but he stopped and put his arm around my shoulder."

"So you talked to him on the phone."

"No, I was there!" He had his assistant bring in some stuff to eat. There were lots of takeout bags on the counter. I mean, he had cold pesto rotini, roasted peppers and eggplant, salads, pickles and olives, roasted garlic and goat cheese. Wine, too, but he didn't drink any. He's off the stuff now."

"You'll blow it," Ginny said, "like you blow everything. Remember when he got you the part in *Scarecrow* but when that actor, Harvey something, who looks like you, walked in, they went with him instead?"

I didn't dare tell her it wasn't true. I had never been offered a role in *Scarecrow*.

I said, "Trust me, when I get the call, I'll be the first one there."

"I'll believe it when I see it."

"Ginny, this is for real!"

"You may be able to live on hope, Ed, but I refuse to do it another day."

"It's a leading role, Ginny! The biggest one next to Al's. I'm gonna do it this time, Ginny. We can be a family again."

"Well, if it's true, then you'll have money for child support." She walked out toward the street. "I gotta go. I'll miss my train."

She hopped into a cab as a man got out of it, slammed the door and never looked back as it pulled out into traffic. I deflated slowly.

I was at home, lying on my back in bed, staring at the ceiling. Like the homeless man said, I need a change. The phone rang. It was Al. Him calling me for a change. He didn't sound too good.

I sat up. "Al? How's it going?"

His voice was hoarse. He sounded depressed. He told me that everything was fine, considering.

I said, "It's never easy, is it? No matter how big you get."

He told me that this was the toughest thing he ever had to do.

I said something stupid, like, "Acting is still an art, and art is painful. But it's what we do. What we gotta do."

He told me not to hate him, but he couldn't get the powers that be to give me the part. I swallowed hard. I thought I was dying. He went on to explain he fought like hell for me, but... Marty Bregman was told by the production manager of the movie that it would cost too much to send all the principal actors to Europe. They could afford to fly only the stars over, and they had a stack of "names" that they would use, to insure box-office drawing power. So, they couldn't use me because they didn't want to pay my way to Europe.

"That's an insult to you," I told Al. "Don't they think your name is enough?"

I was sorry I said that. We agreed that everybody is so damned insecure in this business.

Finally, I said, "I understand, Al. Don't worry about it."

He didn't want that to come between us. He said he'd

make it up to me.

I said, "Like I've told you before, Al, we shouldn't owe each other anything. Let's keep it that way."

He told me I was a real prince of a guy. He must have felt like a pile of dog shit. But I knew it wasn't his fault.

I was hurt, but I said, "You're a great guy, no matter what. Just go out there and win the Oscar this time."

After I hung up, I had to force back tears of disappointment. Then I slammed my fist through the wall, reaming out a hole. My big opportunity was, once again, out the window.

I was livid. I never cried much, but I was doing it now. I finally got a role in a major movie and suddenly I was out because they didn't want to pay me.

The next day, after I calmed down, I went to see my son in Connecticut. On the train, I had a brainstorm. I called my mother in the hospital when I arrived.

"Mom, I got a great idea for a screenplay." I asked her, "What would any actor really die to do? Be in a play where he could play many parts. I'm gonna write a play about an actor, things from my own life. It's gonna be so great that if somebody wants to do it, they'll have to cast me in the lead role."

"You're a good actor and you're a good writer," she said. "You write it and it will be good, I'm sure."

I met Charlie on the street when I got back to New York. He told me Al wanted him to fly to Paris to be with him during the shooting of *Bobby Deerfield.*

I told him to send him my regards. He acted a little guilty and told me he hoped his working with Al hadn't hurt the friendship between me and Al. I assured him it hadn't.

AL

ON THE PLUS SIDE for Al, he stopped drinking — to the point he felt uncomfortable around people who did drugs or who drank to excess. He had become super-sensitive to it and could pick it up easily.

With *Bobby Deerfield*, he was actually returning to work. The gorgeous Marthe Keller was cast opposite him. To prepare for the role Al wanted a real source to study as he did in *Serpico* and *Dog Day Afternoon.*

For *Bobby Deerfield*, he studied films of racing-car drivers. He observed the way a driver got into a car, "like a surgeon putting on gloves." Al liked to imitate, but through character, not caricature.

He categorized an actor as an emotional athlete who "works on his instrument" and finds the heart of the character. He acknowledged it was a painful process and as a result his personal life suffered.

The director, Sydney Pollack, chose Al for the role because *Bobby Deerfield* was a passive character. He wanted an actor whose emotions were close to the surface.

If an inexpressive actor like Clint Eastwood had played the role, *Bobby Deerfield* would have come off as indifferent.

Comparing Al to the real-life Bobby Deerfield, Marthe Keller said, "There's a big similarity. Of all his parts, it is the closest. Something scared me about that."

Marthe was also similar to the role she played — a sophisticated, outgoing European who wakes up Bobby Deerfield to life.

Explaining Al's approach to a role, Pollack said, "He asks questions of a very, very detailed minuscule nature. 'How long has it been since he raced last?' or 'How long does it take for him to come down after a race?' He does not ask broad-stroke questions about what the man wants out of life. Once he starts on the track of a character, it's like a dog picking up a scent."

The clothing a character wore always helped Al with his character. He felt closer to the character in costume. He even wore the wardrobe after the filming was over. *Bobby Deerfield* had an elegant wardrobe including expensive suits by Meledandri. During the stage production of *Pavlo Hummel*, Al wore military apparel.

Al liked to collect pieces of the wardrobe from every production. He had Serpico's jeans, for example, and a pair of Lionel's hobo shoes from *Scarecrow*.

Al did psychological exercises the way a dancer warms up. He didn't suddenly become violent when the camera rolled. He psyched himself up to become violent.

While they were rehearsing in Paris, Al and Marthe didn't get along. He and Sydney Pollack were also at odds. Al and Pollack were different. Pollack had a specific idea for the movie. It meant something to him. Al, meanwhile, had a different view.

In a movie of that scope, the actors and the director need to be together on it. It was a very delicate subject and ultimately became a mess. Al confessed they might have been better off had he listened to Pollack more. The end product would have been more consistent.

The problem was, he didn't quite understand Pollack's point of view.

What Al was after in the movie was "the other side of narcissism," a kind of loneliness that happens to a superstar who is idolized. He wanted to establish narcissistic detachment and depression. His goal was to break that depression, that self-absorption, and open like a flower.

In his own life, he had not gone into or resolved many things, and there were many things he had avoided. To him, that was what *Bobby Deerfield* was about. It was about avoiding — knowing when to duck, when to move, when to hide, when to go in, and when to roll with the punches. It's what Al called his "way of survival."

Al realized that he had experienced many selfish incidents in his life; but one day, he just turned around and said, "I'm a selfish bastard and I don't have to be."

They filmed in Lake Como and Florence, then on to Le Mans. After completion, Marthe moved in with Al in his New York apartment. With Marthe he started to dress better and he learned to drive a car. Before he played Bobby Deerfield, Al couldn't drive. After the production he bought a BMW and became a fast driver.

According to Keller, "He's always working, even if he isn't working — and he doesn't always know it. He talks about characters. He plays so many parts every day."

She said that Al changed in a year. When she first met him, he would walk with his head down. "Now he has gotten taller — or I've gotten smaller. He's opened his eyes. He's starting to see more things."

Al thought of movie stardom as an accident for him. In his own estimation, he was a character actor who played leading roles. His characters, even winners like Bobby Deerfield, were people out of the mainstream, misfits, who were fighting conformity to society.

As one reporter put it, Al's characters were loners, isolated emotionally, but burning with intensity. Within this, Al played a wide range. They were withdrawn, but extroverted. They were illiterate, but articulate. They were indifferent, but commanding. This gave him a certain niche, a unique style.

As Al said, "There should be a stamp on an artist's work. People went to see Junius Booth enact Richard III just as they went to see Toscanini or Caruso."

He felt that too often an actor is put in the position of doing a part he can't really speak through. Al had to connect with his material.

ME

I OWED a lot of money and started to panic. I went to the lender's girlfriend to intercede. She was an opera singer from Italy and wanted to break into acting. I had tried to help her with her acting. Maybe she could speak to Nick and get him to back off for a while. She told me Nick would never listen to her.

You can't play around with loan sharks. They can break your legs.

She said, "I don't know anybody that can get you out of this. I'm going to throw it out to the wind for you. That's all I can do." She meant, to a higher power.

While waiting for a greater power to intervene, the interest on the money was building. Thousands of dollars.

I heard the phone ring and went racing up the stairs. I listened as the answering machine picked up. It was a welcome voice.

"Hi, there. It's Randa... from the *Village Voice.* I was thinking about you, so I—"

I grabbed the phone. "Hi."

She was so cheerful. "Hi. How are you?"

"Great. I mean, terrible. My mother collapsed and had to go back to the hospital. I lost the role in Al's movie... and my last client stiffed me. Other than that, great."

"I'm sorry, really. Anything I can do?"

"Nothing. It's good to hear your voice, though. I feel a lot better already."

"Would you like to come over to my place? That is, if

you're free?"

Would I? It took me just under an hour to get there. Sometimes I think that there's a whole continent between the Bronx and Greenwich Village.

Randa's small studio apartment in Soho was decorated with filmy scarves and throws, cabbage-rose chintz, rocking chairs, dried roses and old lace. It looked just like Randa. Candles flickered around the room and Vivaldi played on the hi-fi. I felt immediately at home. I could picture living with her.

We sat on the sofa together drinking herb tea. A tape recorder was on the table in front of us.

"So Al wasn't very good when you first met him?"

"He had talent, but it was all over the place. I worked with him, helped him develop a sense of direction."

"Then he really owes you a lot."

"Oh, I wouldn't say that. I helped him in the beginning, but Charlie Laughton really got him going. And even if Charlie wasn't there, someone else would have eventually. He inspired that in people. People always wanted to help him."

"Don't negate the part you played in his success."

"I'm not. I'm proud of it. I just wish—"

She read my mind.

"Your day will come. I feel it in my bones."

She eyed me askance. I eyed her back. She got up and stretched, revealing a very slim, well-built little body beneath her flimsy granny dress.'

I couldn't take my eyes off her. "You're really beautiful."

She said humbly, "Oh, no I'm not. I'm not what you'd call the beautiful type."

"Are you ashamed of your body?"

She hunched over immediately. "Of course not! Well, maybe... a little. OK, a lot."

I got up and stepped close to her, studying her. She was acutely uncomfortable.

"You could be a knockout," I told her. "I mean, you already are, but your clothes... Why do you wear those big, baggy things?"

She turned away. "I really don't want to discuss this."

Was I blowing this, too? "I'm sorry."

"It's OK. Really. I like you, Ed. Just being with you makes me feel warm.... and safe."

"I'm glad. I'd like to be closer."

Randa was unable to look me in the eye. "What about your wife?"

"Ginny? I don't know."

"Do you still love her?"

"Yes. No. Both."

"She hurt you, didn't she?"

"She took our son, Dale, and moved to Connecticut when he was just an infant. Was I hurt? Sure. But, I'm surviving. I'm a survivor. I'd survive in a packing crate." I shuddered at the memory.

Randa laughed. "A packing crate? Why in the world would you say that?"

"I ran into an old friend, an actor. He's homeless. He lives in an alley in a packing crate. It almost could be me."

"Never! You've got too much going for you. You're going to make it, Ed. Believe that."

"I could use some convincing."

I questioned her with my eyes. I liked what I saw. I pulled her gently to me and kissed her. She drew back, then succumbed to my kiss. We were both glassy-eyed and dazed when we let each other go.

I felt like I was struck by lightning. "Wow!"

"Yeah!"

I tried to draw her back, but she ducked away.

"I guess I was pushing it a bit, " I said. "I'm not divorced yet, but it's an official separation. I'm a free agent, and she's seeing other men."

"Do you plan to get a divorce?"

"I believe in marriage, Randa. If I could do something to save mine, I would. My son needs a father and a mother pulling together."

"Well, then. That's what you should try to do. But if it doesn't work out, let me know, OK?"

I met a promoter, Gabe Zachary, who convinced me he had unlimited financing available for motion pictures. When he found out I knew Al Pacino, he told me, "I can back all of his movies."

It sounded like something that might interest Al, so I let him persuade me to give him Al's telephone number.

He called Al and told him, "I can finance all of your movies for the rest of your life."

Al diplomatically responded that he didn't need it, he had all the money behind him that he needed for the rest of his life.

Zachary told me what Al said. He wouldn't take no for an answer and wanted me to pursue it further with Al.

"Tell him that instead of his receiving only a salary for his pictures, he could be the producer and keep at least 25 percent of the profits."

I refused. I realized that when you are a superstar, the banks and the studios will finance your pictures. You are "bankable." You don't need wheeler-dealers to help you. I was embarrassed I had given him Al's number and swore I would never do it again.

I completed my screenplay *The Playmaker* based on my taking out ads and playing roles for people. I wrote the script to create a role for myself. Who else could play it but me? I figured if somebody liked it, they would have to cast me in it. The story included another character loosely based on Al. I made him a young student of mine who has suddenly become a superstar.

Because I was away from the apartment so much of the time teaching and going out on my capers, I couldn't give my mother the care she needed. My sisters and I arranged for her to stay for a while at a very nice residential rest home where she could get nursing care. They didn't help her at the home that much. Joan visited her constantly and got her on a diet. She started to look great and got her diabetes under control.

Joan told me, "She misses you and wants to go home. She doesn't think she fits in with all these women."

I said, "What do you mean? They're all her age."

"Yes, but you know Mom, she's one of a kind."

I knew what she meant. She was like Whoopi Goldberg in *Sister Act.* A fish out of water.

So Mom came home.

AL

IN APRIL 1977, Al brought *The Basic Training of Pavlo Hummel* to New York, as staged by David Wheeler's company. He wanted to introduce David Wheeler's company, as well as the play, to Broadway audiences.

At the opening night party at Sardi's, he and Marthe Keller were attended by three bodyguards with walkie-talkies. Two of them were on duty every night at the theater. Al was embarrassed by the attention. These guards walled him off from humanity.

"I don't need any bodyguards. I'm from the South Bronx. I can handle it."

Because of the incident, Earl Wilson, a columnist labeled him the "male Greta Garbo." But Al really didn't want to be alone. He just wanted to choose his own company. That's why he avoided parties and public places where he could be victimized by strangers.

Oddly enough, he and Marthe Keller, went out in public a lot, holding hands and jaywalking, not even noticed by people.

His apartment in the 60s still had no guards or doormen, not even any servants; and it still said "C. Bergen" on the door.

In *Pavlo*, he felt the character growing and changing since it opened. Pavlo had become more unusual, weirder, which acted as a counterbalance to the realism of the play around him. Al was exposing his hurt, his deprivation.

Pavlo was a man with many things against him. The deck was stacked, yet he continued on. Al felt there was a little bit of Pavlo in all of us.

Marthe flew to Europe to film *Fedora* for Billy Wilder. During the production, she started to experience blackouts and was rushed to the hospital. Al closed the play for 2 weeks and flew overseas to be with her.

ME

I CAME UP out of the subway on Broadway at 57th Street. It was an overcast day and I turned up the collar of my World War II Army overcoat as I crossed the street.

I walked around the corner to the Barbizon Plaza Hotel. Many people in show business stayed there, so I was worried about being recognized. I kept my sunglasses on as I crossed the lobby.

The dimly-lit, tapestried dance hall was decorated with U.S.O. banners and World War II posters. A four-piece band was playing a "The White Cliffs of Dover." Elderly couples were dancing the fox trot. The geriatric musicians were dressed in greenish, outdated tuxes from the 40s. As they played, they took turns swigging from a brown, paper-wrapped bottle.

I felt dapper in the French Army uniform I had rented from Eaves Costumes. I danced with a tiny, blue-haired lady, Dorothy Maupin. With a rose in her mouth, she danced as if she weighed mere ounces. I led her through the steps, dancing smartly and expertly, twirling, spinning.

At a table near the dance floor, three other elderly World War II widows sat giggling and whispering to each other as they watched us dance. Their table was set with tea service, sandwiches, scones, petits-fours, and an assortment of chocolates.

Dorothy was having such a blast. She looked up at me gaily. "Oh, you are magnificent, Antoine. Never in my wildest dreams."

With a French accent, I said, "Merci bien, Madame Maupin. I try to make you happy."

She touched a long-gone dimple and said coyly, "Oh, call me Dottie, please."

"D'accord, ma cher Dot-tee."

The band wound up the number. After a pause for a round of bottle-passing, they launched into a waltz.

One of the little ladies, Ethel Ayerling, tapped Dottie on the shoulder. "My turn now, Dottie."

Ruth was not about to give me up. "Oh, please, just one more dance."

Ethel was impatient. "Your time is up. Give way!"

She eyed Dottie hard. Dottie gave way. Ethel slipped into my arms and I waltzed her away.

She almost swooned. "Oh, Antoine, this is divine. I wish there were more of you to go around."

"One of me is all I can feed, Mrs. Ayerling."

"Don't be so formal. I like spontaneity, intimacy. Especially from a Frenchman. Call me Ethel."

"D'accord, ma cher Ettelle."

"I love the sexy way you drop your 'h.'" She imitated my accent. 'Ettelle.' You have such soulful eyes. I could drown in them."

"You are a delight, Ettelle."

"I can see right through you, you darling, through to your very soul."

"You can?"

"Oh, yes, I'm quite psychic, you see."

"What do you see?"

"You are a very sad young man."

She caught me off guard. "Well, really, I..."

"Don't bother to deny it. I know some lady has hurt you very badly."

"You can tell?"

"But don't despair. There is a great change taking place in your life. For the good. Oh, yes. This lady in your life realizes that she truly loves you."

"You sure about that?"

"Oh, yes. All she's waiting for is a sign from you. She's too reticent to say so. But if you make the first move, your life will come together in a most remarkable way."

"Do you know her name?"

She closed her eyes and felt the air with one of her hands. "I sense it begins with... a 'G.' Ginger, perhaps? It's a pet name, no doubt."

"Ginny?"

"Yes! That's it! Ginny!"

The smallest, frailest, of the little old ladies, Anna, tapped Ethel on the shoulder. "Time's up, sweetie."

Ethel didn't argue. "Ah, well, all good things must

come to an end." She clutched my arm, "Now, Cheri, don't hesitate. Take action. A man who takes action can't lose."

She yielded graciously to Anna. I took Anna and danced her across the floor. I looked back and saw Ethel reflecting, as if to say, "Ginny? Could that be the name?" She wasn't sure.

ME AND AL

I WAS WALKING down Madison Avenue with a friend, Glenn Peterson, and bumped into Al. He asked me if I was doing any acting. Suddenly the voice in my head told me to pick up a mike. A mike?

I pantomimed holding a hand mike and, like Sinatra, I said, "No, but I'm taking singing lessons."

Al looked puzzled. He asked me why I did that piece of business with the imaginary mike.

"I don't know, I was just kidding around."

He asked me how things were and I told him I had a few irons in the fire.

"Keep on plugging," he told me.

It was ironic that while Al was a major star, he went from production to production, never knowing what the next project would be. I, meanwhile, had a steady teaching job and no shortage of clients to cavort with, yet there was no order to my life, nothing to look forward to.

In an interview, Al said he chose acting as a profession because it gave him a routine, a way of organizing life. Acting was work and made him feel as though he was "functioning." He compared it to being a craftsman, as if he were making chairs or rugs — or playing baseball. It also involved giving and sharing, something he was still learning about.

"Acting is more than just an anodyne," he said. "It's closest to what I want to do."

He was beginning to understand what technique was — being able to let go of some of the things you're secure with. He had grown secure with his earlier outbursts of emotion. He found that the freer he became, the lighter he was.

"You want to get to the point in acting where you don't have to act. You hope it stays with you like lint."

Al was a great admirer of other actors like Brando, Olivier, Gielgud, George C. Scott and Walter Matthau. He found them all so different, with more variety than in any other profession.

Always the joker, he said, "I can always spot an actor. He's usually looking for work — and he's always dieting."

My mother was back home, but she was constantly sick and it was wearing her down. To cheer her up, I would portray all of her sisters who had died — Lucie, Dolly, Lizzie, Annie.

I'd say, "Tillie, this is Dolly. Don't feel bad. I'm up in heaven with Lizzie and all of our sisters." Then I would interrupt myself in a different voice and say, "I'm Lucie and I'm talking now. You wait your turn!"

I was able to get my mother to laugh hysterically.

She sometimes called for my father who, of course, had died 16 years earlier. I pretended I was him. I would take on my father's voice and use all my acting talent to convince her.

"Tillie, it's Louie. I'm here. Don't worry."

And she would feel better. She would believe it.

"Oh, Louie. Louie, where are you?"

I'd say, "I'm right here, Tillie. Don't worry."

AL

BOBBY DEERFIELD opened in the fall of 1977 and was a disaster. Al's performance was ravaged by the critics.

Hal Hinson said, "Deerfield's character is moody and self-concerned in a way that suffocates the audience's interest. Pacino is so enraptured with his own glamorous brooding that our involvement is superfluous, an invasion of privacy."

John Alfred Avant said, "People will go to see *Bobby Deerfield* because Al Pacino is the star, and many of them won't believe how bad he is in this movie... Among all this year's movie horrors... *Bobby Deerfield* seems the worst, because the embarrassment one feels for Al Pacino is more memorable than anything in the other movies."

Being ostracized by the critics or the public was, in some ways, like being criticized personally by a woman. When Al was in love, he was a one-woman man. His inability to keep relationships on a high emotional level was due to his childhood, when his mother sent him to live with his grandparents. He admitted he feared being abandoned.

"You can depend on women for certain things, but you can't invest anybody with that much power."

He felt it wasn't fair to either party. It was hard for many men to recognize that because they did invest in their mothers. "Mamma doesn't leave you."

One way to deal with it, he surmised, was to leave first. At times, he juggled several women at the same time. If he went out with three or four different women, he figured, he might not necessarily be juggling them. They might be juggling him, going with three or four different men.

Having casual sex with women who worshipped him was not his style. He wanted to be desired for him, not because of his star image.

It was an especially rough time for Al. He was devastated by the death of John Cazale. Cazale had just played a supporting role in *The Deer Hunter* for Michael Cimino and got Meryl Streep, his girlfriend, to be in the movie with him so they could be together. Neither Cazale nor Streep told any of the others the seriousness of John's illness.

ME

IN 1978, I, too, was going through hell. My mother took another turn and needed to have her other leg amputated. I was broke. Her insurance paid for some of the hospital bills, but again I needed money for the 24-hour private nursing and the artificial limbs.

There was no way I was ever going to pay back the money I owed and access all the new money we needed. In order to pay off the loan shark and still have money for the new operation, I had to borrow from another loan shark to pay the first. I had to borrow from Peter to pay to Paul.

I searched my address book for a telephone number. Gino Coccetti. I hesitated. Did I really want to call him. I had no choice.

The Brooklyn Bridge twinkled with lights and traffic as I walked along Manhattan's Lower East Side. I passed Felice's Trattoria, then hesitated. I was nervous. Steeling myself, I retraced my footsteps and went inside.

The maitre d' saw me looking around the gloomy room and came over to me. "Lookin' for somebody, pal?"

I tried to look inconspicuous. "Yes, sir, I am."

I craned my head past his massive body. Then I spotted Gino. "He's sitting over there."

I eased past the maitre d' and walked over to Gino's booth. I slid across the fake red leather and sat opposite Gino. Gino was a dark-haired, ferret-faced man around my age. We had been classmates at Creston High School in the Bronx.

Gino was looking successful, even debonair. "Ed. Sit down, sit down." He lunged across the table and shook one of my hands in both of his. "How long's it been, huh?"

"Gee, since high school."

"So tell me, you still in show biz? I keep lookin' for your name on the billboards..."

"I'm just hanging on, Gino." Lying, I said, "But it looks like the cards are turning up for me now. I'm playing the second lead in Al Pacino's new movie."

"No shit! Man, what a break! Because of you, I feel like he's family."

"He's a great guy, let me tell you."

Gino studied me. "So, how come you call me after all these years? I started thinkin' you forgot old Gino here. It's the 70s awready, fahgodsake."

"Just busy, you know. The wife, the kid, the career..."

"Yeah, yeah, our paths kinda veered off in separate directions. All roads lead outta Rome."

"Gino, I'm not gonna beat around the bush—"

Gino slid the menu over to me. "Try the scungilli, Ed. They really know how to fix it here. The best!"

I couldn't afford to order. "Well..."

Gino yelled to maitre d', "Hey, Patsy, make that two orders of scungilli and bring me another bottle of that Valpolicelli 69." He winked at me. "That was a very good year. They—"

"Gino, listen."

"You were always spoutin' off scenes from movies. Eddie the Mouth, I used to call you." He laughed. "The girls used to love you."

"They did?" I looked him in the eye. "Gino, I got a bit of a problem."

"You got a problem." He addressed an imaginary person sitting next to him, "He only calls me when he's got a problem!"

"I need money fast. To tide me over until the movie starts shooting."

"How much?"

"Three thousand by tomorrow morning."

Gino threw his head back and laughed like it was the funniest thing he ever heard. I was puzzled. Then he said, "Peanuts! Can't help you, Eddie the Mouth."

"I guess I misunderstood. I thought you had connections.

"You didn't misunderstand nothin'. I got the connections. But they don't fool around with no pissy little sums like $3,000. It ain't worth their time. Mine neither.

"Oh, OK. Make it 25 Gs."

"Now you're talkin' sense. That I can do. I'll need your note."

"Whatever you need."

Gino grabbed a napkin, wrote some figures on it. While I scanned it, Gino shouted, "Hey, Patsy, where's that wine? We're ready to celebrate here!"

My mouth dropped open. "This is pretty steep interest, Gino."

"Hey, the Federal Reserve don't set our terms, Ed. You want bank interest, you go to the bank. Do we have a deal or what?

I bit my lip. "I do have immediate prospects."

"So what's to worry?"

I eyed him, hoping he couldn't tell I was trembling inside. I took the pen and signed the napkin note.

After the operation, I took Dale to the hospital to see

my mother. When we looked into the glass cubicle, she was gone. I panicked and ran over to the nurse. "My mother, Mrs. De Leo? Where is she? Is she—"

"Good news," the nurse announced. "We've moved her into a regular room. 806.

I sagged with relief.

We took the elevator up the eighth floor and went to 806. My mother was lying in bed, pale and wan. She was conscious and aware of us. Dale and I sat close to her on the bed.

She touched Dale's face. "I'm so thrilled, Dale sweetie, that you're here. Ed, where're my Gummy Bears?"

"I forgot to bring 'em, Ma. I'll give them to Dale when we get home."

Dale rolled his eyes and looked at me. "I hate Gummy Bears! How many times do I have to tell her that?"

Typical nine-year-old.

"Shh, Dale. Not now."

My mother strained to hear. "Whataya say?"

Dale said, "I don't wanna be here. I hate it here."

I put my finger to my lips. "Think of your grandma. It makes her happy that you're here."

He whispered, "I hate that smell."

My mother tried to sit up. "What? Am I dead? I thought I was getting better."

"You are getting better," I told her. "Dale's acting like a little jerk is all."

She tried to slap my hand. "Don't call your son a jerk. He's a good kid."

"Good kids treat their elders with more respect."

Dale rolled his eyes. "Can we go now?"

"See? They only think about themselves."

He glared at me. "Well, so do out-of-work actors."

I couldn't believe my son.

"Come on," I said. "I'm taking you home."

Dale grinned happily. He got his wish.

"Fine. But Mom said not to come back to the house until 6:00."

"Since you can't behave yourself, I'm taking you home right now."

I leaned over and kissed my mother. I gestured for Dale to kiss her, but he went to the door and turned his back instead.

I smiled at my mother and said, "I'll be back tomorrow, Ma. Keep on truckin'."

I raced Dale up the subway steps back in our neighborhood. As we crossed the street, I asked, "So, Dale, did your Ma tell you about the role I was offered in Al Pacino's movie?"

He was evasive. "Well..."

"Did she, or didn't she?"

"She said she knew all along it was a lot of bullshit."

"He really did try to go to bat for me."

"You're such a dreamer."

"I may be, but that's me, Dale. Like it or lump it."

"Why are you so mean all of a sudden?"

"I'm not mean. I'm just waking up to a few things. Like you. You can be a real brat sometimes. Part of it's my fault.

"It's all your fault. You're just a dreamer, an out-of-work actor. That's all you'll ever be. I hate actors. They're so phony. Always lookin' at themselves."

I stared at him.

"I thought your hero was Clint Eastwood. Isn't he an actor?"

"He's a movie star, not an actor."

"You got me there, Dale."

We walked into the building and waited for the elevator. When it reached our floor, I handed the shopping bag to Dale. "Take this upstairs to Victor. I want to check my messages before your mother gets here." Dale took it and stayed on the elevator.

As I walked into the living room, Ginny and Larry, her boss, sat up on the couch. Ginny's blouse was unbuttoned. Her hair was messed up and her lipstick was smudged. She hadn't expected us back so soon.

"What are you doing here?"

I should have expected something like this. Seeing it first hand caught me off guard.

"Am I too early for the final act?"

Ginny almost blushed. "Ed, you know, Larry... er, Mr. Greenawalt."

"You obviously know him a lot better."

Larry looked like a car salesman who had been accused of selling someone a clunker. "How are you, Ed?"

"You don't really want to hear."

Ginny smiled feebly. She said brightly, "How's your mom?"

"She's conscious."

"Well, that's progress."

Larry put on his jacket. "Glad you showed me those reports, Ginny. See you Monday."

"Yes. Thanks for dropping me off."

I pointed to Ginny's blouse. "Better button up, or they'll fall out."

Larry looked abashed as Ginny hurriedly buttoned her blouse. "I'll just be on my way. No problem."

He reached out to shake my hand. I looked at it and said to myself, "Give me a break."

Ginny escorted him to the front door. She came back and stood looking at me defiantly. "We are separated, you know."

"I know, but this is my place, not yours. So, how long's

this being going on?"

"None of your business. Where's Dale?"

"Dropping something off at Victor's. He'll be right here."

"Good. We can catch an early train back to Connecticut."

"You're not going to see my mother?"

"I saw her yesterday." Hearing the elevator open, she ran to the door, opened it and shouted for Dale to hold the door.

I watched her putting on her coat. "So, I'm out altogether, right? Out for good?"

"I'm sorry, Ed. I've started proceedings. You'll get the papers in a few days."

"I can hardly wait."

And she was out the door. Instead of feeling angry, I felt a flush of relief. I was free.

When Dale was 10, his teachers wanted him to play Scrooge in the school play. They told him he would be a good character actor. He read for it and they cast him. But he never wanted to act. It was no doubt a reaction to my life as an actor.

Dale preferred music and he enjoyed drawing and painting.

AL

IN 1979, Norman Jewison asked Al to star in *...And Justice For All.* Al asked Jewison if he could get some actors together and read it for him. Then he would see how he felt after he heard it. They read it and Al agreed to do it. He thought the screenplay had a nice structure. It was an unusual film because it was very verbal. The audience would really have to pay attention to it.

Al thoroughly immersed himself in the role. What

he liked most about Jewison was his total involvement in the project. Jewison was constantly wrapped up with the movie. He brooded about it. Even after it was over, he mothered the picture. He cared about it. Also in the cast were Jack Warden, John Forsythe, Lee Strasberg and Christine Lahti.

In *...And Justice For All*, Al played a lawyer fighting for truth and justice. It was also a role with flashes of robust humor, in contrast to such past Pacino characters as the icy-eyed Corleone don in *The Godfather*, the bisexual killer in *Dog Day Afternoon*, or the ego-crazed cop in *Serpico*.

Jewison said publicly that other actors adored working wih Al. After he signed for the movie, when they were auditioning the smaller roles, Al insisted on taking part. He would spend hours on the floor, reading opposite even the most minor characters, to help them get the 'feel' of the script. He said it was his responsibility and he seemed to take tremendous satisfaction in it.

Al's compulsive need for precision frustrated even Lee Strasberg, especially his theory about learning dialogue. During the shooting, Strasberg's advice to Al was, "Learn your lines, dollink."

Al was not a quick learner; not because he had a bad memory. He just didn't believe in memorizing lines by rote. He believed in becoming the character first. The closer you get to the character, the better you'll utter the character's lines because that's what the character naturally would say.

But the film opened to bad notices. In the *Village Voice*: "Pacino's performance eventually disintegrates into self-righteous hysteria in a courtroom scene of total renunciation that has to be seen and heard to be believed."

In spite of all the bad reviews, Al was nominated for the 5th time for an Academy Award. Dustin Hoffman won for *Kramer vs Kramer.*

Regarding the characters that Al played, Strasberg said, "Al Pacino becomes them. In fact, he assumes their identity so completely that he continues to live a role long after a play or movie is over."

ME

I WENT BACK to my apartment in the Bronx. All I could do was sit on the bed, feeling the stubble on my face and ruffling my hair. When the phone rang, I let the answering machine pick it up.

I heard the voice of Ethel from the U.S.O. dance. "Antoine, my dear... We girls wanted to thank you for the marvelous afternoon. When can we do it again? Please call us at 555-8787? We love you!"

I smiled ruefully.

Ethel had more to say. "Oh, by the way, Cheri, Ginny wasn't the name after all. It's Ronnie, or something more like that. I'm sorry if I confused you. I'm rarely wrong about these things. Do call us now."

Was my voice speaking to me again? Was it speaking through Ethel? I lay back on the bed. The phone downstairs rang. I jumped up and ran downstairs to answer it.

I was careful. "Hello?"

It was Randa. "Hi."

I was transformed. "Oh, hi."

"How's it going?"

"Professionally or personally?"

"Either."

"Neither."

"I'm sorry. Well, that ad will be running a couple more weeks. Can you tolerate the calls?"

"I'll put up with 'em. I got a callback from the last one."

"Oh. You're going to... to do it again? With the same client?"

If she only knew. "Sometimes it pays."

"Good. Well..."

"I want to see you again."

"Oh?"

"I'm free. Really free now."

"It's all over... with your wife?"

"Finished. End of story."

"Oh, good! I mean, I'm sorry... But I'm happy for me.

"So, when?"

"How about now? I made a great eggplant casserole. It's bubbling away even as I speak."

"I could tolerate it. Can it keep for an hour?"

"As long as it takes you to get here."

New York City was one giant clock and I was the minute hand sweeping from the Bronx to Greenwich Village. Nothing could keep me away from Randa, not doors, not elevators, not subway steps. We continued talking through dinner and we talked as we settled on the couch with our dessert.

"This is really good. What do you call it?"

"Blackberry Jumble."

"And I really liked the eggplant. I swear, honest to John."

"There's a lot more."

"No! I couldn't. I mean, the old waistline. I've got to watch it."

"Let me watch it." She tickled me on the belly.

I pulled her close. She pulled away, then said, "I'm sorry."

I was getting mixed signals. "I don't understand. You say you like me. You seem gung-ho then you back off."

"It's an old war wound."

"What?"

"A scar, really."

"I don't mind scars. I've got a few myself. There's one on my left calf, a really big one. I had this knife—"

"I'm not talking about that kind of scar."

"I'm not picking up the right cues, am I? What's the problem, Randa? Tell me."

"I can't. Not yet."

"Hey, I just got out of a relationship with a woman who spoke in heliographs. I can't hack that anymore. I like you a lot. If we're going anywhere..."

"I've never met a man like you. Men never want to hear woman talk about anything. Especially actors. They just want to talk about themselves, or you to talk about them."

"How do you know so much about actors?"

"I've been around them all my life. My dad is a big-shot producer."

"He is?"

"Don't look so hopeful. He's on the skids. But he was big once."

"Do I know him?"

"Bernard Abbott (a pseudonym)."

"No kidding? He did all those comedies and musicals."

"He can't raise a dime now. It's killing him." She laughed. "He's so bitter."

"Why are you happy about that?"

"What goes around comes around."

"Wow! What did he do to you?"

"You don't want to know."

"I do, if you want to tell."

Randa suddenly jumped to her feet and started to throw the cushions off the couch. "Help me!"

I leaped to assist her. She yanked out the bed hidden beneath. It was already made up, but Randa added more cushions and fluffed it up. She leaped in and hid under the covers, beginning to undress.

She turned to me. "Hurry up, or I'll lose my nerve."

I hesitated, then quickly undressed.

In less than 20 minutes we were snuggling together beneath the covers. It seemed like hours since I got into bed with her. I could hear the ticking of her antique clock on the mantle.

Randa's voice was weak. "I'm sorry."

"It's OK."

"You really mean that?"

I kissed her nose. "When you're ready, you're ready."

"You're a good person. The first minute I saw you, I said to myself, that's a good person."

"I hope I never disappoint you."

"How could you? I don't expect anything from you."

"You don't?"

She replied teasingly, "Well... you are an actor, for God's sake!"

"That just about says it all."

"I didn't mean it as an insult. It's just that I understand. Really I do. Actors are so... helpless."

"I'm trying to learn not to be." I sat up, thoughtful.

Randa sat up, keeping the covers over her breasts. "What's your biggest, darkest secret?"

I turned to eye her, then grinned wickedly. "I never told anybody this."

"Not even Ginny?"

"No. There was this actress in Olson and Johnson's Helzapoppin. She was playing a stripper. She seduced me backstage. I was 13 years old."

She turned away, disturbed.

"What is it?" I asked her.

Without looking at me, she said, "I was raped. When I was 16."

"Oh God, I'm sorry." I pulled her close. "I guess that explains a lot of things. You don't have to talk about it now. But I'm glad you mentioned it. I won't rush you into anything."

"It was my father's co-producer. My mother and I wanted to turn him in, but daddy wouldn't let us."

"Why not?"

"They were doing out of town try-outs and Daddy said it would hurt the show, hurt his image. He put me in therapy instead."

"What a bastard! I wouldn't work for him if he promised to make me a star."

Randa threw her arms around me, pulled me down under the covers. "Ed, I love you! I love you to pieces!" She kissed me and climbed on top of me. Making love to her was like entering an orchard full of ripe, exotic fruit. We couldn't get enough of each other.

I went looking for work as an actor with a passion. I was a new person. I was happening. After the movie, I would return to the stage, like Al.

On my way to an audition, I found myself walking down Broadway, whistling and stepping jauntily. I was feeling good for once. I cut over toward Eighth Avenue and looked for the building that housed Showcase Studios. The building with the actors standing outside, smoking, reading *Showbusiness* and *Backstage*, and studying scripts, was obviously the place.

Up in the rehearsal studio, I entered and looked around. The place was bustling with actors of all ages and types. I went to the desk and handed the lady an 8"x10" photograph, a head shot. She asked me to sign and she gave me a "side" to study.

As I turned around there was Harvey Garr, again, my look-alike. Running into him at auditions was inevitable. The only thing we had in common was neither of us was getting the parts.

He flashed me his fake showbiz smile. “Hey, Ed, how’re you doing? I thought you’d be doing that dinner theater by now.”

“It... fell through.”

We ambled over and sat in folding chairs against the wall.

He didn’t have to ask, but he did, “Don’t have to ask which part you’re reading for.”

“Wall street banker, early 40s.”

“You got it. They get younger every year, don’t they?”

“Who?”

He gestured at the young actors. “Them.”

I glanced at the hard, toned young bodies. They were all preening, exhibiting themselves and flirting.

“Oh, them. Yeah, babies. Thank God, I’m not competing with them anymore.” I laughed merrily.

Harvey eyed me. “I haven’t seen you so “up” in a long time, Ed. What’s happening?”

“Well, I blew off that dinner theater job, my wife kicked me out, I lost a major role in a movie, and my mother had her legs cut off...”

“Have you seen a psychiatrist? Your mental state isn’t natural.”

“My mother has had some heavy operations. Oh, and I think I’m in love.

“In that case...”

An assistant entered from the inner room and called out, “Harvey Garr?”

Harvey jumped to his feet and immediately became a wholly different, jovial, “good fellow” sort of guy. The fatalist evaporated. “That’s me. And how are you today, Eileen. Hey, I love that new hair style.”

Eileen grinned at him cynically. “You’re up. Follow me.”

She held the inner door open for Harvey. He turned,

saluted me, and followed her into the inner sanctum.

I sat in the hot room for a half hour waiting for my name to be called. The ceiling fan didn't give much relief. Finally, Eileen came out and called my name.

The rehearsal studio was air-conditioned and brightly lit. I was asked to read by a face at the far end of the room. He was flanked by several other faces sitting at a table piled with pictures and resumes.

I sat down at a card table in the middle of the room with Eileen who was reading with me. I took a few moments to prepare myself and get into character. The faces cleared their throats impatiently.

I had the lines already memorized, so I embellished them a bit, sure it would grab them.

> *"Let me tell you something, Barry. You can't sit there day after day, manipulating those little old ladies, advising them to buy this and sell that, every few days. Then when they're broke, try going home and sleeping at night, knowing what you did to them."*

Eileen read, without feeling, in a monotone,

> *"Don't tell me you've suddenly developed a conscience, Charles."*

I continued,

> *"I lie there nights thinking about how I'd like to end it all. Just to be free for once. To have a clean conscience—"*
>
> *"You're not saying..."*
>
> *"I won't do it. But I can't say how much longer I can go on like this, doing what I'm doing."*

I paused thoughtfully, close to tears. The producer-face and the writer-face applauded.

The producer said, "Touching. Very moving. Thank you, Mr. De Leo."

The playwright added, "There's more there than I wrote."

"Thank you. Thank you." I bowed low to him.

The producer asked, “Are you available the second week of September?”

“I could be. It depends.” I was fishing to find out what my salary would be... Whether or not I could afford to give up my other income. If I didn’t pay Gino back, I’d be in big trouble.

“We’ve got to have a commitment today. We’ve got to be cast by this afternoon.”

I asked meekly, “Are you Equity?”

I figured if they were signatories to the union, I would at least receive scale.

The producer turned purple with rage. He threw down his script. “Who the hell do you think you are? Are we Equity? Well, fuck you! As a matter of fact, Harvey Garr out there can do the part just as well as you, don’t you think, Elmer?”

The playwright agreed. “By all means.”

“Wait,” I said, “I’m sure we can work something out.”

The producer stood up and waved me away. “Thank you.”

As I walked out I could feel the indignant glares of the faces burning my back.

In the outer room I spotted Harvey lingering by the door, talking to a cute young thing who wore a revealing halter top.

“Hey, buddy,” I said, “you’d better hang around. I think you got the part.”

“No kidding?”

I slapped him on the back and left the building.

When I arrived home in the Bronx, I found Gino standing in the doorway blocking my entrance. I flashed him a smile. “Hey, Gino!”

He looked at me apprehensively. “How’s prospects?”

“Terrific. Coming along.”

“We’re into week two. Interest steps up five points.”

"So does your commission, right?"

"You're not worried?"

"Another week at the most."

"OK, Mr. Mouth. I hope for your sake it all works out. I wouldn't want anything to happen to my old high school chum."

I stared at him. "Gino, that sounds like a... a bit ominous."

"I just wanna make you aware who you're dealing with, Ed. We don't kid around with kidders. OK?"

"OK. Can I buy you a cup of coffee?

"Nah, I gotta see a man about some cement." It worked. I blanched. He added, "See you next week. Same time, same station."

As he trotted away I could here him whistling the theme from *Mission Impossible*. I swallowed hard.

My mummified actor friend, Rich, lumbered toward me. Before I could even lift a hand to wave to him, he darted off. I watched him. His random appearances were beginning to feel like bad omens.

Victor invited me to his studio for dinner. While he stir-fried some vegetables, I sat at the piano, noodling on the keys.

Victor set two plates of rice and vegetables on the table. "Soup's on."

I got up and stared out the window.

"Come on, Ed. It'll get cold."

I sat down and stared at my plate. Victor began to eat, watching me through the corner of his eye. "Find something offensive?"

"No, no! I'm just... I'm a bit edgy."

"How was the audition?"

"They wanted me."

"Great."

"I turned them down."

Victor stopped chewing. "You did what?"

"It's a conflict. How could I take a no-payer when I have so many obligations?"

Vic shook his head. "A bird in the hand is worth two in the bush."

"Exactly. I chose staying alive over a doing a play out in Flatbush."

"And the choice made you edgy."

"Can I use your phone? It's a local."

Victor gestured and continued chewing, slowly, deliberately. I dialed and waited.

His secretary answered. Al wasn't in. I told her I wanted to know if Al was planning to recommend me for another movie. I told her about the role I almost had in *Bobby Deerfield*, but she didn't remember anything about it. She said she'd give Al the message. I hung up and sat back down at the table.

Victor asked, "Tillie's doing a lot better, isn't she? I saw her this morning."

"She's gonna pull through again." I started drumming my fingers. "Can I use the phone again?"

Victor gestured. I went to the phone and dialed again. Randa picked up.

I really needed to talk to her. "Hi."

She had the greatest telephone voice. Bright and cheerful. "Oh, hi. I miss you."

"Can I come over and play?"

"Don't be mad, Ed, but I'm working. Finally."

"Hey, you mean you're doing it? Writing?"

"You inspired me."

"Well, you sure didn't waste any time. How about tomorrow night?"

"OK."

"Hey, would you like to meet my mom? I'll take you to

see her."

"I would. When?"

We set a time and a place to meet. We held hands as we crossed through the main lobby of the hospital and took the elevator to the eighth floor.

My mother looked up when I ushered Randa into the room. "Hi, doll."

I kissed her and dragged Randa closer. "How're you feeling?"

"As light as a feather. Did you know they siphoned 20 pounds of water outta me? My skin looks like it's been pleated by Fortuny."

Randa laughed loudly. I turned to stare at her.

My mother asked, "Who're you?"

"Ma, this is Randa, Miranda Abbott. She's a new friend of mine."

Randa smiled at her and gave a cute little wave with her hand. "Hi, Mrs. De Leo. Ed tells me you're doing great."

"Have we met?"

I said, "I just introduced you. You know who her dad is? Bernard Abbott."

"The Bernard Abbott? How about that! My sisters wanted me to audition for him back in 1938. Before you were born, by the looks of you."

"A little bit. I was born in '40."

"And you tell it, just like that? You're too young to know about Fortuny!"

She and Randa looked at each other and both started laughing.

I asked, "What's Fortuny?"

"It's a who, not a what," Randa explained. "It's girl stuff. Any woman worth two nickels knows who Fortuny is."

My mother added, "And Mary McFadden. She's worth

three nickels."

Randa nodded. "Right you are."

I said, "You're talking about an Old Girls Club, right?"

"You bet. And your mom and I are charter members."

My mother looked me in the eye. "So how're your actors doing, Ed?"

"Uh, fine, fine."

"You used to tell me every detail about every scene you did. Why so close-mouthed all of a sudden?"

"I don't want to tire you. We'd better go and let you get some rest."

Randa took my mother's hand. "It's awfully nice to have met you, Mrs. De Leo."

My mother gave me a hug. "She's got real manners, Eddie. Now if I could only get you to bring me my Gummy Bears."

Randa burst out laughing. I couldn't refrain. And my mother joined in.

Randa and I strolled about Greenwich Village, arm in arm, looking into shop windows. Randa pointed out a long granny dress, similar to the one she wore. At a shop next door, I pointed out a brighter, tighter red dress. Randa didn't care for it. She shook her head and looked away.

That night in her apartment, I read the titles on the stack of books next to Randa's typewriter while she was in the bathroom, changing. She popped her head out.

"Close your eyes now."

I obeyed. I heard her come into the room.

"OK, you can look now."

She was wearing the slim red dress we had seen in the store window. I gaped. She looked drop-dead gorgeous. "Wow! Now, who did you say you were?"

She laughed and slapped me playfully. I pulled her close. "I wish I could take you out somewhere nice and show you off."

She lit up. "I'm free tomorrow night."

"I can't tomorrow. I've got a date. Sort of."

"Is it business or pleasure?"

"Both. It's another one of my capers. It provides my essentials. Like food."

"I'd love to meet one of your "clients." I'll bet they're a gas."

"That's an understatement. One day I'll take you along."

"I don't know if I'm ready for that."

"I hope you never are. Anyhow, it's temporary. It's all gonna change, real soon. Then we'll paint the town red to match the dress."

"I know it."

I held her tight. "Just don't stop believing in me, OK?"

She kissed me and I unzipped her dress. It was never like this with Ginny. With Ginny, it always felt as though the only times we were intimate were when it was with intent to procreate.

AL

TO KEEP UP with his stage work, Al did a workshop performance of *Hamlet* at Joe Papp's New York Shakespeare Festival Theater. Also in the cast were Meryl Streep, Christopher Walken and Raul Julia.

He then did staged readings of Bertolt Brecht's play, *The Jungle of the Cities*, at the Circle in the Square in New York. This was followed by rehearsals of Shakespeare's

Othello at Lincoln Center in N.Y. in the Vivian Beaumont Theater.

Finally, in June, he appeared in another production of *Richard III* — this time at the Cort Theater on Broadway. Penny was in the cast. The production had 25 previews and ran for 33 performances before it closed. Most of the reviews were savage.

People Magazine said Al was now the "toast of Broadway... burnt toast." Walter Kerr in the *New York Times* said Al didn't belong in Shakespeare.

Critically, it was a disaster for him, but he didn't regret doing it. It was a learning experience and very valuable to him. The artist in him said that something challenging, in which you get hit hard and which is not smooth, often illuminates what other people think and alters your own perspective. He found that kind of metamorphosis to be a positive, cathartic experience.

After 70 performances of *Richard*, something started to happen for him. A scene he had thought he would never get or understand, he began to understand. He knew there was still a lot he had to learn. He couldn't wait to get back on the stage.

Repetition was a big thing with Al. Repeating was a chance to practice technique. He remembered someone else saying, "Repetition keeps me green."

Al used to worry about what people said about him, but he was learning not to worry as much. Sometimes he felt critics were wrong all the time, but he didn't take objection to it. It was part of the business. Critics could be wrong, or they could be right. They could be cruel, and they could be kind.

Al considered actors to be outsiders. They were on the outside looking in, interpreting. Their roots were always outside. Actors were wayward vagabonds, minstrels, outcasts. He explained it as the reason why so many actors want to be accepted in the mainstream of life. "And when we are — here's the contradiction — we sometimes lose our outsider's edge."

Diane Keaton talked to Al about doing a movie. They would get together on it, read the script and try to develop it. It needed work, so nothing came of it. Al and Diane were good friends. He thought that he'd like to do a comedy with her.

The kind of comedy he really wanted to do was an all-out Buster-Keaton-type comedy, something slapstick. That's what he had done in the early days. He was a clown at heart. He had always thought of himself as a comedian. He admired comedians, their minds. He found the way they saw the world to be striking, the way they juxtaposed reality, the way the could see humor in people. He found it liberating.

Al continued to be more comfortable with plays than with movies. He found in film a certain sense of control, of holding back. The stage offered more opportunity to act, more experiences to go through. With stage, the play is the source, it is orchestrated with words.

There is less of that in a movie. You are dealing with machines and wires. When you're acting for a camera, it keeps taking and never giving back; but when you perform before a live audience, the audience responds. It's a give and take.

"It's an extraordinary thing. It's wild turf up there."

Al was asked what he looked for in a woman. He said love was very important, but having her as a friend came first. The ideal for him was when the woman he loved was also his best friend. And then there was trust, which took time. He saw love as going through different stages before it could endure.

"Romantic love can be a lot of crap, though, let me tell you. And it can hurt you."

The thought of having children was starting to become more appealing to Al. Fifteen years earlier he almost did, but fortunately nothing happened. Until now he wasn't ready for it. But he still wanted to wait.

"I figure I'll get the dog first. Then the kid."

Marriage was a possibility when the right woman came along. He felt it might be good for him to have that kind of focus. Having the structure of a family was beginning to make more sense to him. It would be a commitment.

One of the things Al missed was being able to walk the streets like everybody else, being anonymous. Having worked as a city messenger when he was a kid for 11 hours a day and then walking the streets for years as a struggling actor looking for work, he knew Manhattan. He knew every bit of it, from Battery Park clear up to Harlem.

I was with him. I know. He knew the traffic lights. He could time himself so he never had to stop for a light. He used to walk from 92nd Street and Broadway right down to the Village and back again, thinking of scenes and characters. He worked out a lot of his role in *The Godfather* that way. Now he was too visible. He couldn't do it any more and he missed it.

He was only 39 and was still afraid of being drafted. He felt that somehow he might get called. He would pass the physical and he'd be taken into the Army.

ME

IT WAS A DARK NIGHT. Dressed in a rented tux, I waited on the corner of 58th Street and Fifth Avenue, around the corner from the Plaza Hotel. I couldn't have them pick me up in the Bronx.

Soon, a long, black limousine eased to the curb and I studied it. Could this be the one? The back window cracked open and a wrinkled hand waved at me. The driver opened the door for me and I got in.

Inside the limo, an ancient, little man, Frank Llewellyn, sat upright, shivering and quaking.

I could only see him in profile. Alfred Hitchcock came to mind. He kept his right hand in his pocket.

"Good evening, sir."

Llewellyn greeted me formally, "Good evening, Hans. I'm so happy you were free this evening."

I sat straight forward like him. "I'm delighted to see you, Mr. Llewellyn."

"There's champagne in the fridge. Do the honors."

I awkwardly opened the mini-fridge, pulled out a bottle of vintage Moet and popped the cork. Champagne spewed all over both of us. Llewellyn didn't react. I hastily wiped Mr. L and myself off. Under the old man's watchful eyes, I poured two flutes. I handed one to Mr. L.

He shook his head. "I've imbibed sufficiently."

I sipped. "Ah... Now, what's the agenda?"

Like a teenager, he giggled. "You decide."

"Any place? Any place at all?"

"Wherever you choose."

"How about Sardi's?"

Llewellyn shuddered. "Oh, no, no, can't go there."

I liked Chinese. "How about Shun Lee Palace?"

"You can do better than that."

"Hmm. OK, how about Le Cirque?"

He shuddered again. "No, no, never again!"

"La Grenouille?"

"Heavens, no. Utter disaster."

"The Four Seasons!"

He smiled. "Very fine. But, no, better not."

I was running out of suggestions. "How about that new place, La Fordice?"

I scored. He said, "Ah, perfect!" He leaned in to the Chauffeur. "La Fordice, Jenkins." He turned back to me. "What's the address?"

"Uh, 40 East 60th. I think."

"You got that, Jenkins?"

The chauffeur nodded and pulled out into traffic.

Driving north, the limo cut in front of a car, causing its brakes to scream. It zoomed up on the left side of another car and cut it off. The driver screamed obscenities, most of which began with parts of the anatomy. I held on for dear life, pale with panic. Llewellyn sat serenely, swaying with the car.

Finally I asked, "Could you, sir, tell him to take it a little easy?"

"Oh, dear, no. I give him his rein. He needs to get certain things out of his system every now and then."

"What is he, a retired race car driver?"

"No, a former New York cabbie."

We arrived at La Fordice, a classy, nouveau French restaurant. It was filled with chic, sedate diners. The ambiance was very elegant and subdued.

I sat with Llewellyn at a table for two, smack in the middle of the room. As we studied the leather-covered menus, I asked Llewellyn what he did, or had done, for a living.

He said, "I've had many professions, but real estate is what made me a fortune. Ironically, a fortune was never what I desired."

"No?"

"Money makes one comfortable, but it doesn't make one happy."

"What is it you wanted to do?"

"I wanted to be a chef."

"A cook?"

"Yes. But my parents thought it was beneath me. I regret deeply that I didn't do what I loved. Whatever you do, young man, do what you love, not what you have to."

"I'll try to keep that in mind, sir."

The waiter came over. "Would you care for something to drink?"

Llewellyn looked at me. I shook my head. The champagne was enough.

The waiter then asked, "Would you like to order?"

Llewellyn looked to me and, with his left hand, gestured for me to begin.

"I'll just take the melon—"

Llewellyn cut in, "The egg aspic with caviar on pate and toast points sounds exquisite."

"That's a good choice."

"Why don't you have that?"

"Why don't you?"

"No. I'm a very delicate eater. I'd better save my very small appetite for the main course. Please have the caviar and egg."

"Well, all right."

The waiter said, "Excellent choice. And for entrees?"

Llewellyn started. "I'll have the Bouillabaisse. Je prends la bouillabaisse."

The waiter showed off his French. "Bon choix, m'sieur." He turned to me. "M'sieur?"

"Uh, the steak in marrons sauce, please."

"Excellent. Some wine?"

Llewellyn ordered, "The Chateau neuf de Pape 69."

The Waiter bowed and left us.

I was impressed. "Wow! I guess you're a gourmet, right?"

Llewellyn responded, "I have, shall we say, a discriminating palate. How kind of you to share my table this evening, Hans."

"It's no trouble at all. Believe me."

My appetizer was delicious. Llewellyn watched me eat it with jealous delight. His right hand was still in his pocket, shaking somewhat.

What is he doing, I wondered, playing pocket pool?

Then the waiter served me my steak. I admired the beautiful presentation. I basked in the luxury of it all. I sipped my wine as the waiter and an assistant placed a giant tureen of fish soup in middle of the table. They added an assortment of sea creatures and shellfish from a large platter. The assistant ladled broth into a large bowl in front of Llewellyn, then the waiter placed lobster tails, shrimps, mussels into the broth. I could see baby squid floating in the bowl. It smelled wonderful.

The waiter stood back with a flourish. "Voila! Bon appetit!"

Llewellyn said, "Thank you! Magnificently done! Oh, could I please have a few more serviettes? If it's no trouble?"

The waiter said, "Certainly, sir." He reached back and placed a couple of napkins at Llewellyn's place. Llewellyn frowned, but remained silent. He gestured to me, "Oh, please begin."

He eyed his bowl of bouillabaisse and slowly removed his right hand from his pocket. He had Parkinson's and it was shaking.

Carefully, he picked up a soup spoon. It started to shake in his hand, hitting the side of a water glass. The waiter heard the clinking of the glass and came running over. As he reached the table Llewellyn hit the glass one more time and knocked it over.

"It's nothing," I said. "Just a little accident here. Too much champagne before."

The waiter mopped up the water with his towel. I raised my hand as if everything was now all right. The waiter backed away and went into the kitchen with the wet towel and the cracked glass.

Llewellyn picked up the large serving spoon and dipped it into his bowl. His hand jerked from side to side and the spoon clanked noisily against the bowl. I reached out helplessly. Broth splashed out onto the table. Llewellyn tried to sop it up with his napkins.

"More serviettes!" He shouted across the room, then sighed. "They never give you enough napkins in these places."

Two waiters came rushing over with a pile of napkins. Llewellyn waited for them to go away. Using both hands, he lifted the serving spoon with great restraint and dipped it into his bowl. His hand shook a little, but he managed to fish out a spoonful of the bouillabaisse. As he brought it up to his chin, he pitched it into my face.

I spluttered, then gaped stupidly at him.

Llewellyn begged me, "Do forgive me."

I dried my face. Another spoonful hit me in the face. I dried it again, then watched in horror as Mr. L tried to get the soup to his mouth. His hand trembled, the spoon gyrated sideways, and the soup sloshed into the lap of a lady at the next table.

She shrieked, then glared at Llewellyn. "Watch what you're doing!"

He smiled at her, "I'm so terribly sorry."

He picked up a spoon filled with baby squids, but before he could get it to his mouth, it rocketed out of his hand and landed in my lap. I leaped up and shook my pants leg. The squids flew every which way. I quickly crawled around and collected them. I laid them near Llewellyn's plate.

Several waiters stood by stunned, looking helpless and utterly appalled.

Llewellyn, losing patience with himself and growing very angry, grabbed a lobster tail, but uncontrollably and abruptly, flung it across the dining room. It landed on a lady's elaborate hair-do.

She shrieked, terrified. "Get it off me! Get it off!"

The maitre d' hurried over and removed the lobster tail from the woman's head and stood stupefied, not sure what to do with it.

Llewellyn got up, tottered over to them, and snatched it away. The lady got up and slapped Llewellyn. Llewellyn turned around and hit her with the lobster tail. She slapped him back. The maitre d' got between them. Llewellyn slammed him in the face with the lobster tail.

I gawked disbelieving. The waiter came running from the kitchen and tripped. He fell smack into the spilled broth on the parquet floor. I hurried to help him up, but Llewellyn dumped the whole bowl of bouillabaisse on both of them.

The maitre d' recovered somewhat and grabbed hold of Llewellyn, but as he did so, he skidded and Llewellyn got away. Llewellyn was livid now. He grabbed his chair and broke it over the table. As if that wasn't enough, he grabbed the table cloth and cleaned off the entire table.

People were shrieking and screaming. It was a madhouse. I grabbed Llewellyn from the midst of irate, close-to-lynching diners and snaked him outside. I found out from the driver of the limo that nobody else would dine with Mr. L, not even his wife, so he resorted to hiring companions to eat with him.

As the limo drove away, Llewellyn sat serenely still, coming down from his ordeal. When we reached 59th

Street, he said, "Well, that was a delight, wasn't it? Perhaps we can do it again? Try a new place?"

I walked on eggs. "Let me check my schedule, all right?"

"Certainly. I wish you good fortune, Hans. You were most agreeable company. A treasure, really."

"Uh, thank you, sir. Good night." I backed out of the limo and waited as they drove off.

I earned my money that night.

I went over to Randa's, still wearing my soiled tux. I rang the bell and her voice blared over the intercom. "Who is it?"

"It's me, Randa. Can I come up?"

She buzzed me in. I could see, when she let me in, that she had been writing. The electric typewriter was still on and papers were all over her desk. She hurried to straighten them out, as if not wanting me to see what she was writing.

I kissed her lightly.

She looked at me. "Don't you look nice! Oops, you have a spot. Gadzooks, what happened to you?"

I scrubbed at my shirt with my fingernails. "Bouillabaisse."

"On you it looks very elegant. Dinner?"

"Almost."

She edged toward the typewriter and shut if off. At the same time, she flipped some papers over face down.

I guess I should have called. "I'm interrupting your work."

"I needed a break. And I'm glad to see you."

I hugged her. Over her shoulder I noticed a page. I broke away and picked it up. "Al Pacino, huh? Reading up on him?"

She sounded nervous. "Uh, sure."

"You're going the second mile for your friend, aren't

you?"

She was confused. "What? Oh. Merrill. Yeah, I am. Actually I have a confession to make. I should have done it sooner. I really want to level with you about this."

I was worried. "Randa, what is it?"

"I'm the one who wants to do a book on Al Pacino, not Merrill. I lied, I guess."

"But why?"

"I don't know. I guess I didn't want you to think I was using you or something."

"So it's not really me you were interested in."

"No. I mean, yes".

"You just wanted to pick my brain about Al."

"Yes, I did. But I'm interested in you, too. Surely you know that by now."

"Just interested? I thought you loved me."

"Ed, I do. I'm very bad with stuff like this. Please believe me."

"Tell me why I should?"

She stared at me, near tears. I was cut to the quick. I started toward the door.

"Don't just walk out like that. Please, lset me try to make it clearer."

"It's already pretty clear to me, Randa. I'll see you around."

I walked out and closed the door after me. I could hear her calling from inside. "Ed! Wait!"

But I didn't. I must have walked the streets of Greenwich Village for hours until my pace slowed down. I then wandered aimlessly, really depressed.

I noticed that I was in the area where Rich lived in his packing crate. I cut through the alley and headed toward the row of crates and boxes. I stopped and looked inside Rich's hovel. I was sure that was his, but another bum, not

Rich, sat up, startled.

I was concerned. "I thought you were Rich."

The bum responded, "I used to be."

"Sorry."

"How about some change?"

"I'm looking for some myself."

He fumbled into his torn pocket and handed me a dollar bill. I stared at it.

"No, you keep it." I handed it back. "You don't usually sleep here. Where's the guy who does?

"Oh, the police ran him over to Bellevue."

"What'd hc do?"

"Nothin'. Somebody split his head open. I thought I'd hold his place... 'til he comes back. If he comes back."

I excused myself and walked away, seriously concerned.

ACT III

"Two roads diverged in a wood,
and I — I took the one less traveled by,
And that has made all the difference."

— Robert Frost
The Road Not Taken

THE HUMAN PREDICAMENT

I WAS AT HOME, trying to unwind, when the phone rang. I let it ring again. After a few more urgent rings, I picked it up. It was the police.

"Ed De Leo?"

"Yeah, that's me. You saw my ad?"

"I'm callin' about your friend, Richard Jaynes."

"Who? Oh, yeah . . . Rich. What about him?"

"He's dead. Victim of a mugging."

"Oh, God! No!"

"He listed you as his friend, to be notified in case anything happens to him. You wannna claim the body?"

I was stunned. "Claim the body? Do I have to?"

"No. You can let the morgue do what they do."

"OK, I'll claim him. How do I do that?"

"You gotta go down to Bellevue and sign him out. Do it, and you got him."

At the cemetery, Victor and Harvey stood next to me at the grave site, over Rich's simple, pine coffin. I wept almost uncontrollably. What a life.

Victor put his arms around me. "He's at peace now,

Ed. Think of that."

"He never gave up wanting to be an actor."

Harvey said, "He's gone to that big casting call in the sky.

I tried to laugh, but it made me only sob harder. The poor mummy bastard.

Victor and I trudged through the streets. The heat shimmered like burning gas on the pavement. I was really down.

Victor broke the silence. "Rich's life is uninterrupted. He's continuing on, you know. His life only seems over to us."

"Vic, I know you mean well, but what you're saying doesn't help."

"I'm very touched that you care so much for an unfortunate fellow human being."

"I wish I could honestly say that's what it is, but..."

"What you feel is natural. Grief is mostly for ourselves, still battling the human predicament."

"Let me tell you about human predicaments."

I was in no mood for Victor's mysticism. I needed to stop the machinery or it would scoop me up with its iron teeth and plant me six feet under without ever having accomplished anything.

When we walked up the street toward the apartment building, I saw Gino waiting by the steps.

"I'm dead this time, Vic."

We approached the building. Gino looked at Vic, then waited for him to go inside. Then he said, "So, Ed, what've you got for me?"

"Gino, I haven't got it. You'll have to give me more time."

"Like, how much time we talkin' about?"

"I don't know. A few weeks maybe."

"You gonna be able to handle it then?"

"I'll handle it, Gino. I keep my word."

Gino eyed me hard, nodded grimly and hurried off.

Victor waited for me in the downstairs lobby. "What was that all about?"

"I did something very necessary, but very stupid. Not to speak of dangerous."

"I'll pray for you."

"While you're at it, ask for a miracle."

"You're not supposed to ask God for things. What you've got to do is listen more."

We went upstairs to my place. The phone was ringing. It was the nurse from the hospital.

She said, "You'd better get over here. You're mother is creating a scene."

At the hospital, the doctor took me aside. "Do you know your mother cheered up all the old patients? She doesn't even think she's disabled. She said, 'Leave me alone! What am I, a cripple? Why are you giving me artificial legs? I'm not crippled.' And she started to get out of bed to walk out of the hospital. I said, 'No, Tillie, you've got to put on the—.' And she interrupted me. She said, 'Give me those damned things! I'll put them on myself.' We've never, in the history of my medical career, ever seen a woman like that."

My mother was sitting on the side of her bed when I walked into her room at the hospital.

"Hey, Ma, you're on your feet!"

"I'm on my duff. Feet's gotta wait their turn."

I handed her a paper bag and she opened it eagerly. "Gummy Bears! You remembered! Where's Dale?"

"He's in camp for the week."

"Yeah? Where's that cute girl you brought to see me?"

"We're cooling it a bit right now."

"She doesn't look Italian, but I like that woman, Ed. She's got a sense of humor, which is more'n I can say for what's-her-name. You know, in 14 years I can't remember ever seeing her smile."

"She tries, Ma."

"People don't try to laugh. Laughter happens. If it's real, it bubbles right up from your gut. Her problem is she ain't got a funny bone. Now, when you gonna get me outta this snake pit?"

"When they say you're ready to leave."

"Doll, I've been ready to leave since before I got here. Now, get me the hell home!"

She walked out of the hospital with two artificial legs. And when she got home, she started walking around.

I got my ability to bounce back from her. I had developed an ability to rebound from some of the difficult stuff I constantly faced. I was able to maintain an affirmative attitude whenever people asked me, "How come Al hasn't put you in one of his pictures?"

Victor helped me bring her home from the hospital. He held the door open and I helped her to the couch. She sat down hard, exhausted from the cab ride.

First thing she asked was, "Where's the remote control?" Victor handed it to her. Her next question was, "Where are my Gummy Bears?" I handed her the bag. Nothing had changed.

Victor announced, "All set? I'm going to the market. What would you like for supper, Mrs. D?"

"Fried chicken. The spicy kind."

Victor and I looked at each other.

"Ma, it's not on your new diet."

"Hey, if you're gonna die, you're gonna die. So why not go out happy and full of spicy chicken?"

Victor said, "You may have made an important discovery, Mrs. D. I'm going to meditate on that.

"Well, while you're meditating I'll be masticating."

Victor grinned and went out. My phone rang. I ran up

the stairs to get it. It was somebody who had seen my ad. This one sounded like it would be fun, judging a beauty contest at Coney Island.

My mother was learning to maneuver herself about the apartment in the wheelchair. She was playing solitaire at the dining room table when I came down wearing a blazer and a bow tie.

She looked at me. "Don't you look scrumptious. I could eat you for dessert. Where're you off to?"

I knew she'd ask. "I've got a coaching session."

"You dress like that to coach now?

"We're doing it on camera now, remember? I'll be in the scene."

"Honey, I don't remember much of anything. Seems like a lot of the past's been wiped out."

"Don't worry about it. It'll all come back."

"I sure as hell hope not. I kinda like starting off new, like a big fat baby."

I was happy she still had a sense of humor. I kissed her goodnight.

"Break a leg, doll."

"Vic'll be down in an hour to see if you need anything."

She waved me off.

I took a cab to an east side townhouse. I bounded up the steps, rang the bell, and announced myself. After I was buzzed in, a well-stacked woman with platinum hair and heavy makeup opened the door. It was a posh apartment.

"Oh, darling, you're divine! You must be Burt?

"Right. Monica?"

Mae West was alive and well. "You know it. Uh, I love a lot of admiration, if you have the inclination."

"Oh, OK. You're beautiful, Monica. Just about the most beautiful woman I've ever met. Honest."

"More beautiful than Raquel Welch?

"Way, way more beautiful."

Monica brushed off the compliment deprecatingly. "We'll see, Burt, we'll see." She picked up her fox stole and handed it to me. "Be a dear. I'm just gaga for men with manners."

I draped the fox around her shoulders. "So where's it to be? Dreamland?"

"As Dorothy says, just put on your ruby slippers and follow the yellow brick road. Our personal tornado is waiting to sweep us away!"

She swept out and I followed.

The event was being staged in the banquet room of the Carlyle Hotel, overlooking the festive Coney Island boardwalk. Monica led me through a crush of glamorous women of all sizes and shapes. Some were statuesque, others more ethereal. They preened and gushed to one another, kissing and cooing.

Monica spotted a raven-haired beauty and smacked her on the lips. "Ricki! You look ravishing!"

Ricki preened. "So do you, darling!"

Monica squealed, "You bitch! You enlarged your tits!"

"Jealous?"

Monica eyed her boobies and seethed. She dragged me to face Ricki. "Burt, this is my dearest friend, Ricki."

My eyes were goggling. Ricki pushed her chest almost into my face. I was in heaven.

I flashed her a smile. "How do you do, Ricki? You're gorgeous. I've never seen so many beautiful women all in one place."

Ricki gasped. "Didn't she tell you? What are you, straight or something?"

"Straight?"

Ricki pressed closer. "As opposed to bent."

Monica pushed her back. "Keep those thunder thighs

to yourself, bitch. We need somebody impartial."

She escorted me away. "There are six seats in the front row reserved for the judges. Introduce yourself, sugar, and I'll see you after the show — for the orgy."

I blanched at the word orgy, but I went into the auditorium. It was festively decorated with balloons and streamers. I picked my way to the front row and introduced myself to the five other judges, two men and three women. We weren't supposed to talk to each other, so I was relieved. All I was required to do was vote by ballot. Two categories, two votes. Easy.

The auditorium started to fill up. Half of the crowd, dressed in flowered prints and wearing beads and bangles, looked like a Carmen Miranda fan club. The rest surely came from nearby all-male nursing homes and seemed to be high on uppers.

An emcee strutted out onto the stage, carrying a mike. He sported a lavender dinner jacket and wore stiletto heels. "Ladies and, er, gentlemen! Let the parade begin!"

He gestured toward the wings, and a bevy of beauties in dazzling evening gowns paraded around, strutting and wiggling their assets. The crowd went wild.

Monica strutted out. She was clearly a favorite by the deafening applause. She did her stuff and exited. Ricki then came out. The crowd went wild. She blew a kiss to the crowd and sashayed off into the wings. Other beauties strutted out and did their turns.

The emcee came back out on stage to announce, "And now we begin the bathing suit category. Eat your hearts out!"

Again the parade started. Monica strutted out in a spangled bikini, followed by Ricki, whose breasts were bursting out of a tiny bra. Ricki seemed to be gaining the edge by the sound of continuous, thunderous applause.

I voted for Monica in both categories. Who would ever know? I think that's what I was supposed to do. After the votes were tabulated, they were given to the emcee in an envelope. He swaggered over to the microphone and opened it. He eyed the audience flirtatiously and announced, "And the winner is... Ricki Mars!"

There was a burst of wild applause. The beauties, all except Monica, crowded around Ricki, hugging and kissing her and weeping. Ricki was crowned, caped and sceptred. She paraded down the runway, bumping and grinding and flaunting every asset she had, blowing kisses.

Monica watched, seething. I thought she would explode. She cast a dirty look at me. I shrugged. It wasn't my fault.

In the banquet room, later, Monica and I shared a round table with several other beauties and their companions. Ricki strutted over, pouting. She bent over Monica. "Be a good sport, sweetie and congratulate me."

Monica eyed her with loathing. "I'd never resort to a cheap tit job to win a title."

"Hey, fair's fair." Rickie edged down next to me and nuzzled my neck. "You are a hunk, you know that?"

Monica warned her, "Take your slimy paws off him!"

Ricki ignored her. "Are there anymore at home like you? I'm wetting my BVDs thinking of the possibilities."

That was all Monica needed. "You vulgar bitch!"

I tried to intercede. "She's only—"

Ricki shouted, "I'm not the vulgar one. I'm a perfect little lady, and I've got a crown to prove it. Which is more than you can say!"

Monica took a flying leap and landed on Ricki's back. They sprawled on the floor. Monica punched Ricki in the nose. Ricki shoved Monica off and grabbed her by the hair. Monica's wig came off in Ricki's hands. Monica howled and slammed Ricki against the floor, then threw herself on top of "her." She yanked off the bra and the falsies came off with it.

I watched, aghast. Other beauties joined the free-for-all. Wigs, bras, gowns, shoes and "tits" flew every which way.

I continued to gape. I must have looked as white as a sheet. "Oh, my god."

Monica ducked out of the fray and came back to join me. Ricki, narrow-eyed with anger, flew after her.

Monica snarled, "Leave me alone. You just spoiled my whole evening!"

Ricki hissed, "You never could've pulled it off. Not in your wildest dreams."

I stared at them, stunned. Guys, please! Just let me get home safely. Please!

"Monica" offered to drive me home. I told him I lived in the Bronx. It didn't matter.

He insisted. His real name was Monroe. When he pulled up in front of my building, I opened the door quickly. Monroe turned off his lights. He eyed me coyly and opened his purse. He counted out five hundred-dollar bills and handed them to me.

I was surprised. "That's too much."

"Take it, big guy. You earned it." He took out a calling card and handed it to me. "Call me. We could spend a nice quiet evening together. Couldn't we?"

"Monica, er, Monroe, I said, "I'm straight. You know I am."

"After all you saw tonight, you're still hooked on the real thing?

"You're real. And I like you, but..."

Monroe/Monica said hopefully, "I promise you, you'd never be able to tell the difference in the dark." He leaned in closer. "I'm real adept at—"

"Sorry. Peace, OK?" I got out.

He/She regretfully blew a kiss at me. I watched the car drive away.

As I turned to go inside, two giant goons rushed me and beat the hell out of me. I crumpled to the pavement, bleeding.

One of the goons pointed to me. "Next time you hit concrete, it'll be real soft. Get my drift, deadbeat?"

They walked off, leaving me on the pavement. I groaned and struggled to my feet. My lip was like hamburger and my left eye was swollen shut. I stumbled into the building.

I didn't want my mother to see me, so I went up to Victor's. He helped me to a chair and washed my eyes. I tried not to tell him too much.

But he had to know. "There's more to this than you're telling me, Ed."

I told him the whole story. "I guess it's a warning to pay up, or else. This is the first of the 'else.'"

"I'd give you the money if I had it, Ed. But you know my situation."

"I wouldn't take it if you had it."

"There must be an answer. There's always a solution, Ed."

"And I'm seriously considering it."

"See? Back to the wall, there's always an answer."

"I'm just trying to decide on the least painful way."

"Ed! I'm disappointed in you."

Ginny called me and insisted I get on a train to Connecticut immediately. Dale was in big trouble and she wouldn't tell me what it was all about.

I took a train to Brookfield to see Ginny. When she opened the door she flinched at the sight of my injuries.

"For God's sake, what happened to you?"

"You should see the other guy."

"That's a joke, right?"

"You're not laughing."

"What's going on, Ed?"

"Where's Dale? What's wrong?"

"He's under house arrest."

"What'd he do?"

"What didn't he do? He threw oranges at people on a bus. He went on a joyride with some kids who were drinking. The police brought him home. They say he's a ringleader."

"Our Dale, a ringleader? That's ridiculous!"

She sighed. "No more New York City for me. I'm giving up my job there."

"Who's going to support you? Larry Greenawalt?"

"I'm a free agent."

"Do what you have to do, Ginny. Just don't stop me from seeing Dale."

"I wouldn't do that. But I can't let him see you in the city any more. You can only see him here. It's for his own good."

I nodded, then went down the hall to Dale's room. Dale lay on his stomach on the jumbled bed. I walked in and sat down beside him. Dale rolled over to look at me.

"So you blew it good, huh?" I said.

"We just borrowed Mr. Campbell's old clunker. We weren't stealing it."

"But you learned your lesson, right?"

Dale made a face and turned away. "Get off my back, OK?"

"What's with the oranges?"

Dale sat up. He looked away, then sighed. "Promise not to get mad."

"I can't promise that, but I won't yell at you."

"You never yell. Mom does the yelling."

"Dale, I love you, no matter what you do. You're a good kid. I haven't been tough enough with you. I guess I haven't helped your mom either..."

"Stop with the guilt stuff already."

"OK, the truth now."

"My friends and me were foolin' around, that's all. We had these oranges, and they bet me I couldn't throw one of 'em into the window of the school bus."

"So you did it?"

"I didn't hurt anybody."

"Dale,even if you didn't hurt anybody, it's wrong. Can you see that?"

"It's that 'do unto others' crap, right?"

"It's not crap. It's a basic rule to live by."

"Mom says you got a girlfriend."

"I don't know. It's kind of cooled."

"What happened?"

"Well... she used me."

"How? You don't have any money."

"She wanted to get to Al Pacino."

"What's so bad about that?"

"You don't use people, Dale."

"Didn't you use Al Pacino to try to get acting jobs?"

"You got me there, Dale."

I had to go to Dale's school and speak to the principal. I assured them he would never do such a thing again.

I was walking in Greenwich Village. Gino came up from behind and fell into step with me. I was startled.

Gino smirked. "So, how're you feeling, ole buddy?"

"I got the message, Gino."

"So when can I expect the remittance?"

I stopped and faced him. "Gino, I don't know. The part in Pacino's movie fell through. I used every cent you gave me to pay for my mom's hospital bill. I have $300 on me. Take it. It's every dime I've got." I thrust it at him.

Gino looked at it and thrust it back. "Keep it. It wouldn't pay one day's interest. I guess we'll have to take the hard line, Ed. Sorry about that."

"Do what you have to do... Gino."

Gino eyed me almost with admiration, then he hurried off. I straightened my shoulders, almost relieved.

I stopped up at the Actors Equity office to check the casting notices on the bulletin board. My old mirror-image, Harvey, was there. Seeing my bruises, he looked me up and down with alarm. "Jesus, Ed... What the hell happened to you?"

"Ran into a door. How's the play shaping up?"

"It folded. Financing fell through."

"Sorry to hear that."

"There's a talent show over at the Whitley tonight. A grand for the winner. Come over and watch me do my shtick tonight."

"Your magic act?"

"Yeah. Hey, you sing. Why don't you enter?"

"A talent contest? C'mon!"

"Don't tell me you don't need the money."

I thought about it. "Maybe I will. I might as well go out singing."

Harvey cast me a puzzled look.

I went home and put on my flashiest clothes. Watch out, Vegas, here I come!

When I went downstairs, Victor was at the stove cooking vegetables. My mother was watching *Jeopardy*. She studied what I was wearing. She was learning not to question me about it.

"They're starting to film the movie with your friend Al. You got your call yet?"

"Not yet, Ma." I glanced at Victor, who remained expressionless, still cooking.

My mother said, "So you're gonna be on home turf tonight. Wish I could be there. Knock 'em dead, will ya?

Victor added, "Enjoy yourself, Ed. Give it all you got."

"Thanks."

At the Whitley Theater, Harvey did his magic act and was pretty darn good. He pulled eggs out of his pockets and made several brass rings interlock and then pass through each other. From the sound of the applause I was sure he would win the contest.

He was followed by a woman who played the accordion, a harmonica and a set of drums, all at the same time. She sang "Seventy-Six Trombones" from *The Music Man*. I was next.

The host introduced me, "Now, folks, you're in for a real treat. We have Ed De Leo. His mother, Tillie De Leo, used to sing here back in the olden days. Little Eddie used to sing with her right on this stage. Now, he's gonna sing a song of his own called "How I Feel About You." Here he is folks, Ed De Leo!"

I sauntered out and bowed low. The mini-orchestra, which consisted of a keyboard, a trumpet player, a string bass, and a drummer, started playing the intro. I grabbed the microphone like it was my lover, and started to sing like Billy Eckstein.

I spotted Randa entering the auditorium in middle of my number. She was wearing a long, slim dress and crocheted hat. She took an empty seat on the aisle.

I finished to a burst of applause. There were shouts of "encore!" I cued the orchestra and launched into "To Dream the Impossible Dream" with intense feeling. It seemed almost my theme song.

I looked through the audience at Randa. She was listening teary-eyed. I didn't care whether or not I won the competition. Her reaction was enough for one lifetime.

But the audience applauded wildly.

The host came out. "Thank you, Ed. The way you sing would make us believe nothing is impossible." He addressed the crowd. "OK, folks, you're now going to vote. See that old-timey applause meter up there. It's gonna tell us who the winner is. So let's make a noise. Hurry on out here, performers. Line up!"

All the contestants drifted out onto the stage and lined up. I looked out at Randa. She was watching, tense and nervous.

As each one of the contestants stepped forward, the audience applauded and the meter registered. When I stepped forward, the meter went all the way to the top and stayed there.

The host announced, "And the winner of one thousand dollars: Ed De Leo! Here's your prize, Ed. Here's your winner, folks!"

The audience went wild expressing their approval.

Later, backstage, a group of people pressed around me, congratulating me. I ate up the adulation. I saw Randa standing around the edges, watching. I pushed my way over to her.

She said, "You were so good."

"Thank you. What are you doing here? How did you know?"

"I called you, just after you left. Victor told me."

"I was going to call you."

"You sure took your time about it."

We went down to the Cafe Figaro in the Village. I told her about my talk with my son and we sat holding hands across the table.

Randa asked, "Your son's name is Dale, right?"

"Yes."

"As in Smith and Dale? He's a pretty wise little guy for a 12 year old."

"He's got a lot of good qualities."

"Like his dad."

"I'm pretty dense. Forgive me?"

"I should've been up front with you. I tend to be too secretive about my life. I'm trying to change that."

"I've been accused of being a dreamer. I'm trying to change that. But I may be a hopeless case." I looked pained.

"What is it? What's wrong?"

"Let's walk."

We went out into the street and started to walk, holding hands. I told her about the loan sharks.

She stopped. "My God! They're going to kill you! You shouldn't even be out here on the streets."

"I can't live in fear any longer. I can't hide out for the rest of my life. What's left of it."

"You're not even scared."

"Hah! I've been scared all my life. Now that I'm facing death, I'm not scared any more. It's almost a relief to stop worrying. If they kill me, they kill me."

"But that's suicidal."

"I love life. I love acting. I love you. I love my son, my mother. But I seem to have no control over anything. I guess I'm doomed to just be a 'poor dumb player who struts and frets upon the stage then is heard no more.'"

"Ed, my God! We've got to do something!"

"I've done everything I know."

"At least come home with me."

"That I can do."

She stared at me, then started to giggle. We both laughed like two crazy people. Pedestrians noticed and stopped to watch us. We fell into each other's arms, just laughing hysterically. We skipped off down the sidewalk like two demented children.

The next morning I marched up the street, whistling. I didn't have a care in the world; not after a night like I had with Randa. At the stoop, I leaped into the air and clicked my heels together.

Gino stepped out of the entrance and waited for me to come up the steps. "Man, I don't believe you. You crazy or something?"

"What do you mean, Gino?"

"This could be your last day on earth. Can't you take it seriously?"

"If it's my last day, I'm gonna spend it happy. Even people on death row get a happy meal, don't you think?"

"Man, you are one fucked up customer. With one dropped dime you're on your way to a construction site, man."

"Gino, I'm tired of your threats. Just do it why don't you and get it over with."

I reached into my pocket, took out my wallet and peeled off ten hundred dollar bills. "Here, take it. It's a grand. It oughta buy me at least one day's reprieve. Now, if you'll excuse me, I gotta go cook breakfast for my mother. See you around."

I went on up the steps to the building. I turned to see Gino lingering, looking shaken beyond comprehension. I could see he was impressed, but his look quickly turned to anger. He was on a short fuse.

I called Al. I needed $15,000 to repay half of the money to the loan sharks, or it was over for me. It was like a scene from one of Al's movies, maybe *Dog Day Afternoon*. I was cornered, waiting to be gunned down.

Al bailed me out of my debt to the loan sharks. Within a week the money was there for me. What a relief! I could have found myself in the Hudson River wearing cement sneakers.

Life has its ironies. The phone rang. Without picking it up, I knew what the call was. I had rehearsed it so many times in my head, I was prepared for it. It was the hospital.

Gloria flew in from California. She, Joan and I were with mother every day, trying to boost her spirits. She died in December.

Al sent flowers to the family and money for funeral costs.

I tried to keep busy. I thought I might have a better chance of getting The Playmaker produced if I did it as a stage play instead of a movie. If I could get a director attached to it, I might be able to impress a backer.

I heard about a director, Lamar Livingston, who was supposed to be very good with new material. Livingston had dated several big stars. I did a reading of the play for him, two weeks after my mother died.

While I was reading one of the lines in the script, about the mother, I looked up to heaven and started to cry. My own mother came to mind and the dam broke.

I was embarrassed and said to Livingston, "Oh, God, I've never done anything like this before."

He said, "Don't apologize. That was one of the best pieces of acting I've ever seen."

The unexpected is what makes good acting exciting. It's what I always told Al. I was "playing against the situation." With my mother having lost both legs and then dying, I was an emotional volcano.

AL

IN 1980, Al needed a good, meaty film role. He was intrigued by Cruising to be directed by William Friedkin of

The Exorcist fame.

Also written by Friedkin, Cruising was a murder mystery based on a series of brutal killings of homosexuals from 1962 to 1979 in New York City. Al played a young policeman who had to go undercover into the S&M underworld of the gay community to track down a psychotic who was killing homosexuals.

When they started filming in Greenwich Village they were picketed by the gay community. They were being accused of being anti-gay. Al told the press he had never wanted to do anything to harm the gay community, or the Italian-American community, or the police community, or any group he portrayed on-screen.

When he read the script, it never occurred to him the movie would be termed anti-gay. He felt his responsibility to the picture was as an actor, to the character he was playing, not to some issue he was not qualified to discuss.

The protests focused on the sadomasochistic fringes of gay life rather than on the gay mainstream. After the film was finished, Al hated it.

The New York Times said, "Cruising is a homosexual horror film." The New York Daily News called it "...a depraved, mindless piece of garbage that should never have been made."

What did he do about it? Back to the theater. He and director Arvin Brown wanted to do something together and agreed to do a revival of David Mamet's stage play, *American Buffalo* in which Robert Duvall had starred in 1977, with Ulu Grosbard directing.

The Pacino role was that of a psychotic, foul-mouthed punk. They decided to mount it at the Long Wharf Theater in New Haven. Long Wharf had a policy of not billing any actors. It was a good move.

Critic Mel Gussow said the production was "easily the

most amusing *American Buffalo* I have ever seen. When Mr. Pacino makes his entry on the Long Wharf stage, the play accelerates in a fresh direction. It is not that he is better than Duvall; he is different, as different as they were in *The Godfather.* In Pacino's hands his character becomes street-smart, cocksure and self-mocking... The actor has chosen wisely. In each case (including *Pavlo Hummel*) he has confirmed a player's position in our dramatic literature, and he has staked out an impressive claim to a challenging contemporary role."

Al's juices were flowing again.

ME

I HAD TO MOVE from Parkchester. There were too many painful memories of my mother in the apartment. Finding a suitable and affordable new place wasn't easy.

My biggest hardship in renting other apartments on a month-to-month basis was moving all of my belongings each time. Ginny, meanwhile, was not getting along with her parents. They loved Dale, but wished Ginny would either remarry or go back to work. She had no social life. All she did was stay in the house or go on shopping sprees. Between her and Dale, the house was always in turmoil.

Ginny's parents owned a couple of cottages adjacent to their house in Connecticut. They offered to rent one of them to Ginny and me for only enough to pay the overhead. There were four acres of wooded grounds surrounding the houses and it was a beautiful setting. I seriously considered it, but I knew I couldn't pursue my acting from Connecticut. We took the house, though, so Dale would have a nice place to grow up. I would find a way to pay the rent.

Al AND ME

IT WAS 1982. Al agreed to star in *Author, Author!* for Twentieth Century Fox, co-starring Dyan Cannon and his old flame, Tuesday Weld. The script was by Israel Horovitz, based on his own experiences.

Al's character was a playwright and the harried father of five. His wife had run off with another man in the midst of rehearsals for a play that would either make or break his tenuous toehold on Broadway.

I visited Al on the set. It was being produced by Irwin Winkler, who had been one of the producers of *Rocky*. The director was Arthur Hiller, who directed some classic pictures such as *The Americanization of Emily and Love Story.*

Al asked me how I was doing and told me my mother was still in his prayers.

"Life goes on," I told him.

He said, "You're so up, I don't believe it. It took me a long time to get over my mother's death."

"I still think about her," I said.

"I've helped so many people, but I haven't helped you that much, have I?"

"You've helped me more than I can say, Al. You've been the best friend."

"You're the one person I really want to help. More than anyone."

I smiled. "Watch out or I'll be coming around for handouts."

He laughed. He must have had dozens of old friends asking for favors, introductions, or loans.

He could see that, behind my cheerful facade, I was really depressed. He said there were a few roles still open in the picture. He sent me to see Cissy Corman, the casting director.

Cissy arranged an audition for Arthur Hiller. I read for a role she thought I was right for.

My first line was "Yes, I'm screaming."

I asked Arthur, critically, "You don't want me to actually scream the line, do you?"

He replied that I was the first actor to understand the part. He didn't want any screaming. So I read it for him realistically, no shouting. He told me he liked me and I thought I had the role. The producers wanted a star, however, and the part went to Alan King. But they cast me in another role.

I had a scene with Al and Dyan Cannon. Tuesday Weld and Alan King were also in the cast. It was a good scene set at Roseland, a famous dance hall in Manhattan. I played a fan of Dyan Canon who was there with his wife. Dyan was an actress going to a premiere with Al, the author.

My first line this time was, "Oh, my God, here they come!"

I did it without screaming. Then I continued with, "She looks skinny, doesn't she?" But Dyan didn't like the line. So I changed it to, "She looks different in person."

We did a lot of takes and I had some nice close-ups. Arthur liked me a lot. I could tell by his laughter. Al was on the floor laughing. Arthur said to me, "I don't know why Al hasn't told me about you earlier."

After the scene was in the can, Al gave me a big hug and said, "I told Arthur and Dyan and everybody that you're great."

I wondered if I could get an Academy Award for being in only one scene.

Dyan Cannon came up to me after the shoot and said, "You really are good. What's your name?"

I said, "Ed De Leo."

"Oh, yes, Al was raving about you. He says you're one

of the best actors in New York."

Al later told me that though the dailies looked great, my scene was cut out of the picture. He explained to me on the set that the lighting was screwed up, or something, and the scenes didn't match. So I wound up on the cutting room floor again. If there was ever a plot to destroy my career, this was it. One blow after another.

But I wasn't the only one with problems. Rewriting went on during filming under Hiller's direction. The temperature in Gloucester, Maine was near zero. That plus location problems resulted in big arguments between Al and Hiller.

Word spread that Al was a troublesome actor. On the last day of filming, Al arrived 90 minutes late and got a loud chewing out by director Hiller. Al walked off the set, and it took producer Winkler to coax him back. The filming resumed.

Al said his lateness was a misunderstanding. He didn't know he was supposed to work that day. He had been ready and wanted to work, but had not been informed. Al acknowledged he and Hiller had different tempos.

He said, "My struggle was the same as his struggle, to get the movie made."

A month or so later, while I was out walking, I bumped into Arthur Hiller coming out of the Director's Guild headquarters. He remembered me immediately.

"You're a wonderful actor," he said.

I asked, "What about my scenes? Why did they have to get cut?"

"Don't feel bad. My daughter was in some of those scenes and now she won't talk to me."

He explained that all the beautiful stuff he had wanted never got captured on film.

Reviews were not so hot and it was a bomb at the box-office. That was four busts in a row for Al. Thank God he had distinguished himself in The Godfather, Serpico, and Dog Day Afternoon. He needed to take time out to recoup and to plan his next move.

ME

WHILE RANDA AND I still saw each other from time to time, it was never the same. She had been trying to change me into somebody I simply wasn't. Like Ginny, she couldn't take my life-style, running from job to job, failing at auditions, always chasing after that "big break."

I had no doubts I eventually would be discovered. Making it as an actor, as everyone told me, was a matter of "being in the right place at the right time."

For Randa, it was too painful for her to watch. She was having her own struggles as a writer and needed a fresh start. When we were together it became obvious we were both thinking, "Whose problem is it today, yours or mine?"

My trips to Connecticut on the weekends to see Dale didn't help. Randa suspected there was a bond between Ginny and me that she couldn't compete with. Perhaps she was right. Finally, we agreed to start seeing other people.

Ginny's father died, and her mother followed him in less than a year. Dale now had no grandparents. Ginny, like me, was an orphan. Her brother inherited the houses. Rather than making it easier for Ginny to live there, he made it more difficult by not maintaining the property and increasing the rent. This, of course, put more pressure on me to send her more money each month.

AL AND ME

LATER IN 1982, I ran into Al in the crowded lobby of an off-Broadway theater where we were both attending a play. He gave me a big hug and told me his production of the David Mamet play, *American Buffalo* was going to open at the Downtown Circle In The Square in Manhattan in February. He was really excited about it.

The critics loved it. They agreed that this was Al Pacino's first fully rewarding performance since *Dog Day Afternoon*. Primo critic, Walter Kerr, called his performance "astonishing and mesmerizing."

I took Ann Bancroft's sister, Phyllis Wetsel, to see the show. Phyllis and I were joining forces to manage actors. We tried to go backstage to see him after the show, but nobody could get in. So I sent him a little note: "Tried to get to see you. Too many people. You were excellent, as usual. Your good friend, Ed."

Al came running out of his dressing room to catch me. "I'm so glad you came."

I was surprised that he was so warm. Sometimes people forget their friends. They get busy. But Al is always good to his friends. He's consistent.

Al was taken by Phyllis and told me she was pretty.

I said, "She's Anne Bancroft's sister. We're both trying to manage some clients now."

"So, now you're managing. Once you were trying to raise money for films. Why don't you go back to the one thing you were great at ... the acting?"

How right he was. I was still going off on tangents.

"Let the other guys raise the money," he said. He was thinking like a star, the way Herbert Berghof had described him.

But I was a different kind of person. I loved acting,

but I also wanted to write. I wanted to produce, I wanted to manage, and I wanted to teach. I wanted to do so many things. I loved it all. And that, obviously, was my big mistake. I didn't have the tunnel vision that Al had to be a star. I wanted it, and I wanted it bad; but wanting is not enough. You have to zero in on the goal and keep your eyes focused on it.

Al was more like Marlon Brando than I. He focused on the acting, I did many different things. Brando was once asked why he was such a great actor. He replied, "I had to be. I'm not good at anything else."

Maybe that's the huge difference between me and Al. Al just wanted an acting career. He did have something else as well — a great capacity for making friends. Normally, that doesn't make you a lot of money. It doesn't pay your rent or put food on the table. But that depends on how you choose your friends.

That same year, Al did some workshop rehearsals of Eugene O'Neill's *The Hairy Ape* at Circle in the Square.

Lee Strasberg died and it was a tremendous blow to Al. Strasberg had really believed in him. Al accepted the post of artistic director of the Actors Studio along with Ellen Burstyn. Soon, though, he withdrew to leave Burstyn as sole artistic director, stating, "I believe that the turmoil following Lee's death has ended and the situation has been stabilized at the Studio. I make this decision with every warm feeling towards the Studio, which is my alma mater and which gave me so much as a young actor."

According to Al, Strasberg hadn't been given the credit he deserved. Marlon Brando didn't give him any credit. The Actors Studio had such a bad name, Al felt it was unfair. It had done so much for him. He felt it had launched him and was a turning point in his life.

"I'll be grateful to the Actors Studio forever," Al said.

"I'd like to marry that place."

Al wasn't sure that actors had many places to go, to develop early on. He thought the Strasberg approach had been very instrumental to a lot of the acting seen in films all over the world. The Method seemed to translate to movies more readily than to theater because it was more of an internal approach. A movie gets close to the actor so that you can see him working internally.

Strasberg had been Al's mentor. It wasn't what he taught him about acting, as much as knowing him, working with him, and hearing him express his feelings about acting and work. At the Studio, actors who had to deliver and produce had a place to experiment and expand.

You could do a lot of different roles you wouldn't normally get cast in. By doing them, you could find out more about yourself in relation to your work. Al compared it to his repertory experience in Boston when he was younger. He had gone there specifically for one role, but he had to do several roles as well. He dreaded the other roles.

The irony was, the role I was brought up to do didn't turn out too well, and the roles he thought were wrong for him turned out well. He learned from it that an actor should always keep trying different things.

ME

WHAT AL SAID to me about focusing on the acting, finally got to me. It was 1983 and I had been teaching with the Board of Education for 15 years. I was 52 years old. I figured if I didn't do something drastic to get involved in the Broadway or Hollywood scenes, it would soon be too late. I made the big move and retired from teaching.

An acting student of mine, Mario Jensen, who worked

for the New York City Transit Company, told me about a manager, Irene Kearney, who worked with new people and might be interested in me. I got together with her and she agreed to help me with my acting career. In return I would coach several of her clients in her office.

I had fresh photographs taken and new resumes printed. Irene tried to get me an agent, but nobody was interested. She also sent me to see several casting directors, but nothing came of it.

AL

AL BECAME INTERESTED in doing a remake of the Howard Hawkes movie, *Scarface*, that Paul Muni had starred in back in 1932.

When he was in Los Angeles, he had gone to see the original film at an old theater on Sunset Boulevard. He was very taken with it and mentioned it to Marty Bregman. After Bregman saw this classic on late-night television, he got excited because of Al's passion for the role. He realized immediately what Al could bring to it.

Bregman got Oliver Stone to write a screenplay and Sidney Lumet to direct. Lumet came up with the idea to set the story in present day Miami instead of the 1930s in Chicago and make the character, Tony Montana, an outcast from Castro's Cuba. Because of artistic differences, however, Lumet was replaced by Brian De Palma.

When the production was announced, Irene's son, who was an agent, sent me up for a role in it. I was right for one of the parts and I was sure Al would recommend me if he was told I was being considered.

But history repeated itself. Alexis Gordon was the casting director. She said I wasn't cast because they didn't want to fly actors to Florida where they were shooting. But, then they cast Steven Bauer in the role I was up for. She thought I was more of a Jason Robards type.

The picture was shot on location in Miami. Al was on screen in virtually every scene. He had two accidents on the set. One was getting burned by grabbing an M-14 machine gun that was hot from having fired many rounds. The other was getting his fingers caught in the slamming of a telephone booth door.

One way to bring a sense of danger to film acting, he believed, is to stop being a censor, to let your impulses take over and let the director be the censor.

When Al was about to do a project, he would dream constantly about the character. He continued to stay in his roles 24 hours a day. Once he was able to find the truth of the character, he just couldn't switch it off like other actors did when the scene was over.

If he played a crazy, he'd be crazy all day, not just in the scene. Even an attack dog couldn't scare him while he was doing *Scarface*. He faced it down and made it back off. A tough way to live.

Strasberg used to tell him, "Darling, you know, you have to let it go sometimes."

While acting was hard work for him, he found it both energizing and enervating. He described acting as "childish, responsible, illuminating, joyful, bizarre, diabolical, and exciting."

He referred to Eleanor Duse who said "acting" is a horrible word, but it's an attempt to get at some truth, to show emotions and motivations which are both believable and natural. She's also the one who said the most important thing to learn in acting is how not to act.

Acting also frustrated Al. He realized, as an actor, you're always waiting for someone to offer you a part.

You're not at the helm, you're a component. You would like to be offered projects rather than having to create the whole thing yourself.

The position is a difficult one to be in because what you'd really like is for people to come to you. They did come to Al, but not always with something of interest to him. He wished people would offer him comedies. So, since he didn't create his own projects, he resorted to doing plays.

When an actor starts out, Al observed, there are many plays out there and the producers look for actors to appear in them. When an actor joins a repertory company, he's told what plays and what parts he's going to do. That's how the actor is first oriented. If he becomes successful, it all suddenly changes. People are no longer telling him what to do. They're looking at him and asking him what he wants to do and say. Al missed the luxury of having no choice.

Al was turning down almost everything. Being selective had its advantages, but he didn't want to be selective to the point of not doing anything. He felt as if he had not done enough work over the past few years. He thought he could use more work in the theater, just to experience and learn more.

The selection process with film was different from the stage. Choices were more commercially based. It was something he didn't like, but had to live with. Brilliant scripts, certain to be box-office winners were hard to find. *Serpico* and *Dog Day Afternoon* came in as ideas. That doesn't happen very often.

Personal fame had changed things for Al. He tried to do more things now than he normally would do. Coping with success was an occupation in itself. He constantly found himself dealing with it, living with it, and learning to adjust to it.

It wasn't easy. It affected normal things he would have done. He wished he could ride the subway again. Growing up, nobody ever mentioned the difficulties of being a success. It was only great to be a success.

Many people mistook Al's desire for privacy for snobbism or aloofness. Actually it had more to do with his thinking he might not be an interesting personality. Al was still basically shy.

In a role it was different. Acting transformed him. He wanted to live his life, not think about his image. He didn't want to have to start watching himself all the time. He thought it could be damaging. It could take away the spontaneity. "I'm in this business to do good work," he said, "not to be a star."

ME

IN AN ATTEMPT to de-escalate the capers, which were taking up too much of my time, I started teaching acting classes to young professionals. This time, however, I was working for myself.

I rented space for the classes at the Harlequin Studios on West 47th Street, a popular showbiz hangout in the Broadway area, used for classes, auditions and rehearsals. Through word of mouth, I was able to assemble a nice group of student actors. I directed them in scenes and coached them as I had done with Al.

Ginny and I decided to get back together. I gave up the apartment in the city and moved in with her in Brookfield Center in Connecticut. Dale was 14 years old and needed a fulltime father.

No more ads. No more kinks, no more kooks. That

was the end of the capers. I would put the blinders on.

Ginny gave birth to Jason on August 29, 1983.

I called Al and told him, "I have two sons, just as my little voice had told me 15 years ago."

AL

In the fall, *American Buffalo* was remounted at the Booth Theater on Broadway. Three weeks into the run, James Hayden, a young actor in the play, was found dead in his apartment. He died of a drug overdose. He was a good friend of Al's and Al took it very hard.

Hayden was the fourth death of a friend — Bruce (Cohen) Gregory, Cliffy, John Cazale, and now Jimmy — three of them from drug overdoses. Hayden, ironically, had been playing a young junkie in the play.

Al had to shoot promo footage that afternoon out at his country house, along Palisades Parkway. That same night he had to perform in the play with Hayden's understudy in the role.

A romance developed between Al and actress Kathleen Quinlan who had been outstanding in *I Never Promised You a Rose Garden* in 1977. They started living together.

Once *Scarface* was edited, it was difficult to get an R rating for the picture because of the gore and violence. Many viewers were turned off by it.

The *Village Voice* called Al's performance "studied and mannered." N.Y. critic David Denby called the movie "a sadly overblown B-movie." Said Rex Reed, "When it's over you feel mugged, debased, like you'd eaten a bad clam." Yet Rick Corliss, in *Time*, said, "Pacino creates the freshest characterization in years. There is poetry to his psychosis that makes Tony a creature of rank awe. And the rhythm of that poetry is Pacino's."

Charlie Laughton, who continued to work with Al on everything he did, thought most people didn't get it. He thought Al had given the greatest performance of his career.

There were always two sides to Al, the tragic and the comic. He said of himself, "I'm just a fun-loving depressive."

He needed to have a certain amount of fun, otherwise he would have chosen a different career. He had tried to incorporate a lot of humor in *Scarface*. He felt the movie's intentions were misunderstood. It had been intended to be larger than life and was a metaphor, addressing excess and avarice.

Brian De Palma, the director, deliberately exaggerated everything — the language, the cocaine, the fighting and the shootings. He didn't want to, as Shakespeare said, "hold a mirror up to nature." His vision was to magnify nature, in a more Brechtian way, a more operatic way.

American Buffalo was taken to London, at the Duke of York's Theater, where it was well-received. It was a great boost to Al's spirits.

ME

I CONTINUED to teach acting. I directed a stage play called *It Had To Be You* with my students. We rehearsed it at the Harlequin Studio in mid-town Manhattan and then performed it at a dinner theater in Buffalo, New York.

I met a promoter, Pat Powers, who offered to help me recruit more students. He earned commissions by recommending actors to teachers and photographers. Pat found a studio for me at 250 West 57th Street, where I set up my own acting workshop.

An agent, Steve Carson, who was married to Elizabeth Taylor's daughter, started to find acting jobs for many of my students. One of my students was given a leading role in the Broadway musical *Cats*. When the producers of the popular soap opera *All My Children* couldn't find the right girl to play Julie, one of my student actors was sent up for it and got the job.

Mari Lynn Henry, head of casting at ABC, was impressed. She asked me, "Who are you? You must be good. All your students are getting work."

A potential student once asked me what was my relationship with Al. I told him we had both studied with Herbert Berghof and Charlie Laughton. We had done a lot of scenes together and I coached him. I chose to think I had inspired him.

This kid somehow got to Al and asked him if I had taught him how to act. Al replied we were great friends. He didn't comment on the teaching. It was a fair response because, officially, I had never been his teacher. And I like to think my friendship was more important to him than the training. What a wonderful response. We were "great friends."

One of my acting students, Jodie Harris, and her husband, Alan, liked my work so much, they went into business with me to run the workshop.

Bill Hickey started to send me some students. I heard from one of them that Hickey said I helped a lot of his students. I took the young hopefuls he couldn't reach, the ones that needed extra help.

He said something like, "Ed De Leo gets to them and brings them out. He sends them back to me and they're great. Whatever he's doing, he's doing something right."

What a great man. You can see why everybody loves him.

My students were working, but I was still struggling. I still had no apartment, so I slept at the studio on 57th Street until I could locate a place. Then, I found a terrific apartment on West 96th Street. The living room was enormous and I was able to use it for classes and rehearsals. I stayed there during the week and took the train to Connecticut on the weekends.

One of my students, Victoria Maxwell, informed me her husband, Ron, was going to direct a new movie, *The Pope of Greenwich Village.* Ron had directed *Little Darlings* with Tatum O'Neal and Christy McNichol, *Kidco* (which Victoria was in), and *The Night The Lights Went Out in Georgia* with Christy McNichol, Mark Hamill, and Dennis Quaid. She told me Al Pacino and James Caan were going to star in it.

I figured between Al and Ron, surely I could get a part in it. But could I stand another rejection? Eternally hopeful, I looked into the possibility of getting a role myself. With Al in the movie, he would be there if I needed him as a reference. But Al and Jimmy Caan, I was told, were both asking $4,000,000 a picture and a profit participation, so a deal couldn't be struck.

Instead, Eric Roberts and Mickey Rourke were cast, along with Daryl Hannah.

Victoria arranged for me to see the casting director, Bonnie Timmerman. I found out the story was about a young hustler in Little Italy who was unable to separate himself from his cousin who constantly screwed-up everything.

Ron told Timmerman he liked me and she should give me something juicy; but she offered me the role of a bartender with only one line. Insulted, I wanted to turn it down. A bartender? Me, who played Willie Loman? It was unthinkable. But Ron convinced me it would be good exposure for me... and a screen credit. He really wanted me on the set.

Ron was having trouble controlling Eric Roberts. Eric had a great face and a lot of talent, but Ron felt he was overdoing it, "pushing it" too hard. Aware of my background as a teacher and coach, Ron suggested I coach Eric privately to calm him down. So, I agreed to be Tony the Bartender.

I walked into a minefield. Ron wanted Eric off the picture, and Eric wanted Ron off the picture. Howard Koch, the producer, was forced to choose between the two. Since he had so many of Eric's scenes already in the can, he figured it would be easier to fire Ron than Eric.

Stuart Rosenberg was brought in to replace Ron as director, an unfortunate choice for me. There were two bartender roles in the picture. I was to play the second one, later in the story.

Rosenberg sent his assistant over to me. He said, "No hard feelings, young man (I was over 50), but we're gonna shoot only your hands pouring the drink... because if your face gets on the camera, nobody's gonna watch the stars. They're gonna watch you."

I was flabbergasted. I was acting only as I thought the character would act.

Long ago, when I was studying with Herbert Berghof, I played a bartender in a scene with Joe LaBrese and an actress. I was so involved in the scene, Herbert said afterwards, "You were fantastic. We never watched the other two people."

It was their scene, but I had inadvertently upstaged them. Now the same thing was happening in *The Pope of Greenwich Village*. It was complimentary, but trying for me, all the same.

Herbert had been surprised, even though I had done

what he had taught me. I had done only what a bartender would do, pour the drinks, listen to the music, and react to the other characters. I had felt it a successful scene. I had been beginning to really develop as an actor.

The past repeated itself and I was cut out of *The Pope of Greenwich Village.*

Ron later told me, "They didn't want your face on camera. They were threatened by the way you work and your reactions."

I received screen credit on the picture as Tony the Bartender, but all that was seen on screen was my hands pouring a drink. You never saw my face. I felt sabotaged, primarily because I was a friend of Ron's. Ron told me not to take it personally; all of his allies on the picture were given a rough time.

After the class at Berghof's, back in 1959, when I played the bartender, one of Berghof's favorite students, Olga Bielmeyer, came up to me and said, "Honey, what you have, no acting teacher can teach."

And I said, "Thank you, but Herbert did teach me. He's a good teacher."

Olga said, "You're going to make it in Hollywood because you have star quality. You don't need a teacher."

Some prophecy.

AL

THE MORE SUCCESSFUL Al got, the more difficult it became to maintain that success and, at the same time, maintain his original enthusiasm. It was the work, the craft, the getting out there every day, doing roles that made him stretch, that gave him the strength. He didn't want to lose that.

Yet there was another side to it. As he became more well known, he became more bankable and he could get a picture made. Sometimes the filmmakers wanted him for a reason, while Al wanted to be wanted for what he could do, not because he was bankable. It started to get confusing and sometimes got him involved in projects he shouldn't have taken.

In 1985, director Hugh Hudson sought out Al to star in an historical epic, *Revolution*, being produced by Irwin Winkler. The picture was filmed in England during a period of horrendous weather. It was constantly cold and rainy and it took its toll on the cast, including co-star Nastassja Kinski. Al caught low-grade pneumonia and shooting had to stop for a week while he recuperated. Kathleen Quinlan was not with Al. Their relationship had dissolved.

The critics generally found *Revolution* to be a shambles. It didn't make any sense.

Vincent Canby in the *New York Times* said, "Pacino has never been so intense to such little effect. It's like watching someone walking around in a chicken costume. It's sloppily written, edited and dubbed. Pacino's very first speech in the film is spoken as if he were a ventriloquist. At the climax, when Pacino explains, 'In this country, ain't no one ever gonna treat nobody like a dog in the dirt,' some critics literally screamed with laughter. It's England's answer to 'Heaven's Gate.'"

Other critics found his performance "naturalistic" and "riveting."

His career now in jeopardy, Al financed and filmed a movie of his own based on *The Local Stigmatic*, the play he had performed in 1976, with David Wheeler directing. Most of the people who viewed it didn't understand it, nor could they understand why he did it.

He would continue to edit it over a period of seven

years, pouring hundreds of thousand of dollars into it. He thought it was too raw ever to be released. He sometimes showed it at colleges. He screened it once for a group at the Whitney Museum.

His experiences with *Revolution* and *The Local Stigmatic* made him pull back even more. He was cautious about meeting new people. He remarked that in the old days, when he met somebody, there would be a natural evolution. When two people met, there was either something there or not. They took the time to find out.

Now, he observed, "People just think they know you right away." Fame, he concluded, is not an easy thing to understand unless you've experienced it. Al didn't care for instant intimacy. He needed time to get to know people, whether they were writers, co-workers or friends. When he does make friends — and I can only speak for myself — he remains loyal to them in good times and bad.

Two years passed for Al with no film roles. Two producers from Israel, Menacham Golam and Yorum Globus, who ran a motion picture production and distribution company in Hollywood, offered Al the starring role in an American remake of *Investigation of a Citizen Above Suspicion* and a film version of *American Buffalo.*

Because the idea of portraying the characters in these plays on screen appealed to him so much, Al turned down a number of other offers. Unfortunately, however, Golam and Globus were unsuccessful with their plans and the pictures aborted.

Al and Diane Keaton became very close friends. When she became pregnant it was assumed Al was the father. But she had a miscarriage.

Al disappeared from the public for four years. As he admitted himself, he became his own worst enemy by being overly careful.

Lee Strasberg had once told him, "Dahling, you have to adjust."

But Al found it was not so easy when you were a star. The dangerous thing about success is not being able to take risks. You are type-cast in certain kinds of roles, like tough cops. The powers that be in the motion picture industry do not want you to do anything in which you could possibly fail. As a result, they inhibit your development as an actor. If an actor doesn't take risks, all he's doing is keeping himself afloat.

Al was aware he was not always the first choice for a role. He was a "valuable element," and he made sense to the project, but the director may have wanted him for the wrong reasons.

Certain projects that would not normally get put together, could get put together because of "elements" that are attached — like the star. The public does not always know if the star was the first choice, even when the casting seems strange.

One thing Al did during his four years away from movies was perform in *Julius Caesar*, directed by Stuart Vaughan, at Joe Papp's New York Shakespeare Festival Theater. Martin Sheen and Edward Hermann appeared in it with him. He followed it with *Crystal Clear*, a workshop experiment directed by Phil Young, that soon was abandoned.

ME

DALE GRADUATED from Brookfield High School in the spring of 1987. He was 18 already and almost an adult. In spite of the ups and downs in my life, I felt blessed.

The graduation was a festive ceremony and we had a party afterwards at the house. Jason was four years old. I didn't have a career, but I had a family; and that was an accomplishment! I knew how much Al would have loved to have a family.

Because my student actors were doing such good work and were getting jobs in the theater, on television and in movies, I organized a theater company and called it "Actors Creating Theater." I rehearsed plays in my apartment and we performed them at the American Theater Academy off Times Square.

Tony Andresakis joined me as a partner and we shared the business management, as well as the artistic affairs. I started to direct as well as produce the plays.

We did *Hatful of Rain* in a number of theaters including the Royal Court Theater, with Tony playing the father and me directing.

Finally, we rented a little theater, formerly a church, on West 58th Street. We did productions of plays that had played on or off Broadway, like *Barefoot in the Park*.

Ron Maxwell, original director of *The Pope of Greenwich Village*, came to see our production of *The Last of the Red Hot Lovers*, which starred his wife, Victoria. She was outstanding in it. Ron wanted to re-cast the production, put some money into it and, with me in the cast, do it as a full off-Broadway production. But we never did it.

I rented a couple of rooms in my apartment to actors. It helped them out and provided me with extra money. It created too much traffic, however, and the landlady evicted all of us. I had to sleep at the theater during the week, while I looked for another place.

AL

IN 1988, Al did an on-book reading of a play called *National Anthem* by Denis McIntyre in New Haven. Arvin

Brown directed. It was Al's only work that year.

There were a million reasons why Al delayed making movies for four years. It's rare for a script to come to any star's attention that makes him say, "This film is for me" and he dashes off to shoot it. It takes a long time and much work before any script becomes satisfactory film material. It can take months or years. Another reason Al preferred the theater was that there was always a ready-and-proven script available or he could do a classic.

He had been doing movies for 18 years and acting on the stage for almost 30. He needed to escape, even momentarily. After so many years, he developed a way of coming into and going away from a part, even while he was working on it.

He sometimes felt the need to escape from a role in middle of interpreting it. He learned ways to detach himself. He even gave himself tasks he normally would not do in his personal life, just to get distracted. In earlier years he didn't have that ability.

When he was playing a lawyer in *...And Justice For All*, for example, he was in a real court surrounded by a group of real lawyers discussing a case.

He instinctively jumped in and said, "Let me see that file!"

The lawyers looked at him like he was crazy. That sort of thing wasn't happening very much any more.

While he liked the idea of growing and adapting in the theater by repeating the same character day after day, year after year, he now found the most exciting thing about motion pictures was not having to repeat the same character night after night.

A script called *Sea of Love* was sent to Al by Universal. He consulted with Marty Bregman and they both agreed to turn it down. Universal then asked Marty to produce it. They promised they would fix the script.

Al loved the character of the burned-out cop who faced a mid-life crisis; and certainly could relate to the drinking problem. Harold Becker was signed to direct and Ellen Barkin was cast. Richard Price's revised script appealed to him as a new challenge.

In *Sea of Love*, Al played Frank Keller, a lonely, divorced New York City police detective who got involved with a woman played by Barkin, a sultry, dangerous woman he met through the personal ads.

Once again, Al knew preparation was everything. He observed that many actors avoid preparation because they don't want to leave what they are. They don't want to leave their lives to go and prepare for somebody else's. Al found he had to do it; and when he did get involved, it was rewarding. It became a blend of him and the character he was playing.

In the movie, Al and Barkin really steamed up the screen, but according to people who were there, they weren't so hot on the set.

There was a rumor that mischievous Al would drink coffee and eat a muffin just before a kissing scene, so he'd have crumbs in the corner of his mouth. Ellen Barkin commented that if she were to arrive naked to do a love scene, Al would wear a raincoat.

Al really got into this role. In a scene in which he is drunk and yells at Barkin, he scared her so badly her rings vibrated from her shaking.

In another scene, two hoods recognize Frank as a cop while he is visiting his lover in a shoe shop. He's lied to her that he is a printer. She follows him angrily outside. He flies into a rage about the public's conception of the police.

Al needed to discuss the scene before doing it because it was so complicated. His character never told her he was a cop, and Al thought he deliberately provoked those guys so he'd be found out. On one level he explodes over how cops are treated, but at the same time he's covering his lie.

Sea of Love was given a test screening at a mall in Sherman Oaks. Al warned the others he might attend in disguise. The idea of wearing disguises fascinated Al. He often spoke about how the great Shakespearean actor Edmund Kean ended his life. Kean had been a superstar in his day. Someone said watching him act was like watching bolts of lightning cross the stage.

Al spotted many parallels between Kean and himself. Kean couldn't get work at first. He was short and had dark features. He rose to the top as an actor in London; but, because of a scandal he came to America. When the theater he was to appear in was burned down, he fled to Canada and joined a tribe of Indians. When he came back he wouldn't speak to anyone unless he was in disguise in his Indian attire.

Al enjoyed the experience of putting on glasses and a mustache and blending in. He had gone to a concert once in New York in a disguise. It made him feel free and he was excited by it.

In April of 1989, *Entertainment Tonight* blew his 49th Birthday, saying he was 50. It depressed him.

Sea of Love opened in September and Al got rave reviews. *People Magazine* called him "terrific," "vital," "charming," "funny," "tough," and "touching." The *Village Voice* said, "Pacino is amazing."

This was a new, mature Pacino.

By playing the part now, as opposed to 10 years earlier, he had a closer, more tactile understanding of the character. He understood the situation in which his character was involved. He started to look at new parts that might have excited him five years earlier, but now other values were starting to excite him. To Al, it came down to what he wanted to address at this point in his life — the things he started to find relevant.

Al made some really funny statements that were also very profound. He said, "I probably got into acting so I wouldn't have to think. The reason I acted was for a relief from thinking."

Another time he said he wished, in some ways, the government would force him to make a movie once a year. "There would be a sort of regularity, a kind of consistency in the output so that your movies don't become blown all out of proportion."

He observed simple movies become epic events if you make them only every few years. He decided not to let so much time lapse between them in the future.

ME AND AL

1989 WAS A year of crisis. Tony and I didn't see eye to eye on anything, so I pulled out of Actors Creating Theater. Tony continued with it.

At the same time, trouble was brewing in Connecticut. Ginny was being harassed by Social Services after several complaints about the condition of the house. She was obsessed by collecting things and would never throw anything away. The house was piled to the rafters with junk.

Social Services were also on her case for not taking proper care of our child. They decided to inspect the premises and assigned a social worker to Ginny. I knew Ginny would not take this gracefully, so I resolved to move them out before it got too complicated.

I had an offer to teach acting at a dramatic workshop called Total Entertainment, in Bayonne, New Jersey. It was based in a store that had been converted into a school. I took a train to Jersey to meet with the director and I got the job.

Ginny and I packed our belongings and moved to New Jersey with little Jason, who was five. Dale stayed behind at the house we had been renting in Brookfield. He paid the rent from a trust set up by Ginny's parents.

We took an efficiency apartment at a welfare hotel in Jersey City, which was not too far from Bayonne. I commuted to the workshop by bus. In a very short time, we were kicked out of the apartment because again Ginny was reverting to a pack rat. I tried to talk the manager into letting us stay, but I failed. We had to move again.

When we were departing from the hotel, there were so many pieces of luggage, I couldn't carry them all in one trip. I told everybody, "Please, don't let anybody touch my black bag."

"Nobody'll touch the goddamn bag," Ginny said.

She left it alone, but didn't keep her eye on it. When I went back upstairs for more boxes, somebody stole it. I was furious. It held all my tapes and scripts.

I pointed to the mound of luggage and boxes and said to Ginny, "You can have it all, everything, just give me my son." Of course, she refused.

Using most of my pay check as the deposit, I took a single room at a hotel in Bayonne, closer to the workshop. It cost us $100 a day. There was just enough money left over for food. Ginny stayed at the hotel with Jason while I taught my classes. Daily, as soon as I got home, she started to fight with me. She was sorry she had agreed to live with me again. She wanted to pack up and leave.

When I arrived home one day, I was arrested. Ginny had reported me to the police for domestic abuse. When the case went to court, she admitted to the judge she was lying. I couldn't understand her behavior any more. Something had to change.

Dale called to say he wanted to move to Denver. He planned to work in a ski shop with a friend and to look around for a college to attend, but he needed money for the trip. I wanted to help him, but I was broke.

One day I met a young entrepreneur, Ron Galuccio, in a pizza restaurant. When I told him about my unproduced screenplay, he suggested he might be able to raise financing for it. He knew of my financial predicament and, knowing about my friendship with Al, insisted on calling him to help me. I just couldn't bring myself to do it myself. Al had helped me out so many times before.

When Ron called him, Al told him I should just call him myself. I did. I told Al I had lost everything, I had been forced to move into a welfare hotel, I was teaching classes in Bayonne, New Jersey, and Ginny was miserable.

He wanted to know how he could help me. I told him if I had the money, I would move to California to look for work. There were more acting opportunities in films and television in Los Angeles than in New York. With so many television shows being produced, so many new cable networks doing movies in Hollywood, maybe that's where I should be. I would also be closer to Dale.

Al said he thought it would be a good idea. He might be able get me work if I went there. I told him I'd like that. He said to come to New York to pick up the money. It was enough to cover our trip, help Dale with his, and have some left over to cover our expenses until I found work.

Ginny was opposed to going to the Coast, but went along with the plan, since she had no other options, and no place to return to in Connecticut.

Jason was now six years old. On the refrigerator, Ginny had pasted a picture of him holding a can of Coke. My voice told me he would be doing commercials in Hollywood. Wow! I had never thought of that. He was very cute and animated. He would probably do well.

In December, we packed up and flew out to California. We took a room in a hotel in Hollywood on La Brea and Sunset and started looking for an apartment.

Ginny had a friend, Barbara Cox, who had five children and was brought to Hollywood by Pat Power to get them work in television. He was managing them. Ginny moved in with Barbara to baby-sit her girls.

Jason and I shared an apartment with Pat's nephew, Michael Cacciotti, on Hobart and Third. Pat's real name was also Cacciotti, but he used "Powers" as a professional name. He was still a promoter.

Al had told me to see an agent, Cary Wood, at the William Morris Agency, one of the top three talent agencies in the world. When I met with Wood at his office on El Camino Drive in Beverly Hills, he said Al should have known not to send me to him. He explained he did motion picture packaging. He was not representing new actor-clients.

"I guess Al isn't aware of that," I told him, "or he'd never have arranged this."

I called Al's home to tell him what had happened. Perhaps he could set me up with another agent. Penny, Charlie's wife, answered the phone, and it took me by surprise. I hesitated. She said, "Ed? This is Penny. Don't you remember me?"

"Of course, I do. How are you?"

We hadn't spoken in years. She wanted to know why I was calling their number. I explained I had lost Al's other number. I stuck my foot in it by telling her Al had financed my trip to California. I didn't say how much he had given me. For some reason, she and Charlie didn't approve of

Al's helping me. They were his family now, and perhaps I was a threat of some kind.

The next day, I called Al's secretary, Marissa. She told me Penny complained because Al gave me money to go to California, saying he was helping me get acting work but not them.

When I was able to reach Al, I thanked him for his help in making the move. I mentioned that all my acting demo tapes had been stolen in New Jersey.

"The agents and casting directors in Hollywood all want to see your work on tape. It's more important now than pictures and resumes."

"You oughta have new tapes made anyhow," Al said. "After all, you're a little older now and you should have something more representative."

"You're right," I said. "I'll rehearse some new scenes and put them on tape."

Al offered to pay for them, but I told him, "I've got enough money to pay for a video. Don't worry."

He was always very giving and I didn't want to take advantage. "I think I'll do a scene from *Death of a Salesman.*

He said, "You're a perfect Willy Loman now."

"God, when I met you, I was perfect for Biff. Now I'm Willy. So many years have gone by."

But now I was exactly like Biff, always drifting.

Al told me he had a daughter, Julie-Marie. "She was born on October 16, Ed. Your birthday."

He never mentioned the mother of the child. Al, of course, was not married. The baby was the result of a brief love affair. Al said he loved Julie-Marie and he swore he would always be there for her.

He said to me, "Boy, you're lucky, you've got two sons. That's what I'd like. I miss not having a son."

I mentioned the voice in my head, that it had told me

I would have two sons. I asked him if he remembered the time on the street corner, when the voice told me he was going to become a big star. He didn't remember.

Victoria Maxwell moved to Los Angeles to seek work as an actress. She informed me she and Ron were divorced. Because she was a fine actress, I asked her if she would like to act in a couple of scenes with me for a demo tape. We did a scene together from *Death of a Salesman*; one from *Middle of the Night*, an original script Victoria had written; and a scene from the teleplay, *Verna: USO Girl*, which her husband, Ron Maxwell had directed on television.

I read in the *Hollywood Reporter* that Herbert Berghof had passed on. It made me sad. Herbert was such an important part of my life. If not for him, I would never have met Al. Al may never have become a star. Even though Al was not that enthralled with Berghof as a teacher, his being there resulted in his working with Charlie. This, to Al, was the best thing that ever happened to him. Uta Hagen continued to operate the HB Studio and Herbert's daughter was on the staff.

To keep busy, Al did a workshop production of the play, *Chinese Coffee*, by Ira Lewis, directed by Jack Gelber. Then, he let Warren Beatty talk him into appearing in the movie *Dick Tracy*.

It was a wise decision. Al, in my opinion, was the best one in the movie. He played Big Boy Caprice and was hilarious. His comedic roots shone through. His early flair for doing comedy routines paid off.

Because Al was now being acclaimed for his comedy, I thought he might be interested in doing my screenplay. When I told him about it, he asked me to send it to him. After he read it, he told me he liked it. My heart started to race. I thought for sure I was going to have a deal. But he added that it wasn't for him.

"But it is, Al," I said.

"It's a little too heavy."

"Too heavy? You've done so many heavy, dramatic parts." I wanted to know why he found it too heavy.

He said, "Well, for instance, you could make it a little lighter with the mother and the son."

That's what David Sheldon and other readers had told me. I said, "You're right. There's too much down-and-out stuff, money, alimony. It should be more up."

"Yeah, you need more humor."

"That's so ironic. I've been told I am very funny, by so many people."

He said, "You weren't funny here, Ed."

I knew he was right. I knew I wasn't being true to myself. The story needed more humor, especially in the scenes with the mother. I started to rewrite it in an attempt to lighten it up.

AL

THE GODFATHER, PART III completed a full circle for Al. He played Michael Corleone who was now in his 60s. His salary was $8,000,000.

Off screen, his off-again-on-again relationship with Diane Keaton was rekindled. He was even seriously contemplating getting married. He thought perhaps, after all, he could be a husband as well as a father . Why not? But he waffled. Al and Diane had a fight over Al's continuing refusal to make a commitment.

Al was questioned by the press about what it was like to work with a lover. He responded he preferred not to. He explained it was wonderful when it worked, but sometimes things that happened between them in their day-to-day life could affect their working life. By being confined together in close quarters, the least little thing might upset one of the partners.

He said people think that living together enables you to infuse personal things into the work, but it isn't true. He said it's more of an interference than an asset. In order to work, you need to be objective and use your imagination; and, he added, "you need a little peace."

Working together on *Godfather, Part III*, was a bitter-sweet experience for Al and Diane. It was the end of the line for them.

During shooting, Al's grandmother, Kate, died. Diane flew to New York with him for the funeral.

The production was falling behind schedule. Al sensed it was a different Francis Coppola from the man who did the first *Godfather*. Coppola was still mourning the tragic death of his son. Winona Ryder got sick and had to drop out. Coppola replaced her with his daughter, Sofia. Insiders were upset by it. Al felt the strain. Sofia may have been too inexperienced.

Alexander Walker, leading London critic described Al's acting as a "seamless portrait of a man being inwardly devoured by something more fearful than the diabetic stroke that fells him, frighteningly, at a crucial part in the story... one of the finest pieces of acting ever seen in American cinema." Critics were generally cruel about Sofia Coppola's performance.

Al didn't get nominated for an Academy award for *Godfather*. Instead, surprisingly, he got nominated as Best Supporting Actor for his role in *Dick Tracy*. This was his 6th Academy Award nomination. Joe Pesci won for *Goodfellas*.

Al's inevitable 50th birthday arrived in April. He started to become more philosophical about his acting career. He said when you don't make many movies, and he never did, each one becomes overly important.

"The ups are too up and the downs are too down, because there's too much riding on them psychologically." He found himself coming back to reality. Five years earlier, it would have been unthinkable for him to make three movies in a row as he had just done.

Al never bragged about his performances. In fact, he was always hard on himself. He was always afraid if his reviews were negative he would agree with them. He finally realized it's OK to make lots of films, and not worry about each one being a hit. His life did not depend on it. He became less afraid of making a movie and taking a chance. If he failed in a role it wouldn't be the end of the world.

ME

IN DECEMBER 1990, after I made a few changes in my screenplay, I called Arthur Hiller at the Raleigh Studios in Hollywood and asked him if he would be interested in reading it. Maybe my face on the cutting room floor was not in vain. Hiller was a real live director who knew me. He was gracious and agreed to read it.

Hiller's said, "I found the premise intriguing, but I wasn't attracted to the character and situations enough to feel it would make a compelling movie. I wish you well with it in other directions, and have your photo in my Friends File for future reference."

AL

AL DID STAGED readings of Salome by Oscar Wilde at the Circle in the Square, directed by Arvin Brown. Molly

Ringwald was in the cast with him.

In 1991, he signed to star in *Frankie and Johnny* with Michelle Pfeiffer, directed by Garry Marshall. An offbeat love story, it was based on a play, *Frankie and Johnny in the Clair de Lune*, by Terrence McNally, who also wrote the screenplay. It was for Paramount Pictures.

Since Al was going to play a short-order cook, the first thing he wanted to find out was what a short order cook did. He had a few actor-friends who had worked as short order cooks and they helped him with his research. He went to a restaurant and hung around to pick up some atmosphere and behavior.

During rehearsals, to loosen Al up, Michelle Pfeiffer would try to act immature and giggle. She would say things to him to make him laugh before doing a love scene. Al would roll over laughing.

Michelle noticed the difference in Al since they acted together in *Scarface*. He seemed to be a happier person. He didn't let his roles mix in with his personal life any more.

There was a party for *Frankie and Johnny* at the Roxbury, one of Hollywood's fashionable niteries on the Sunset Strip. I hadn't seen Al since I moved to Los Angeles, so I thought it would be a good opportunity for us to get together.

I missed meeting Michelle because she had already left. Al and I sat at a table together, away from the rest of the crowd, and brought each other up to date. He reminded me that acting in movies is grueling work. He didn't enjoy having to report to make-up calls at 5:00 in the morning. It shouldn't be necessary to have such long hours.

One of my acting students, Con Horgan, was a waiter at the Roxbury and was impressed to see me sitting alone with Al Pacino.

Al wasn't sure how to label *Frankie and Johnny*. Was it

a drama? Was it a comedy? Was it a comedy-drama? Even in drama, Al felt, you tried to find as much comedy as you could. It made drama more palatable, easier to take.

Frankie and Johnny was, of course, a love story. Al knew love was different for everyone. It had a lot to do with where you were in your life and what's happened to you. What happened in *Frankie and Johnny* was not something he had experienced himself, but he understood it. People sometimes recognize somebody else's need and that's what they fall in love with. Then, once they do, the question is, how long will it last? There are so many phases to love.

Al started to feel burned out, so tired he couldn't possibly do another movie, getting so old. Yet he had boundless energy.

ME

PAT POWER told me his brother, Tony Cacciotti, was producing a new sitcom for CBS called *City*, starring his wife, Valerie Harper. He and Paul Haggis were the executive producers. Haggis had created some big shows like *Mork and Mindy*, and had written shows like *L.A. Law* and *Thirtysomething*.

Tony was receptive to my call and invited me over. He looked to be in his 30s, attractive and muscular. He obviously worked out. I did a monologue for him and he liked it. He wanted to know a little more about me. We chatted about New York and I explained how I had met his brother, Pat. Finally, he said he was going to take a chance and use me, in the one small role that was open in the first episode. If I was any good, he would give me a running part.

I was in the main office scene. It was a bull pen, like the office in *Murphy Brown*, with people sitting at desks and others walking in and out. I was thrilled to meet and work with Valerie Harper who had achieved so much fame on *The Mary Tyler Moore Show*, later starring in the *Rhoda* series. Not only is she a fantastic actress, but she's also a wonderful person.

Also in the cast was Todd Susman, a big television star who had starred in the Neil Simon movie, *The Star-Spangled Girl.* I found out Todd got his first break in Hollywood when my friend, David Sheldon, directed him in the West Coast premiere of Murray Schisgal's stage play, *Jimmy Shine.* He was signed up by the William Morris Agency as "the next Dustin Hoffman."

After the first show, Tony said to me, "Kid, you know, you're pretty good. We're gonna start measuring you for the series."

They were going to fit me for suits. That meant I had a running role. I was ecstatic!

With a role in a television series, I felt I had arrived. I put Jason in a private school I had to pay for every week. My salary for the role was minimal, so it was still a struggle.

Tony knew I was down on my luck and asked me, "Hey, kid, you have enough money to eat?" I was in my 50s and he was calling me "kid."

I told him I was all right, but he insisted on giving me extra money.

They measured me for 15 suits. Tony said, "We're gonna give you many different looks." In the dressing room, he directed the hairdresser to create an eccentric character with crazy hair styles.

On the set one day, Valerie, out of the clear, blue sky, said, "There's only one performer in this show I fear. He's the biggest scene stealer in the world." Everybody laughed. "Once he comes on screen, nobody watches anybody else."

Did she mean that I had star quality? She wasn't jealous. She didn't have to be, she was so great herself. She would laugh and say, "There's only one person in the scene — Ed De Leo." She was really cute the way she said it, but I trembled, fearing the bartender syndrome and getting axed.

Pat called me from New York, "Ed, you're fabulous."

I had only a few lines here and there, but when I was on, I was totally involved in what I was doing. When I was busy at my desk, the other characters would talk to, and react to me.

I saw some of the daily rushes and was amazed. The man I saw on the screen reminded me of Charles Laughton, the actor. But it was my face up there. I couldn't believe it. I came alive on screen simply by being totally involved with the action, using objects, doing all the things Herbert Berghof, Lee Grant and other great teachers had taught me. Now I was doing it on national television!

When I told Tony how funny Valerie had been when she talked about me, he told me flat out what she had been trying to say. I said, "I thought she was kidding."

"Are you trying to steal Valerie's thunder?"

"No, no," I assured Tony, "She's only kidding. She likes what I'm doing."

But that wasn't the case. The producers and writers gave me less and less to do.

Still, I worked for the full 15 episodes. I loved the show, and working on it with Valerie, but it wasn't picked up by the network for the next season.

Again, I was out of work and walking the streets. I scouted around for some teaching work. I looked up Madame Oleska who was still running her acting school, Theater of Arts. She had moved to Wilshire Boulevard in Hollywood. I taught acting for her and did some directing.

To conserve our funds, since Ginny was not living with us, I moved with Jason into a back room in Madame Oleska's theater, using it as temporary living quarters. After saving a little money, I rented an apartment in West Hollywood on Fairfax, off Santa Monica Boulevard.

I stayed in touch with Al. He asked me how I liked L.A. I told him I liked the climate, but not the intense hot season. He wanted to know how Ginny and Jason were doing. I told him Ginny wanted to go back to New York, but Jason liked California. He wanted to work in television, maybe do some commercials, but he needed pictures. I couldn't afford them. Al sent Jason a check to pay for pictures and resumes.

I began taking Jason around to agents who represented children. An agent agreed to work for him on a trial basis. To her amazement, the first time out, he was cast in a Krylon Paint commercial.

Bob Yuker, a former sports hero, who was in Mr. Belvedere, was in it. The producers had been conducting an extensive search for the kid. Jason had everybody laughing at the audition and was given the part.

AL

AL HAD PERFORMED Ricky Roma in *Glengarry Glenn Ross* on Broadway. It was now going to be produced as a movie for New Line Cinema.

Cameras rolled in the fall 1991 with Alec Baldwin, Ed Harris, Jack Lemmon, Kevin Spacey and Alan Arkin also in the cast. David Mamet wrote the screenplay, adapted from his play which had won a Pulitzer Prize. Al played a sleazy, fast-talking real estate salesman with a pinky ring.

Al wasn't sure how the film would be received, since it

didn't have the usual sex and violence.

When Al's daughter, Julie-Marie, was three, I asked him what she would like for her birthday. He said she liked comic books; so I sent her a nice set. Al bought her a piano for $25,000 dollars. He said he could never afford to do those kinds of things in the early days.

Al was still living in Sneden's Landing, just outside the city. He considered buying a farm so Julie-Marie could have a horse. He went to see her constantly. He took her to the movies, Central Park and Playland. He showed off her paintings, photographs and toys in his office in Manhattan. She had a room in his house for when she was with him.

Having a daughter made him see things differently. It was a major consideration. He couldn't "take that turn at 80 miles an hour any more." Since Julie-Marie lived with her mother, not with him, it was difficult. After six or seven days without seeing her, the pangs started and he had to see her. He needed to be close to her.

Whenever a role was offered to him, he would ask himself, "What would my daughter think of this?"

Al started to date Lyndall Hobbs, a tall, slim blonde from Australia. They had met a long time ago then bumped into each other again. She had been a television fashion reporter in London and became a film director. She directed Back to the Beach in 1987 with Annette Funicello and Frankie Avalon. She and her young daughter moved to Manhattan to be closer to Al.

Al was asked to star in *Scent of a Woman* for Universal Pictures, directed by Martin Brest. He played a blind, bitter army veteran who agreed to go on an outing in New York City with a teenage boy, a scholarship student, who had been paid to watch over him for the weekend. In it he displayed great authority as an actor. His famous "Oooh-Haaah!" was imitated all over the world.

He had played blind characters before, but not in a movie. At first, they were thinking about putting things over his eyes, but he knew it wouldn't work. He wanted to use his own initiative. There were films he could get and books he could read, but he knew unless you are really blind, you never fully understand it.

He would take a scene and act it out in the dark. He would think about what it was like for a blind person to enter a room, how they would do basic things.

He didn't think the blind were different from everyone else. Some could cope and some couldn't. Just like in life. While blind people seemed to depend more on emotion and their senses were keener, they were still the same kind of people. He met with people from the Associated Blind and the Lighthouse, two of New York's best-known organizations that work with the blind.

Bonny Graham, media manager for Lighthouse, said, "What impressed me most about Al was his attention to detail. He was always eager to hear our advice and suggestions and he was obviously giving tremendous thought about how to render a realistic portrayal of a blind person."

Al built his role around the testimony of people who took him through the whole story, from rage and self-pity, to helplessness, to bitterness, to self-acceptance and resignation. And back.

He found the role to be like the character in *The Loneliness of the Long Distance Runner*, the guy who almost reaches the famous brass ring, who almost makes it, but doesn't go on. He had talent, he found the right path, he was in the military, and he was a natural leader; but he had an impulse to blow it all and he let it influence him. He became a could-have-been.

Al created a multi-leveled characterization. His failure with women was at the root of his misery. He had a hurt "at the deep core of his soul." He danced a mean tango with passion and finesse, he raced in a wild car-spree, he barked out orders like a warrior, and he gave a speech at the end about morals and manners. But the role was also that of a man preparing for suicide.

In February of 1993, Al was honored by the American Museum of the Moving Image. A gala charity event was thrown in the grand ballroom of the Waldorf Astoria in Manhattan.

Seven hundred celebrities attended, including Alan Arkin, Lauren Bacall, Debra Winger, Kevin Spacey, Tony Roberts, Christopher Reeve, Tony Randall, Jack Klugman, Marthe Keller, John Leguizamo and Carly Simon. They showed clips from Al's films. Speakers honoring him included Ron Silver, Sidney Lumet, Brian De Palma, Garry Marshall, Ellen Barkin, Alan Arkin, and Alec Baldwin.

Scent of a Woman opened in March to great reviews for Al, and there was no doubt in anyone's mind he would be nominated for an Academy Award.

Since he continued to go back and forth between the stage and film, Al was still being asked to compare the two. He said the difference between acting in the theater and in movies was that in motion pictures you were an acrobat on the wire but there was a safety net, and in the theater there wasn't a net at all. Consequently, your whole being was wired up a different way. It was hard to act with the concentration you have in the theater in a movie where there are so many disruptions, breaks, physical problems, and where everything is so drawn out.

"You can't beat a long, uninterrupted period of performing on stage."

Again going back to the stage, Al performed both *Chinese Coffee* and *Salome* at Rich Forum at the Stamford, Connecticut Center for the Arts, with Christopher Reeve.

The two one-act plays were moved to the Circle in the Square in New York, to help the theater raise funds.

The critics liked him in *Chinese Coffee* but berated him for the other. He could never get good reviews for material with "thee" and "thou" in the dialogue.

David Richard in the *New York Times* said, "Did I say that Mr. Pacino's two performances have nothing in common? I take it back. In both roles the actor demonstrates an uncanny ability to communicate the gathering tension in characters who, to behold them, appear merely discombobulated or spent. He's a master of the sneak attack, and you don't want to be looking elsewhere when he strikes."

ME

GINNY DECIDED to move back in with us; but in the interim, Jason had caught the acting bug. Doing the commercial whetted his appetite. Submitting his photos and resumes paid off. He got cast in the award-winning Richard Marx video, Hazards. They needed a kid with a sad look who resembled Marx. Robert Conrad and Jennifer O'Neil were in it.

Jennifer O'Neil was doing a movie, *Invasion of Privacy*, and she recommended Jason. He got cast in the part of Robby Benson as a boy. Then he did a Buick commercial. After that, a Cheer commercial. I, of course, coached him. I also sent him to a speech teacher, James Weldon. At age 13, he had an agent, a manager, and, of course, a live-in coach.

Ginny didn't like Jason's being in show business. She hated it. She was afraid he'd wind up just like his father. God forbid.

While Ginny was standing on a street corner, she got hit by a car. She flew up in the air and came down on her butt. It sounds comical, but it really happened. She didn't get hurt, but the car got dented.

The driver gave her his name and address and his license number. Ginny threatened to use the insurance money to get away from me. Unfortunately, the man who hit her was unemployed and had no insurance. My phone calls cost us more than the man could afford to pay us.

It had been six years since Al suggested I move to California. Ginny said, "If he was your friend, he would have recommended you for a few movies. If he knows how good you are, why are we hurting out here, struggling so hard? Can't he push you more?"

I, of course, defended him. "He's doing what he can. You can't just stick somebody in a part. The director has to want you. Everybody in Hollywood — the stars, the writers, the producers — everybody has a cadre of friends who want to be cast in their movies. At one point, they have to draw the line. What's Al going to say to his people? 'I refuse to do *Godfather IV* unless you use Ed De Leo?' I mean, let's get real."

Ginny hated the climate in California and the phoniness of Hollywood. She wanted to go back to New York. She stayed away from the apartment for long stretches at a time, always returning with thrift shop gems to add to the clutter. None of this bothered Jason. He loved his parents, and this was his home.

Victoria Maxwell told me her ex-husband, Ron, was going to be directing a two-part mini-series for Turner Broadcasting, based on a Pulitzer Prize winning book, *Killer Angels* by Michael Shaara, for which he had written a screenplay.

Since Victoria had originally read the book and helped Ron option it, she was certain both she and I could get good roles in the movie. The producers were Robert

Rehme and Mace Neufeld who had produced many motion pictures such as *The Hunt for Red October.*

Ron had always been impressed with my acting and arranged for me to read for Joy Todd, the casting director. I was cast in a role as the Town Mayor and I would have a scene with Sam Elliott. My son Jason was also invited to read and was cast in the production.

I was ecstatic. I was going to appear in an "event movie" with a large group of wonderful actors — Tom Berenger, Jeff Daniels, Martin Sheen, Sam Elliott, Maxwell Caulfield, Kevin Conway, C. Thomas Howell, Richard Jordan, Royce D. Appelgate, John Diehl, Patrick Gorman, Cooper Huckabee, James Lancaster, Brian Mallon, Andrew Prine, Stephen Lang, Richard Anderson, Bo Brinkman, Kieran Muroney, George Lazenby, Vee Gentile, Dwier Brown, and Buck Taylor. Good company.

The title of the mini-series was changed to *Gettysburg.* The production was an awesome dramatization of the events leading up to the most famous battle of the Civil War. The movie was filmed on the battlefields of the Gettysburg National Military Park with thousands of extras and huge battle scenes.

The entire movie was six hours long, but was cut down to four hours for a two-part airing on TNT. As my fortune would have it, my scene was cut out of the two-part television version, but appeared in a six-hour home video version. In the editing, my role was changed to an irate citizen. This version was also aired on TNT.

AL

AL WAS CAST in *Carlito's Way* as a savvy Puerto Rican gangster who finishes a five-year jail term and tries to turn over a new leaf. Like Michael Corleone, just when he thinks he's out, they pull him back in. His loyalty to his sleazy lawyer, played by Sean Penn, and his failure to accept the fact that "the street" has changed, bring him down.

Carlito's Way was directed by Brian de Palma, who had directed him in *Scarface*. Also starring were Penelope Ann Miller and John Leguizamo.

Penelope Ann Miller created a big buzz by telling the press she had a romance with Al. She said, "It's not a secret and I'm not ashamed of it. Al is a very passionate person, and he brought out a certain womanliness, a sexuality, a passion in me. I think I always knew I had it in me, but he brought out a real fire."

The story broke in the newspapers and tabloids.

Al's next picture was *Two Bits*, produced by Arthur Cohn and directed by James Foley. Child actor, Jerry Barone, and Mary Elizabeth Mastrantonio also starred in the picture. It was a nostalgic depression-era memoir about growing up on the streets of South Philadelphia in 1933. Al played a grizzled and rumpled old man sitting in an overgrown garden, giving advice to a 12-year-old kid.

He finally won the Academy Award as Best Actor for *Scent of a Woman*. He reached the summit!

He did an interview with Barbara Walters. Aware that Al is a very private person, Walters tried to probe deeper and get some insight into what made him tick.

She asked him, "Do you know who you are?"

He replied something like, "Of course I don't. That's why I'm an actor."

I was stunned by the depth of his answer. He summed it up so well. Luigi Pirandello had written a play called *Six Characters in Search of an Author*. In contrast, we actors are wandering souls in search of characters. We're not valid unless we're playing roles.

Al told me he had 10 pictures lined up. There was talk about his doing *The Ruth Etting Story* with Winona Ryder. He was looking forward to doing Oliver Stone's *Noriega*, but the picture fell apart over budget. There were also discussions between Al and Warner Brothers to play Pablo Picasso with James Ivory directing. He bought the rights to *American Buffalo* so it could be made into a movie.

Al and Lyndall Hobbs lived together and Lyndall adopted a baby boy. Al could finally play father to a son. Now in his 50s, he said "It's never too late to raise a family."

Will he ever get married? Al feels marriage is a state of mind, not a contract. In thinking about the law and marriage, he once asked, "How did the cops get in on it?" Marriage to Al was a matter of commitment, an emotional thing. He knew what that feeling was, and he didn't rule out marriage as an option.

A childhood friend of Al's, Ken Lipper, gave Al a screenplay he had written, called *City Hall*. Ken, who had also grown up in the Bronx, told Al he was producing the picture with Ed Pressman and he had Al in mind to play the role of the fictional New York City Mayor John Pappas.

Al and Ken hadn't seen each other since they were 15; though they did stay in touch from time to time over the years. Lipper, a former deputy mayor of New York City and a Harvard Law School graduate, was the founder of Lipper & Company, an investment management firm that manages over three-and-a-half billion dollars in assets.

Al read the script and agreed to star in the movie. Lipper and Pressman were producing the movie for Rob Reiner's company, Castle Rock, which is now owned by Ted Turner. Lipper's screenplay, which he started writing in 1989 on weekends, was rewritten by Paul Schrader, Nick Pileggi, and Bo Goldman (who wrote *Scent of a Woman*).

With its New York City setting, *City Hall* was full of

good roles for actors with my background. Al sent me to the director, Harold Becker, for an audition. Becker had directed Al in *Sea of Love.*

I gave a heartfelt reading and seemed to impress everyone, but I was offered only a small role that involved one day's work. I told the casting director I wished there was something bigger, even a one-week role. Unfortunately, I didn't get cast at all, even for the one-day part. They wanted somebody in his 40s.

I found out later that nobody on Al's "friends list" was cast in the film. I really wanted to be in that picture because one of my former teachers, Martin Landau was going to be in it. Between Al and Martin, I figured I could get some good exposure.

John Cusack, Bridget Fonda, Danny Aiello (another Bronx classmate of Al's), David Paymer and Anthony Franciosa were cast to co-star with Al. The production cost $50 million and the film was scheduled to open in the winter of 1995-96.

Al went right back to work starring in *Heat*, with Robert De Niro, for Warner Brothers, directed by Michael Mann. Al was cast as an obsessed cop, De Niro a smart killer who eluded him. Pacino and De Niro had wanted to do a picture together for a long time, ever since they co-starred in *The Godfather Part II*, but had no scenes together.

Between acting assignments in studio pictures, Al and his actor-friend Michael Hadge, who had performed as an actor in *The Local Stigmatic*, produced a movie called *Looking For Richard*, which combined scenes from Shakespeare's *Richard III* and documentary footage of how people are affected by Shakespeare's words, including everyone from classical actors such as John Gielgud to street kids in New York.

Al financed the film himself, and Fox Searchlight Pictures acquired worldwide distribution rights. The idea of the film was Al's creation and he directed it. He cast Winona Ryder, Kevin Spacey, Alec Baldwin, Harris Yulin, Estelle Parsons and Aidan Quinn. Actors like James Earl Jones, Rosemary Harris, Kevin Kline and Derek Jacobi, as well as truck drivers and hardhats, give their thoughts about Shakespeare.

Two Bits, which he shot two years earlier, had its world premiere on October 12 at the Chicago Film Festival. The distributor, Miramax, had retitled it *A Day to Remember*, but went back to the original title.

The review in *Variety* said it "has the impact of a sweet little short story or one-act play rather than a fleshed-out drama." and "There's nothing wrong with Pacino's almost entirely sedentary, underplayed turn as the benign, philosophical old codger who's ready to call it a life, but there is an element of showboating about it, and it's the sort of performance any number of talented character actors could have given."

Other reviewers felt quite differently. Guy Flatley in *Cosmopolitan* said, "Al Pacino is pure perfection! He gives a sweet and flamboyant performance." Sheila Benson in *Cinemania* said, "A very nice surprise! Al Pacino has erased that line between acting and essence. This is a delicate etching done with the most tender reserves of humor and irony."

Jack Mathews in the *Los Angeles Times* found *Two Bits* to be a "slight but earnestly told tale." Regarding Al's performance, Mathews said he "brings enormous sympathy to a man sizing up his life on what he is certain is the day it will end." But Susan Granger on *American Movie Classics* topped them all, saying, "Al Pacino gives a passionate Oscar-contending performance."

WHO IS ED DE LEO?

WHERE DID I go off? Did I lose it? I thought I had something special as an actor. I think I've always been true to what I wanted to do. Shakespeare said, "This above all, to thine own self be true."

I was always a natural actor, but I was also a natural teacher. I coached many young people in New York. I helped them get soaps (some, with three-year contracts), and television series, and motion pictures. I liked seeing them make it. I liked the teaching, but I didn't really want to be a teacher. I wanted to be an actor.

I taught acting, not because I was a bad, unsuccessful actor. In fact, a friend Roger Morgan said to me, "Remember when we were all having trouble with our scenes and you got up and showed us how to do it? We were all amazed at what a good actor you were."

If you are that good and that natural, and have early applause and early acceptance and people are telling you how good you are, you've kind of made it in your own way. You aren't always striving to achieve. In a way, you're already satisfied you've arrived.

While Al only had tunnel vision, I had a number of different things I was very good at. Lee Grant had said in one of her classes, "There are people who make it with tunnel vision. There are other people who take the wide, wide way. They get there, and have so much more to offer the world."

There are people who just want one thing and have blinders on, like a horse. But there are people without blinders, and they, they become richer in the long run.

Those people, when they do make it, have such a broader experience. They can bring many more sides to their characters, eventually.

Why wasn't I more successful in acting? Perhaps underneath it all, I didn't really want to be an actor as much as I wanted to be a teacher. They say people do what they really want to do, regardless of what they dream about. I wanted to work in Special Education when I did it. When I coached acting, it was because I wanted to do it. I didn't have blinders on, but perhaps I didn't want to.

Ginny, has had serious emotional problems and I feel really sorry for her. It would be too easy for me to say she sidetracked me. She got what she wanted, and I got what I wanted. As they say, be careful about what you want, you might get it.

Ginny thinks, as do my sisters Gloria and Joan, I pursued a career that was not worth it. Maybe they're right. I did have artistic satisfaction whenever I performed, even when I did the capers. But I also liked to teach acting.

Like Mr. Chips, I've taught thousands of students over the years. Perhaps it is the art of acting I love, whether it's me doing it or somebody else. I took pride in the people I taught, not only when they went on to fame and fortune, but when they were good in class. I also love the beauty of acting when I see it well done on the stage, in movies and on television.

The voice in my head talks to me and leads me on. It cheers me up when I am rejected and, like my teacher, Herbert

Berghof, I have been rejected as an actor for many years.

My greatest happiness comes from my family — my parents, my sisters, cousins, nephews, nieces, and especially my two boys, Dale and Jason, whom I love deeply. I have a ball watching them grow.

Jason has the same vulnerable quality Dale had when he was a pre-teen. Ginny's mother once said, "Dale is too generous. He's so good to the other kids, they're gonna push him aside and get ahead of him."

Ginny said, "Oh, he did that at camp the other day."

I worked with Dale quite a bit on that. I taught him to take care of himself and not let people get ahead of him. I said, "Raise your hand and go to the front. Be the first one, not the last."

After that, I watched him in football games. He was very aggressive. Now he's a ski instructor in Denver. He turned out just fine.

Who is Ed De Leo? The voices I've been hearing all my life may be angel voices, messengers from God, talking to me. I heard voices, but did I listen to them? There is a difference between hearing and listening. Sometimes I listened and sometimes I didn't. When I did, I reaped the benefits. When I didn't, I suffered the consequences.

AL

AL MOVED TO Los Angeles. He gave a seminar at Paramount in the summer of 1995 and helped Charlie and Penny set up an acting school in Venice, California. Al enjoyed sitting in on some of the classes.

Heat premiered in the Steven J. Ross Theater at Warner Brothers Studio, in Burbank. It was followed by a gala party on the lot, attended by 700 VIPs and guests. The movie opened nationwide on December 15, 1995.

Bill Higgins at the Los Angeles Times said, "The film is an action/crime drama that would make even Newt Gingrich think twice about repealing the assault weapons ban."

"It's the season of testosterone," said Kevin Pollak. "Guys and guns, boys and toys."

The critics loved it and Al came out on top once again. "Awesome," "truly epic," "a masterpiece," "wholly original," said Richard Schickel in *Time Magazine.*

"A powerhouse!" said Paul Wunder of WBAI-FM radio.

"Pacino and De Niro are great," said David Ansen in *Newsweek*. "Pacino is electrifying," said Peter Travers in *Rolling Stone.*

Variety reported, "*Heat* occupies an exalted position among the countless contemporary crime films. Stunningly made and incisively acted... extraordinarily rich characterizations... Pacino and De Niro are undiluted pleasure to watch in their top form here."

According to Mike Caccioppoli on WABC Radio, "Al Pacino and Robert De Niro deliver two of their best performances."

Guy Flatley in *Cosmopolitan* said, "Al Pacino is pure perfection. He gives a sweet and flamboyant performance."

But you can't please all the critics all of the time. Rex Reed, who seemed to be on some personal vendetta, said, "Pacino has resorted to phoning it in. I haven't been moved by anything he's done since the *Godfather* trilogy, and his eye-rolling gum-sucking, staccato mannerisms are so old they're growing hair... Pacino seems to be acting for the ghost of Lee Strasberg, busying himself with facial ticks and vocal tricks and so many appalling accents we've forgotten why he's even doing them in the first place."

This proves how personal movies are, how they affect

people different ways. In my opinion, Al, like Picasso, illuminates every role he undertakes.

"Acting comes out of chaos," he told the New York Post. "You have to be always open for new stuff to happen, always keeping the antennae out... so you can then select and make the right choice."

He reminisced about the early Bohemian days in Greenwich Village. "We had the theater. There was this energy. It was a very fruitful time, a very rich time and I've never quite felt that again. Even with all the success that came."

He admitted he owed a large percentage of his success to his dramatic father figures. "I got a lot of help. You bet." I feel proud to have been part of it.

On January 25, 1996, *Looking For Richard*, which Al wrote, produced and directed, premiered at the Sundance Film Festival in Utah. Variety praised it as "high-spirited and infectiously energetic." The review said, "Al Pacino's *Looking For Richard* is a master class in Shakespeare and acting conducted by an uncommonly passionate and delightful teacher." It went on to say, "Remarkably cohesive," the picture is "nervy, personal, funny and emotionally charged throughout, a compelling tribute to the Bard and the players who make his words live."

This was a triumph for Al, who finally received approval for his interpretation of *Richard III*. It's been a life's mission for Al. He put together an all-star cast including Harris Yulin, Penelope Allen, Alec Baldwin, Kevin Spacey, Estelle Parsons, Winona Ryder, and Aidan Quinn. Other appearances included Kevin Kline, Kenneth Branagh, James Earl Jones, Rosemary Harris, Peter Brook, Derek Jacobi, John Gielgud, and Vanessa Redgrave.

In February 1996, *City Hall* finally opened and to favorable reviews. Al's performance was hailed by the critics as "spellbinding," "first-rate," "superb," "smoldering," "brilliant," "masterful," and "spectacular." Also appearing in movie theaters all across the country and overseas in *Heat*, *Two Bits* and *Looking for Richard*, he was now starring in four movies at the same time!

But Al didn't stop there. Why should he? More in demand than ever, he continued on with his 26th film *The Devil's Advocate* in which he was cast as the devil.

How do you play Satan? Al studied old movies like *The Devil and Daniel Webster*, *The Witches of Eastwick*, and he read *Dante's Inferno* and *Paradise Lost*. But the devil he was to play was a contemporary man who ran a law firm.

The director, Taylor Hackford was interested in a devil who was sardonic, fascinating, charming, sexy and seductive, but not all powerful. This devil had a philosophy of pure evil, but Al tried to find stuff that's funny, too. He knew he had to go for that to make it palatable. The idea of being able to run the gamut, to go from being sincere to being flamboyant to being coquettish to being enraged was a challenge, and he had lot of fun doing it. Bodda-bing!

After portraying the devil, what do you do next? A mafia killer, of course. Al went on to star in *Donnie Brasco*, playing hitman Lefty Ruggiero. The director, Mike Newell, called Lefty a gangster for the 90s, a constantly broke gambler whose sleeves get more threadbare as the story progresses.

Al swore that this would be his last movie.

He added a lot of humor to his character, cooking pasta, spending Christmas Eve wearing a red leisure suit and watching nature documentaries on TV.

But did Al Pacino really stop? Of course, not. Bodda-boom! He returned to the stage to direct and star in Eugene O'Neill's *Hughie*. Performed at the Mark Taper Forum in Los Angeles, Al played a two-bit Times Square hustler and horse player. He gave an unusually low-key performance with exquisite nuance.

Al was still working with Charlie Laughton. Their production company Chal Productions (CHarlie and AL) had offices in Manhattan and Santa Monica. Al's movie, *Chinese Coffee*, which he financed himself, was still being edited.

In September of 1999, with the Millennium getting closer, Al took a long shot, appearing in *The Insider*, directed by Michael Mann and written by Eric Roth, who had written *Forest Gump*.

In this very complex story about the tobacco wars, Al played Lowell Bergman, the *60 Minutes* producer who persuaded Jeffrey Wigand to blow the whistle on the Brown & Williamson tobacco company and then fought to restore Wigand's reputation. It was a forceful performance that almost earned him another Academy Award nomination.

By now, Al was no longer the brooding actor he used to be. He no longer paced like he used to. He was more accepting of things.

"You keep going, I guess," said Al, "and pretty soon you just count whatever blessings you've got. I've found that happiness is cool. I like it. You enjoy it more when you can spot it."

Al still considered himself a slow learner. "I don't think I've made as many mistakes in my life as I've made this year. Take my word for it. And yet, I feel I'm learning.

Whoops. Another movie. *On Any Given Sunday*. In this Y2K movie, directed by Oliver Stone, Al played an aging football coach who had to contend with a changing sports world. Among the changes were a new breed of worldly young players and a team inherited by a widow (Ann Margret) and her daughter (Cameron Diaz).

To prepare himself for the role, Al had to jump into the world of pro football, meeting a number of top football coaches and assimilating them into his character.

Al started building a family. He and the beautiful actress

Beverly D'Angelo fell in love and started living together. Beverly gave birth to twin babies, Anton and Olivia. They say it's hereditary and I believe it. Al has twin sisters. Now Al had three children. He was finally a family man like me. We now had that in common.

LIFETIME ACHIEVEMENT

AL'S MOST OUTSTANDING roles have been dangerous people – gangsters, addicts, maverick cops, even the devil. Yet the Al that friends and people in the motion picture industry know is a sensitive, generous, and funny person. It's odd that he's made a career out of such extreme characters.

Director Oliver Stone hit the nail on the head when he said, "His characters operate out of need. They need, they want something. They need and they'll do anything for it. So those are often his best roles, when Al's life is on the line."

Yes, that's the Al I know. A man who will do anything to get what he wants.

Al was interviewed by *Daily Variety* and said "To me, it's always life and death. That's probably a problem, although I haven't thought about it. But it's too damn much life and death for me. I'll tell you, I wish I could cool it a little bit!"

What else can happen in the life of a superstar? A tribute, of course. In January of 2001, he was given the Cecil B. De Mille award at the Golden Globes. The Hollywood Foreign Press Association called him "one of the defining actors of the cinema" and presented him with a lifetime achievement award.

"A small measure of our appreciation of what a great actor he is and what he's contributed to the art of acting."

When Al was asked about receiving the award, he replied, "I was overwhelmed in a way. I put the phone down and I thought, 'Well, what did I do?' And I thought about it a while and was deeply honored, as I am now. It's nice to wake up and find you're going to be getting an award, any award. But the Cecil B. De Mille Award, that's sort of like, I don't know, am I awake?"

Al's next movie was *Insomnia* in 2002. It was a psychological thriller directed by Christopher Nolan, who had directed a wild movie called *Memento.*

Al played a celebrated but troubled Los Angeles homicide detective who gets sent to Alaska to investigate the murder of a teenage girl. Since accidentally killing his police partner, he suffers from insomnia. Awake day and night, he is constantly fatigued and has to work with the local law officer played by Hilary Swank. The killer is a local writer played with quiet dignity by Robin Williams. The movie got mixed reviews, but Al's performance was painfully believable.

Then he went right into *Simone*, a sci-fi comedy-drama, a very different type of movie for Al. Under the direction of Andrew Niccol, Al played a down-on-his-luck producer-director whose film is endangered when his star walks off. So he assembles some software and digitally creates an actress to substitute for her. The beautiful virtual actress becomes an overnight sensation and a hot property who everyone thinks is a real person. As with Insomnia the movie got mixed reviews, but for the discriminating, the movie was received well as a clever and witty satire on the emptiness and shallowness of Hollywood.

There was no way I could keep up with Al or reach

him. He went from one movie to the next. He was attracted to *People I Know*, written by Jon Robin Baitz and to be directed by Daniel Algrant.

Al's role was a New York press agent who has to scramble when his major client played by Ryan O'Neil becomes involved in a career-threatening scandal. The film also starred Kim Basinger, Tea Leoni, Richard Schiff, Robert Klein and Bill Nunn.

Al gave one of the best performances of his career. It was a brutally honest and shocking movie about people in power and how they use that power to control the lives of other people from politicians and CEOs to blue collar workers and how far they will go to hold on to their power.

Al carried the movie with a sensitive and tragic portrayal of a man so absorbed in the good he was trying to do he didn't see the evil all around him. He only noticed when it was too late.

He's a worn-out, pill-popping, haggard, unhealthy, chain-smoking publicist whose idealism goes back to his involvement with the civil rights movement. It's a dark, depressing film with an unhappy ending (the story of my life). It takes place over a hectic period of 24 hours.

Al played the role with an accent that set him apart from the other New York types in the scenes. Roger Ebert recommended the movie on his television show.

The year 2003 came fast. I was still looking for work and Al was already doing another movie. More power to him. *The Recruit* was a thriller directed by Roger Donaldson and written by Roger Towne and Kurt Wimmer.

The story was about a brilliant young CIA trainee, played by Colin Farrell, who is asked by his mentor, Al, to help find a mole in the Agency. A very twisty plot, but nevertheless entertaining. The Colin Farrell character is a computer hacker and barman who is enticed by mysterious

CIA recruiter Pacino to train at the CIA "farm" where he learns everything is not as it seems, the world is full of deception, and everyone, including friends and lovers, is concealing some type of treachery. Al is good in the lead but the role was not much of a challenge, nothing that stretched his range as in his other movies.

The best thing I can say about *Gigli*, also in 2003, is that Al was on the screen only briefly. He played a blustering cameo but the lackluster performance was not entirely his fault. There was no way for him to find a center in a movie that basically didn't work.

Directed by Martin Brest, who scored with *Scent of a Woman*, the movie starred Ben Afleck, Jennifer Lopez and Christopher Walken. The success of the film was damaged by an overblown pre-release publicity campaign.

I was at Cedars Sinai Hospital for treatment of a stroke when *Angels in America*, a six-hour mini-series, aired on HBO. My room had a TV set but we could get only local channels. I got to see a videotape of it after several months of physical therapy in a nursing facility.

Directed by Mike Nichols, *Angels in America* was written by Tony Kushner, based on his Broadway play.

Al starred in it along with Meryl Streep, Emma Thompson, Mary Louise Parker, James Cromwell and new actors Justin Kirk, Ben Shenkman, Jeffrey Wright, and Patrick Wilson. They all gave stunning performances.

The story is all over the place, but the scenes and dialogue are, for the most part, brilliant. Some of it is on the pretentious side, perhaps too faithful to the stage version, but it's worth the ride.

It's 1985 and God has abandoned Heaven. Ronald Reagan is in the White House people are dying of AIDS. When a young man tells his lover he is ill, the lover splits only to find himself guilt-ridden. A young Mormon Republican is pushed by right-wing attorney Roy Cohn (Al) toward a job in Washington while at the same time coming out of the closet to the torment of his psychotic wife who is yearning to escape a sexless marriage.

Several of the cast play a number of different roles including Meryl Streep as Ethel Rosenberg who Roy Cohn had helped put to death. Al gives the most outstanding performance of his career. It was ironic for me to watch him sick and dying in a hospital while I was so close to death in a similar environment.

Angels in America not only won a record 11 Emmy Awards, taking the award for Outstanding Miniseries and all four best acting awards, it also won the same awards at the Golden Globe presentations plus four SAG acting awards. It won practically every award it possibly could.

So, who is Al Pacino? He doesn't sail, he doesn't cook, he doesn't garden or spend time with any hobbies other than maybe baseball — at least he never used to. He has said he envisions himself sitting around the Duomo in Florence, sipping anisette, watching the girls and having a great life, not acting. But he'll never do it. He'll never stop acting.

Playing a role, creating a character, is his "anodyne" (a favorite word of his). He defines it as "something soothing, something you enjoy that's just for you."

He has soared to the top, but he has also flopped. It's impossible for an actor to succeed 100 percent of the time. He's dependent on scripts, on directors, on studios, on other actors, on schedules, on time, on location. Al wants to keep acting, but would like his roles to custom-fit him as much as possible.

Still shy and vulnerable, Al is an innocent, even though he's played the wildest roles imaginable. An artist striving for perfection, he is always asking for more rehearsal time and extra takes. He'd love to have a glass of wine to mel-low with, but he refrains. Hard liquor doesn't tempt him any more. It hasn't for a long time.

Al's relationship with his father, Sal, has never been close, but he has seen him periodically throughout his life. When he was younger, Al stayed with him for a while. His father has visited him from time to time. Sometimes four or five years would go by before he saw him, but his father always tried to communicate with him.

Al gets annoyed with his father sometimes. He said to me once, "He goes on all these talk shows and he talks too much."

I replied, "He's just proud of you. And he's not a bad looking guy." I added, "Be good to him, Al. After he's gone, you won't have another chance."

Sal remarried back in May 1995 to Katherine Covin. The next August, he closed his restaurant, Pacino's, in West Covina, after run-ins with state liquor control officials and city code enforcement officers. Even though Al and Sal were estranged for many years, they are very close now.

Al has always had charisma, that's for sure. Charisma is a person's soul expressing itself outwardly. This is something that can't be taught. The greats in any field make their art appear so simple we are constantly filled with the misconception it can be taught, which of course it never can be. It can only be nurtured. This is what Lee Strasberg did so successfully.

Al has achieved his dreams. He likes to leave big tips now, sometimes up to 80 percent. He can relate to the kids who wait on tables, remembering the odd jobs he had to take while struggling to become an actor. He contributes generously to causes such as AIDS research and hungry children. He's a sucker for street hustlers and gives them $5 bills.

I keep wanting to call him, but I hate to bother him.

Sometimes he doesn't take my calls and has his assistant talk to me. I have mixed feelings about Al. I know he appreciates how much I helped him in the early days. He recently expressed this to a group of students who attended one of his acting workshops at the Actors Studio in New York. He acknowledged I was his first acting mentor.

Al is the success he is because he would never compromise. And me? I took too many side roads. I tried to play it safe by working too much outside of the acting arena. I thought it was the right thing to do for my family. Somehow, along the way, I guess I lost my vision. My great satisfaction in life, though, is my family. If I had to choose between a career and my family, I would choose my family.

FINALE

2004 WAS TO BE Ed's final year. He was in and out of hospitals and nursing homes for complications of diabetes, which he had been fighting for a number of years. He had been gaining weight over the last few years.

When we first met him in New York in the 70s, he weighed around 160 pounds. By 2004, his weight had ballooned to almost 300. It inhibited his movement so that he could barely walk. He was living in a small apartment off of Sunset Boulevard on Fairfax, owing months of back rent, supporting himself and his family on Social Security and a meager income from teaching private acting classes.

During one of our visits to Ed in the hospital, after his coming out of intensive care for therapy, we mentioned Al Pacino was about to star in a new movie. Ed, barely able to sit up in bed, responded, "Oh, could you call him for me? Maybe there's a part in it for me."

We tried to contact Al, to let him know about Ed's condition, but the telephone numbers and fax number Ed had given us turned out to be old numbers. We found out later Al never got the messages.

Ed passed away June 29, 2004. He was buried at the world-famous Forest Lawn Cemetery in the Hollywood Hills where he shares the lush greenery with stars such as

Lucille Ball, Bette Davis, Steve Allen, Buster Keaton, Liberace, Telly Savalas, Ricky Nelson, Jack Webb, Stan Laurel and Gene Autry.

We watched *Angels In America* for the second time recently on DVD. Seeing Al's portrayal of the dying Roy Cohn was like revisiting Ed in the hospital. The look and speech pattern were almost identical. It was like Al playing Ed as Roy Cohn. Talk about foreshadowing.

In spite of everything, Ed never lost his faith in God and believed that life goes on. He suspected he might be dying and wanted to be sure his share of income from this book would be distributed to his family. He continued telling us his story to the very end.

"Don't forget to put in the part about my role in *Gettysburg*... and mention all my students who have become successful."

"We won't, Ed. It's all in the book."

Ed's son Dale is doing well with his own landscaping company in Denver. Jason, after a stint as an actor, is working at a good non-show business job in downtown Los Angeles, lives in a modest apartment with his mother Ginny and has a steady girlfriend.